Pittsburgh Series in Bibliography

EDITORIAL BOARD

Matthew J. Bruccoli, General Editor

William R. Cagle
Charles W. Mann
Joel Myerson

MARJORIE KINNAN RAWLINGS

Marjorie Kinnan Rawlings

A DESCRIPTIVE BIBLIOGRAPHY

Rodger L. Tarr

UNIVERSITY OF PITTSBURGH PRESS
Pittsburgh
1996

Published by the University of Pittsburgh Press, Pittsburgh, Pa., 15260
Copyright © 1996, University of Pittsburgh Press
All rights reserved
Manufactured in the United States of America
Printed on acid-free paper

Library of Congress Cataloging in Publication Data

Tarr, Rodger L.
    Marjorie Kinnan Rawlings : a descriptive bibliography / Rodger L.
Tarr.
       p. cm. — (Pittsburgh series in bibliography)
    Includes bibliographical references and index.
    ISBN 0-8229-3920-7
    1. Rawlings, Marjorie Kinnan, 1896–1953—Bibliography. 2. Women and literature—United States—Bibliography. 3. Florida—In literature—Bibliography. I. Title. II. Series.
Z8725 23.T37   1996
[PS3535.A845]
016.813'52—dc20   95-24171
                                                                                                                              CIP

A CIP catalogue record for this book is available from the British Library.

Eurospan, London

For Carol Anita

Contents

Acknowledgments		xi
Introduction		xv
A.	Separate Publications	1
	AA. Collections	157
B.	First-Appearance Contributions to Books and Pamphlets	169
C.	First Appearances in Journals, Magazines, and Newspapers	177
D.	Blurbs	237
E.	Translations	243
Appendix 1. Movie Work		267
Appendix 2. Films Made from Rawlings's Work		268
Appendix 3. Radio Address		270
Appendix 4. Unlocated Poem		271
Appendix 5. Principal Books About Rawlings		272
Index		273

Acknowledgments

THIS BIBLIOGRAPHY demonstrates the diversity of Rawlings's canon, much of which until now was undocumented and/or unknown. The debts owed in a descriptive bibliography of this kind are many. I am especially grateful to Norton S. Baskin, Rawlings's husband, who let me intrude into his retirement and who answered my many questions. There is little question that this bibliography would be different if it were not for Philip S. May, Jr., who in every conceivable manner has contributed to this book. My Rawlings research is made so much easier by Phil May's knowledge, library, and friendship, a friendship given greater meaning by Gloria May, whose graciousness is exceeded only by her understanding. I am also delighted that this bibliography led me to new friends, two of them collectors of Rawlings's works. To Robert Middendorf, attorney-at-law in San Diego, I owe specific debts to his collection and to his acumen. To Margaret A. Levings of Monticello, Florida, I owe a debt in kind for her collection and her enthusiasm. Patricia Nassif, Lady Acton, professor of law at the University of Iowa, provided important information. David Nolan of St. Augustine, Florida, was ever vigilant for the hitherto lost Rawlings item. A special thanks to Richard Young for making available to me the Rawlings material that appeared in his family magazine the *Dumpling*; and to Mike and John Blauer of San Marco Books for their information on the Rawlings facsimiles. My thanks to Wilam Baker of Northern Illinois University, Dale Trela of Roosevelt University, and Kevin M. McCarthy of the University of Florida, who contributed in divers ways.

The librarians and caretakers of Rawlings's life and works are no less important. I must particularly acknowledge Carmen Russell Hurff, curator of the Rawlings Collection at the University of Florida, who was never without an answer to my questions. Sally Morrison, former caretaker, and Ginger Blinn, caretaker of the Rawlings home at Cross Creek, provided invaluable information. The guardians of the Scribner Archives at Princeton University were most helpful, and I am especially indebted to Jean F. Preston, former curator of manuscripts. My thanks to the librarians at the British Library, the National Library of Scotland and the Bibliothèque Nationale. Victoria Buser of the Bodleian Library, Oxford University, provided important documentation. The archivists at the University of Wisconsin were immensely helpful in locating many of Rawlings's contributions to university publications while she was a student. Lynda Edwards, news librarian, was helpful in locating Rawlings's childhood contributions in the *Washington Post*, as was my graduate assistant Anita McCormick. My entreaties to the editors of the *Louisville Courier-Journal* were answered promptly. The work of Barbara Gallucci and Wayne K. Arnold of the Rochester Public Library was most appreciated in the effort to confirm Rawlings's contributions to Rochester newspapers and to the weekly *Five O'Clock*, as were the efforts of Elizabeth Norris who located Rawlings's work for the YWCA in New York, and Sherrill Redmon of the University of Louisville and Dorothy C. Rush of the Filson Club for the YWCA in Louisville. Ellie Chucker, Richard Hurlbut, and Anatol R. Steck proved invaluable for their persistence in locating Rawlings's work in her high school magazine *The Western*. Deborah W. Walker of the Rollins College Archive sent information about the *Animated Magazine*. Mary E. Bowling of the New York Public Library kindly searched the *New Yorker* archives. Bernard Schermetzler and Jill Rosenshield of the University of Wisconsin archives and rare books library provided documents and information on Rawlings's student days. Sharon Inamoto and Diana R. Brown of Turner Entertainment answered questions regarding the MGM files. Clark Evans and Willam E. Sundwick of the Library of Congress supplied material. Linda D. Surles shared information about Rawlings's election to Phi Beta Kappa, and Mary E. Arnold for Rawlings's membership in Kappa Alpha Theta. I want especially to acknowledge Michael Perry Dean of the University of Mississippi, who shared his thesis on Rawlings's writings with me, and Louise S. Bailey of Marshall University, who offered contributions. William B. Todd supplied information on the Tauchnitz edition of *The Yearling*.

Many others answered my litany of requests: Jean Katona of the Girl Scouts of the United States of America; Ben H. Love of the Boy Scouts of America; Donald Roe of the National Film Archives in Washington; Chauncey B. Jessup of the Nation Archives in Washington; C. H. Harris of the Jacksonville Public Library; Laura V. Monti of the Boston Public Library; Margaret E. Jaffie of the Voice of America; Patrick F. Gilbo of the American Red Cross; Mary M. Egle, Editor of Mockingbird

Acknowledgments

Books; Jerrold B. Spears of the Department of the Treasury; Eric Rothstein of the University of Wisconsin; Anne M. Blythe of Columbia, South Carolina; James B. Meriwether of the University of South Carolina; John R. Ward of the Louisville Free Public Library; Edna Saffy of the Florida Community College of Jacksonville (South Campus); Sidney Ives, former rare book librarian, and Dave Lashnet and Bruce Chappell of the University of Florida; Charles A. Hand of Paris, Illinois; Edith Golub of Macmillan Publishing Company; Charles Schlessiger of Brandt and Brandt, New York; John Patrick of St. Thomas, U.S. Virgin Islands; Louis D. Silveri of Assumption College; E. Noble of the Indiana State Library; Jill D. Wright of the Johnson County Public Library, Franklin, Indiana; Dale Sheehy of the Public Library, Bridgewater, Connecticut; Nancy Boerner of Indiana University; Robert C. Davis of Indialantic, Florida; Mary Ellen Brooks of the University of Georgia; Jake Glisson of Evinston, Florida; Roy Hammock of St. Augustine, Florida; Suzanne Zambito of Tampa, Florida; Michael Christie of Crawfordville, Florida; Sue Logan of the *Louisville Courier-Journal*; Mrs. Barry Bingham, Sr., of Glenview, Kentucky; Yvonne Schofer of the University of Wisconsin; Alison McCuaig, Ann VanArsdale, and Margaret M. Sherry of Princeton University; Linda D. Surles of Phi Beta Kappa; Mary Edith Arnold of Kappa Alpha Theta; Ronald R. Randall of Santa Barbara, California; Sandra L. McKinley of the Franklin Mint; Leland Hawes of the *Tampa Tribune*; Elinor Fillion of the University of Toronto Library; the librarians at Grace College; Chris Berry of the National Library of Canada; Judith Brooker of the National Library of Australia; Heather Moore of the University of Virginia; David Widmer of ISBN; Patrick Morrissey of Barry University, Helga Whitcomb, former interlibrary loan librarian, and Carol Ruyle, Interlibrary Loan Librarian of Illinois State University.

I owe a debt to the editors and the staffs of the following presses who answered in spirit my persistent questions: Walda Metcalf of the University of Florida Press; Robert I. Fuerst of the University of Miami Press; Lara Rice Bergen of Grosset and Dunlap; Jean Rose of the Octopus Publishing Group Library; John Bodley of Faber and Faber; John D. Allen of Thomas Allen; and Charles Scribner III of Charles Scribner's Sons.

For the translations of certain foreign languages I am indebted to Irene Brosnahan (Chinese), Keiko Hawkins, Hiroshi Tsunemoto, Yasuyo Moriya (Japanese), Diane Urey (Spanish), Bill Bohn (Hungarian), and Rati Ram, Vaishali Sonak, Basudeb Biswas, Sarathy Bharani, and Joseph Jeyaraj (languages of India). I am especially indebted to Paul Wadden, who searched the libraries of Japan for me, and to my esteemed friend Longming Li of Shanghai, who supplied me with his own translations into the Chinese language.

I am much indebted to the many rare book dealers who helped build my collection and who answered my questions.

This work was supported in part by research grants from Illinois State University. I am also grateful to Virginia Lee Owen, former dean of the Colleges of Arts & Sciences, and Ron Fortune, chair of the Department of English, for their support.

I am especially grateful to William R. Cagle, who checked the entries against the Lilly Library copies; to Joel Myerson for his careful reading and infinite patience; and to Matthew J. Bruccoli, whose stern but nurturing stewardship informs entirely this work.

My dedication to Anita says little of my actual debt. Together, we found Rawlings at Cross Creek, and our lives have been strengthened by the experience.

These individuals deserve my special acknowledgment:

    Norton S. Baskin
    Carmen Russell Hurff
    Philip S. May, Jr.
    Robert Middendorf
    David Nolan

Introduction

THIS DESCRIPTIVE BIBLIOGRAPHY of Marjorie Kinnan Rawlings's writings is limited to writings by Rawlings. It does not describe writings about Rawlings. However, there is an alphabetical list of principal books about Rawlings in the Appendix.

FORMAT

Section A lists chronologically all books and pamphlets wholly or substantially by Rawlings, including all printings of all editions in English through 1994. At the end of this section there is an AA Supplement that records collections of Rawlings's work that do not include any material by Rawlings published for the first time and were not edited by Rawlings.

The numbering system for Section A indicates the edition and printings for each entry. Thus, for *The Yearling*, A3.1.a indicates that this is the third title published by Rawlings (A3), and that the entry is for the first edition (1), the first printing (a). Printings for all first editions are listed separately: A3.1.a, A3.1.b, A3.1.c, and so forth. There are no multivolume works of Rawlings's writings. Issues are indicated by subscript numbers; thus, $A7.2.a_2$ is the second issue of the first printing of the second edition (first British edition) of *The Sojourner* (A7). States are discussed in the text. A complete binding description is given for all first editions, and an abbreviated description for subsequent editions.

Each A entry begins with a facsimile of the title page (with dimensions and other relevant information given), followed by a facsimile of the copyright page. Next comes the pagination information and then the collation formula. A list of contents follows, which includes a full list of the preliminaries, insertions such as illustrations, and appendixes and indexes. Book and chapter divisions within the text are not noted. Quasi-facsimile transcription under any of the rubrics is indicated by single quote marks. Information on typography and paper includes the dimensions of the printed text, the kind of paper, the number of lines per page, and a quasi-facsimile transcription of the running heads. Thus, 19.0 (18.4) × 9.8 cm. means that the height of the printed material from the top of the running head to the bottom of the last line is 19.0 cm., that the height of the text from the top of the first line to the bottom of the last line is 18.4 cm., and that the width of the text is 9.8 cm. Whether the paper is laid or wove is noted, and if laid the distance between and the direction of the chain lines are also noted. All paper is assumed to be white, unless otherwise indicated. Binding cloth descriptions, with some modifications, follow the systems advanced by G. Thomas Tanselle and Philip Gaskell.[1] When there are two or more bindings listed, alphabetical designations (A, B, C) are given, which would mean that B is the second variant binding listed. Unless specified, no priority of bindings is implied. Binding information also includes notes on flyleaves, endpapers, page trimming, and page-edge gilding or staining. All wrappers are paper, unless otherwise indicated. Stapled and perfect bindings are specified. General color designations are used.[2] Dust jackets are fully described and usually reproduced. Locations are provided for libraries and private collections holding copies of each title described. Library symbols are from the *National Union Catalog*. The notes provide information not discussed elsewhere in the entry. Information on publication is taken from Scribners Records and Scribners File-Cards located at the Firestone Library, Princeton University, from records of Brandt and Brandt, Rawlings's agents, located at the University of Florida, from published and unpublished letters of Rawlings located at the University of Florida and the University of Georgia, as well as in private hands, and from contemporary book trade announcements and publishers' records.

For most subsequent editions a quasi-facsimile transcription of the title page is given. Epigraphs are identified within brackets. Publishers' logos and/or other devices are also described within brackets.

---

1. See G. Thomas Tanselle, "The Specifications of Binding Cloth, "*The Library*, 21 (September 1966), 246–47; "The Bibliographical Description of Patterns," *Studies in Bibliography*, 23 (1970), 72–102; and Philip Gaskell, *A New Introduction to Bibliography* (New York and Oxford: Oxford University Press, 1972), pp. 237–49.

2. General color designations, instead of Centroid numbers, have been used because of the inexactness of the Centroid system. For a defense of this position, see Joel Myerson, *Ralph Waldo Emerson: A Descriptive Bibliography* (Pittsburgh, Pa: University of Pittsburgh Press, 1982), p. xvi.

Introduction   XVII

Rules are horizontal, unless otherwise noted. Colored lettering and unusual type fonts are noted, but no measurement or description of the font is given. A brief description of the binding is given. Locations for copies examined are provided.

Section B lists chronologically all titles in which material by Rawlings appears for the first time in a book or pamphlet through 1994. Items that were previously unpublished are so identified. The first printings only of these books or pamphlets are described in quasi-facsimile. Bindings are assumed to be cloth, unless otherwise indicated. Locations are provided.

Section C lists chronologically the first publication (and republications) in journals, magazines, and newspapers of material by Rawlings through 1994. This section includes fiction, poems, editorials, essays, and letters. All entries are signed 'Marjorie Kinnan Rawlings,' 'Marjorie K. Rawlings," or 'Marjorie Rawlings,' unless otherwise indicated.

Section D lists chronologically blurbs by Rawlings on the dust jackets of books by other authors.

Section E lists chronologically by title translations of Rawlings's writings. Languages are listed alphabetically.

Appendix 1 lists Rawlings's movie-writing assignments; Appendix 2 lists the movies made from Rawlings's work; Appendix 3 lists a radio address by Rawlings; Appendix 4 lists an unlocated poem by Rawlings; and Appendix 5 lists the principal books about Rawlings.

TERMS AND METHODS

Edition. All copies of a book printed from a single setting of type—including all reprintings from standing type, from plates, or by photo-offset processes.

Printing. All copies of a book printed at one time (without removing the type or plates from the press).

State. States occur only within single printings and are created by an alteration not affecting the conditions of publication or sale to some copies of a given printing (by stop-press correction or cancellation of leaves). There can be no first state without a second state.

Issue. Issues occur only within single printings and are created by an alteration affecting the conditions of publication or sale to some copies of a given printing (usually a title page alteration). There can be no first issue without a second issue.

Edition, printing, states, and *issues* have been restricted to the sheets of the book. Binding and/or dust jacket variants have no bearing on these terms.

Binding variants in this bibliography are treated simply as binding variants; however, it can be assumed that deposit copies at the Library of Congress, the British Library, and the Bodleian Library are early copies.

Dust jackets in Section A entries have been described in detail because they are part of the original publication effort and sometimes provide information about how the book was marketed. There is, of course, no certainty that a dust jacket now on a copy of a book was always on it.

All Scribners first edition, first printings, are identified by an 'A' and a Scribners seal on the copyright page, with the exception of *Cross Creek* (A4), *Cross Creek Cookery* (A5), and *The Secret River* (A9), where the first edition, first printing, is identified by an 'A' only on the copyright page.

The spines of bindings or dust jackets are stamped or printed horizontally, unless otherwise indicated. Vertical-stamped or vertical-printed spines are stamped or printed from top to bottom or from bottom to top, and are so indicated.

In descriptions of title pages, bindings, and dust jackets, the color of the lettering is always black, unless otherwise stipulated. The style of the type is roman, unless otherwise stated.

The term *perfect binding* refers to books in which the pages are held together with glue or adhesive along the back edge after the folds have been trimmed off—for example, most paperbacks.

Dates provided within brackets do not appear on the title page. Usually—but not invariably—they are taken from the copyright page.

Sheet bulk is provided when such information is necessary to differentiate printings. An electronic digital Mitutoyo micrometer was used to measure the bulk in millimeters.

In addition to the abbreviations used from the *National Union Catalog*, the following abbreviations or short titles are used throughout the bibliography:

BL	British Library
BMC	*British Museum Catalogue*
CBI	*Cumulative Book Index*
DLC	Library of Congress
MGM	Metro-Goldwyn-Mayer

Introduction

MKRH Marjorie Kinnan Rawlings House, Cross Creek
NUC   *National Union Catalog*
PC   Private collection
PM   Collection of Philip S. May, Jr.
RM   Collection of Robert Middendorf
RLT   Collection of Rodger L. Tarr

The following are additional symbols:

Scribners Records: Scribners publication records at Princeton University

Scribners File-Cards: Scribners publication file at Princeton University

Scribners Records contains an accounting of stock ordered, delivered, sold, and on hand, together with receipts. Scribners File-Cards record publication information. Scribners Records and File-Cards are not always complete—for example, they seldom list BOMC printings.

For the Bodleian Library, British Library, and Library of Congress copies, the phrase *deposit-stamp* is used to distinguish the date stamped in the book from other library records. Copyright numbers are from the DLC Copyright Office.

The Scribners code is given for printings in which it appears. The first letter in this code designates the printing (or what Scribners regards as a new printing); the digits indicate month and year; and the bracket letters indicate the printer. Thus *C-1.65 [Col]* means that the book is the third printing dated January 1965, and that it was printed at the Colonial Press.

For paperbacks, the serial number provided is that of the first printing. Paperback publishers often change the serial numbers in later printings; but such changes have not been noted in this bibliography.

Freak copies—that is, books with gatherings out of order or with repeated gatherings—are without bibliographic significance and have been ignored in this bibliography.

This bibliography does not attempt to indicate the relative scarcity of Rawlings's works.

A bibliography is outdated the day it is published. Addenda and corrigenda are earnestly solicited.

Illinois State University
June 1995

A. Separate Publications

A 1 SOUTH MOON UNDER

A 1.1.a
First American edition, first printing (1933)

SOUTH MOON UNDER

By
Marjorie Kinnan Rawlings

NEW YORK · LONDON
CHARLES SCRIBNER'S SONS
1933

A 1.1.a: 18.8 × 13.0 cm.

A 1.1.a *South Moon Under* 3

[i–viii] 1–334 [335–336]

[1–21]⁸ [22]⁴; 172 leaves.

Contents: p. i: half title: 'SOUTH MOON UNDER'; p. ii: blank; p. iii: title page; p. iv: copyright page; p. v: 8-line explanation of the historical basis of the novel; p. vi: blank; p. vii: section title: 'SOUTH MOON UNDER'; p. viii: blank; pp. 1–334: text; pp. 335–336: blank.

Typography and paper: 15.5 (14.9) × 8.9 cm.; wove paper; 35 lines per page. Sheet bulk: title page: .187 mm.; p. 183: .199 mm. Running heads: rectos: pp. 3–9, 11–29, 33–47, 51–53, 57–75, 79–85, 89–109, 113–119, 123–141, 145–147, 151–157, 161–165, 169–175, 179–203, 207–217, 221–231, 235–243, 247–261, 265–271, 275–281, 285–289, 293–297, 301–309, 313, 317–333: 'SOUTH MOON UNDER'; versos: pp. 2–38, 42–58, 62–68, 72–98, 102–134, 138–184, 188–226, 230–252, 256–322, 326–328, 332–334: 'SOUTH MOON UNDER'.

Binding: Light green calico-textured cloth. Front cover: goldstamped thick-thin-thin-thick vertical rule along spine top to bottom; '[at bottom third: goldstamped thin-thin rule] | [in bluish gray, partly covering the rule] South Moon | [goldstamped thin-thin rule] | [in bluish gray, partly covering the rule] Under | [goldstamped thin-thin, thin-thin rule] | [in bluish] MARJORIE KINNAN RAWLINGS | [goldstamped thin-thin rule]'; spine: '[goldstamped thin-thin rule] | [in bluish gray] South | [in bluish gray] Moon | [in bluish gray] Under | [goldstamped thin-thin, thin-thin rule] | [in bluish gray] RAWLINGS | [goldstamped thin-thin rule, then four sets of goldstamped thin-thin rules aligned with the rule on the front cover] | [in bluish gray] SCRIBNERS | [goldstamped thin-thin rule aligned with the rule on the front cover]'. Top edge trimmed and stained bluish gray. Bottom edge trimmed. Fore-edge rough trimmed.

Dust jacket: Front cover: Florida woods scene in grayish brown and black, with a dark blue sky and white moon; '[the title is at the bottom third in white] SOUTH MOON | UNDER | [in dark blue with white outline] MARJORIE KINNAN RAWLINGS | [in white at bottom right] CARROLL SNELL'; spine: scene continuous with front; '[all lettering in white] SOUTH | MOON | UNDER | RAWLINGS | SCRIBNERS'; back cover: on a white background in brown frame: '[in bluish gray] SOUTH MOON UNDER | [in brown] *by Marjorie Kinnan Rawlings* | [in brown frame with bluish gray lettering at left] *The* | *Setting* | [in a brown frame with brown lettering at right: 10-line description of the setting] | [in a brown frame with bluish gray lettering at left] *The* | *Title* | [in brown frame with brown lettering at right: 12-line description of the title] | [in a brown frame with bluish gray lettering at left] *The* | *Women* | [in a brown frame with brown lettering at right: 16-line description of the women]'; front flap: '[on a white background in brown at the top right] $2.00 | [title in bluish gray] SOUTH MOON | UNDER | [in brown: 35-line description of the novel] | [in brown and underlined] *A Selection of the* | *Book of the Month Club* [in brown and underlined]'; rear flap: on a white background: '[in bluish gray] *The author says of the* | *country about which* | *she has written:* | [in brown] 26-line description of The Scrub]'.

Publication: 2,945 copies published on 1 March. Listed in *Publishers' Weekly,* 123 (4 March 1933), 859; and as a best-seller in *Publishers' Weekly,* 123 (8 April 1933), 1,215. $2.00. Copyright A60498.

Printing: Printed and bound by the Scribner Press.

Locations: FU (dj), InU (dj), PM (dj), RLT (advance copy, dj with promotional wrap), RM (2, dj).

Note one: Galleys were ready on 29 December 1932 (Scribners File-Cards).

Note two: The plates were altered between the first and second printings. The first printing, p. 184, l. 20, describes the alligator: 'The big bull was all of thirty feet'; in all subsequent printings the length is changed to 'of twenty feet'. The question of length was raised by Joseph F. Marron, librarian at Jacksonville University Library, who in an undated letter to Maxwell Perkins said he had read "an advance copy bound in page proofs" [not located] and claimed that "13 feet would describe a mammoth alligator while 30 feet would indicate an impossible size." Perkins responded, 26 January 1933: "We are taking up the question with Mrs. Rawlings and although we have printed 3,000 [2945] copies which cannot be changed, the greater part of the first copies to be issued, by far, will be changed if, as we expect, she agrees that the estimate of the alligator's length was an error." In a telegram to Rawlings, 26 January, Perkins

Dust jacket for A 1.1.a

South Moon Under Printing Flow Chart

Publisher	CSS	CSS	CSS	CSS	G&D	G&D	CSS	G&D	G&D	G&D	G&D	G&D	G&D	G&D
Printing	1st	2nd	3rd	4th	5th	6th	7th	8th	9th	10th	11th	12th	13th	14th
Sheet Bulk TP	0.187	0.178	0.162	0.164		0.173	0.169	0.161	0.182	0.146	0.125	0.118	0.156	.160 mm.
Sheet Bulk 183	0.199	0.175	0.163	0.159	0.168	0.142	0.171	0.176	0.173	0.154	0.126	0.122	0.146	.148 mm.
Plate Change														
p. 184, l. 20	No	Yes	Yes	Yes	Yes	Yes	Yes	Yes	Yes	Yes	Yes	Yes	Yes	Yes
Sewing	8's	8's	8's	8's	8's	8's	8's	8's	8's	8's	16's	16's	16's	16's
Copyright Page	'A' + S	Seal	Seal	Seal	No	No	Seal	No	No	No	No	No	No	No
Batter:														
'vibrant' 11:27	Yes	Yes	Yes	Yes	Yes	Yes	Yes	Yes	Yes	Yes	Yes	Yes	Yes	Yes
'him' 24:35	No	No	No	No	No	No	No	No	No	No	Yes	Yes	Yes	Yes
'myrtle' 2:25	No	No	No	No	No	No	No	No	Yes	Yes	Yes	Yes	Yes	Yes
'mildly' 306:35	No	No	No	No	No	No	No	Yes	Yes	Yes	Yes	Yes	Yes	Yes
'8' in p. 328	No	No	No	No	No	No	Yes	Yes	Yes	Yes	Yes	Yes	Yes	Yes
War Statement	No	No	No	No	No	No	No	No	No	No	No	No	Yes	Yes
Sheet Size TP	18.7	18.6	18.6	18.7	18.6	18.8	18.7	20.3	20.3	20.3	19	19	19	19
	X 13.0	X 13.0	X 13.0	X 13.0	X 12.6	X 12.6	X 13.0	X 13.4	X 13.4	X 13.4	X 13.3	X 13.0	X 13.0	X 13.0 cm.

Flow chart for A I.I.a

A 1.1.a *South Moon Under*

asked to change the length from thirty to thirteen. In a telegram, 28 January, Rawlings responded: "Thirty intentional[.] But make it twenty to avoid questioning." In a letter to Perkins, 4 February, Rawlings wrote that "thirty feet is the size of about the biggest alligator caught on the Ocklawaha of late years. . . . But it does strain credulity, doesn't it? . . . I am glad you changed it" (Scribners Archive).

Note three: Scribners Records gives sheet stock orders as follows: 18 January: 2,945; 25 January: 44,000, designated 'B.M.C.'; 25 January: 10,000 (listed as 10,600 in another part of the Records), designated 'Reg.'; 27 March: 2,300, designated 'B.M.C.' A Scribners file copy of the novel, owned by James B. Meriwether, gives a partial record of the number of copies published. Notes in this file copy confirm the two trade printings of 2,945 copies and 10,600 copies. These notes combine the two printings of the BOMC and list the total as 46,300 copies, which agrees with the Records. All printings subsequent to first trade printing, including all BOMC printings, contain the plate change discussed in *Note two*. An advertisement in the *New York Herald Tribune Books*, 5 March 1933, claims 'Sixty Thousand in Sixty Days', even though the book was published three days before. Scribners Records does not record any additional printing dates after 2 March 1938, although it does record deliveries and receipts through 1943.

Note four: Scribners Records indicates that 3,200 dust jackets were printed for the first printing, and then 13,000, presumably for the second printing of the trade edition. Scribners routinely ordered more dust jackets than printed copies, then used the excess dust jackets on subsequent printings. Such a practice makes even more problematic the association of dust jackets with printings. In the case of *South Moon Under*, all the dust jackets for all printings seen, including BOMC, have '$2.00' at the top of the front flap and '*A Selection of the | Book of the Month Club*' at the bottom of the front flap.

Note five: Scribners Records indicates that the plates were melted on 18 August 1955.

Note six: An advance copy with a promotional wraparound band (11.4 × 50.8 cm.), placed over the dust jacket, has been seen. On an orange background: front cover: '[in a oblong circle at upper left] A BOOK | *that is being* | TALKED ABOUT | [underneath the circle] *don herold says:* | 11-line description of the novel] | [to the right of the description is an illustration of a man holding a rifle and an alligator] | [underneath the illustration] SOUTH MOON | UNDER | *by* Marjorie Kinnan Rawlings'; spine: '[in a circle] A | Book | *that is being* | TALKED | ABOUT'; back cover: advertisements for three novels; front flap: '*don herold says* | Brush your brains once a day, | See your bookseller once a week'; rear flap: blank. *Location:* RLT.

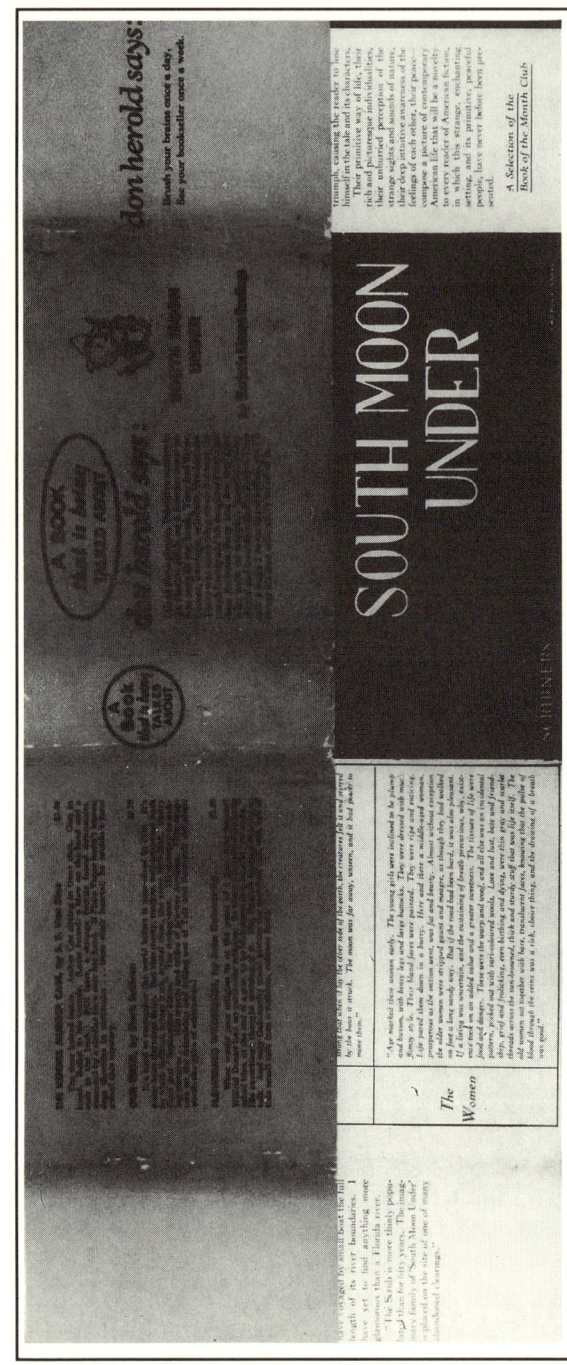

Wraparound band for A 1.1.a

A 1.1.a *South Moon Under*

> **Memorandum of Agreement**, made this - twenty-first - day of - November - 1932 between MARJORIE K. RAWLINGS
> of Hawthorn, Florida, - - - - - hereinafter called "the AUTHOR," and CHARLES SCRIBNER'S SONS, of New York City, N. Y., hereinafter called "the PUBLISHERS." Said - - Marjorie K.Rawlings - - being the AUTHOR and PROPRIETOR of a work entitled:
> SOUTH MOON UNDER
> in consideration of the covenants and stipulations hereinafter contained, and agreed to be performed by the PUBLISHERS, grants and guarantees to said PUBLISHERS and their successors the exclusive right to publish the said work in all forms during the terms of copyright and renewals thereof, hereby covenanting with said PUBLISHERS that she is the sole AUTHOR and PROPRIETOR of said work.
>
> Said AUTHOR hereby authorizes said PUBLISHERS to take out the copyright on said work, and further guarantees to said PUBLISHERS that the said work is in no way whatever a violation of any copyright belonging to any other party, and that it contains nothing of a scandalous or libelous character; and that s he and her legal representatives shall and will hold harmless the said PUBLISHERS from all suits, and all manner of claims and proceedings which may be taken on the ground that said work is such violation or contains anything scandalous or libelous; and s he further hereby authorizes said PUBLISHERS to defend at law any and all suits and proceedings which may be taken or had against them for infringement of any other copyright or for libel, scandal, or any other injurious or hurtful matter or thing contained in or alleged or claimed to be contained in or caused by said work, and pay to said PUBLISHERS such reasonable costs, disbursements, expenses, and counsel fees as they may incur in such defense.
>
> Said PUBLISHERS, in consideration of the right herein granted and of the guarantees aforesaid, agree to publish said work at their own expense, in such style and manner as they shall deem most expedient, and to pay said AUTHOR, or - her - legal representatives, TEN (10) ----------------------- per cent. on their Trade-List (retail) price, cloth style, for the first three thousand (3000) copies of said work sold by them in the United States and FIFTEEN (15) per cent. for all copies sold thereafter.
>
> Provided, nevertheless, that one-half the above named royalty shall be paid on all copies sold outside the United States; and provided that no percentage whatever shall be paid on any copies destroyed by fire or water, or sold at or below cost, or given away for the purpose of aiding the sale of said work.
>
> It is further agreed that the profits arising from any publication of said work, during the period covered by this agreement, in other than book form shall be divided equally between said PUBLISHERS and said AUTHOR.

Contract for A 1.1.a

Note seven: Rawlings acknowledged receiving an "advance copy" on 6 February: "I like the inside cloth cover particularly" (Scribners Archive).

Note eight: There is an inscribed copy at the University of Florida: 'For my good friends | the Fiddias— | with my deep thanks | for their assistance in | gathering and preparing | the material for this book | affectionately, | Marjorie Kinnan Rawlings'. Leonard Fiddia was the prototype for Lant (see *Selected Letters*, pp. 339–340).

Note nine: The two DLC deposit copies (both with deposit dates of 7 March) are later printings; each has a Scribners seal but no "A" on the copyright page, and each has the plate change discussed in *Note two*.

Note ten: On 1 April 1933 Perkins wrote to Rawlings, "The actual royalty sale to date is a little short of 5000." On 10 April, he wrote that 6,000 copies had been sold and that the novel was listed as a bestseller in the *New York Herald Tribune Books*. On 12 April, he sent Rawlings $1,000. In a letter, 15 April, Rawlings complained to Perkins about not knowing the sales figures and said that to her knowledge 56,000 copies had been sold, about 50,000 being Book-of-the-Month Club sales. On 17 April, Perkins sent $8,000. A memo, 10 August, in the Scribners Archive indicates that 9,696 copies of the trade printing had been sold.

A 1.1.b
First American edition, second printing, for the Book-of-the-Month Club, 1933

New York: Charles Scribner's Sons, 1933. 44,000 copies. *Copyright page*: Seal only. *Binding and dust jacket*: Same as A1.1.a. Sheet bulk: title page: .178 mm.; p. 183: .175 mm. *Location*: RLT.

Note one: The second and all subsequent printings contain the plate change, 'of thirty feet' to 'of twenty feet', described in A1.1.a, *Note two*.

Note two: The first BOMC printing is identified by a double crimp at the bottom left edge of the back cover of the binding.

Note three: On 17 January 1933, Maxwell Perkins wrote Rawlings that the Book-of-the-Month Club had picked up *South Moon Under*, and "at worst it should be $4,000 for you, and $4,000 for us," and he estimated that the "edition will number between thirty and forty thousand copies" (Scribners Archive).

Note four: In a letter, 23 January 1933, Perkins informed Harris Powers, editor of the *Ocala Morning Banner*, that there were no advance copies of *South Moon Under*: "We did make up a certain number of rough copies from the proofs for the Book of the Month Club, . . . but even these did not have the final corrections of the author, . . . we shall not publish until the first of March" (Scribners Archive).

A 1.1.c
First American edition, third printing (1933)

New York: Charles Scribner's Sons, 1933. 10,600 copies. 2 March 1933. *Binding and dust jacket*: Same as A2.1.a. Sheet bulk: title page: .162 mm.; p. 183: .163 mm. *Location*: RLT.

A 1.1.f *South Moon Under*

Note one: The 'A' is dropped, but the Scribners seal is retained on the copyright page.

Note two: Scribners Records lists the third printing (second trade printing) after the first BOMC printing. However, the order number (4471) indicates that it was ordered before BOMC (4197). If the order number rather than the entry sequence is considered, the second trade would be the second printing and the first BOMC the third printing. Both were ordered on the same day, 25 January. No difference in the texts between the second trade and the first BOMC has been noted.

A 1.1.d
First American edition, fourth printing, for the Book-of-the-Month Club (1933)

New York: Charles Scribner's Sons, 1933. 2,300 copies. 27 March 1933. *Binding and dust jacket*: Same as A1.1.a. Sheet bulk: title page: .164 mm.; p. 183: .159 mm. *Location*: RLT.

Note: The second BOMC printing does not have the double crimp on the binding.

A 1.1.e
First American edition, fifth printing [1934]

[in frame, title in hollow font] SOUTH MOON | UNDER | By | Marjorie Kinnan Rawlings | [device] | GROSSET & DUNLAP | PUBLISHERS NEW YORK

viii + 334 + 10 pp. 19.1 × 13.0 cm. *Binding*: Gray calico-textured cloth, with maroon rules, stamped in dark blue, in a style imitating A1.1.a. *Dust jacket*: Not seen. Sheet bulk: title page: .173 mm., p. 183: .168 mm. *Publication*: 2,500 copies published October 1934. 75¢. Listed in *Publishers' Weekly*, 126 (27 October 1934), 1590. *Location*: RLT.

Note one: 10 pages of conjugate Grosset & Dunlap advertisements comprise pp. [335–344].

Note two: The Grosset files contain an invoice, 20 June 1934, for the purchase of 2,500 copies from Scribners. There is no record in the Grosset or Scribners files for subsequent Grosset printings.

A 1.1.f
First American edition, sixth printing [1934]

New York: Grosset & Dunlap, n.d. [1934]. viii + 334 + 10 pp. *Binding*: Same as A1.1.e. Sheet bulk: title page: .173 mm.; p. 183: .142 mm. *Location*: RLT.

A 1.1.g *South Moon Under*

Note: The sheet bulk and part of the contents of the 10 pages of conjugate advertisements, pp. [335–344], are different from A1.1.e. The priority of A1.1.e and A1.1.f have not been determined.

A 1.1.g
First American edition, seventh printing [1933?]

New York: Charles Scribners Sons, 1933. *Binding:* Same as A1.1.a. Sheet bulk: title page: .169 mm.; p. 183: .171 mm. *Location:* RLT.

Note: Typographical evidence (e.g., the batter '8' in p. '328') indicates that this printing follows the Grosset printings, A.1.1.e–f, which do not have batter in the '8', and precedes A1.1.h. This and all subsequent printings contain the batter '8'. The title page date of 1933 is incorrect. The date of printing would have to be 1934 or after.

A 1.1.h
First American edition, eighth printing [1937?]

New York: Grosset & Dunlap, n.d. [1937?]. *Binding:* Light green cloth. Sheet bulk: title page: .161 mm.; p. 183: .176 mm. *Location:* RLT.

Title page is the same as A1.1.e, except '*By arrangement with Charles Scribner's Sons*' follows 'PUBLISHERS NEW YORK'.

Note: Typographical evidence (e.g., the batter in 'mildly', p. 306, l. 35) indicates that this printing follows A1.1.g. The batter in 'mildly' is found in all subsequent printings. Listed in *CBI* and *Publishers' Weekly* as published in December 1937 under the series title 'NOVELS OF DISTINCTION'.

A 1.1.i
First American edition, ninth printing [1938?]

New York: Grosset & Dunlap, n.d. [1938?]. *Binding:* Light green cloth. Sheet bulk: title page: .182 mm.; p. 183: .173 mm. *Location:* RLT.

Note: Typographical evidence (e.g., the batter in 'myrtle', p. 2, l. 25) indicates that this printing follows A1.1.h. The batter in 'myrtle' is found in all subsequent printings. The statement on the arrangement for royalties on the front flap of the dust jacket is different from A1.1.h.

A 1.1.j
First American edition, tenth printing [1938?]

New York: Grosset & Dunlap, n.d. [1938?]. *Binding:* Green cloth. Sheet bulk: title page: .146 mm.; p. 183: .154 mm. *Location:* RLT.

Note: Typographical evidence (e.g., the shift in the letter 'l' in 'low', p. 1, l. 1) indicates that this printing follows A1.1.i. The shift in 'l' is found in all subsequent printings. The advertisement on the back of the dust jacket for Ernest Hemingway's *To Have and Have Not* (1937) suggests that the date of printing is 1937 or after. The statement on the arrangement for royalties on the front flap of the dust jacket is different from A1.1.i.

A 1.1.k
First American edition, eleventh printing [1938?]

New York: Grosset & Dunlap, n.d. [1938?]. *Binding*: Light green cloth. Sheet bulk: title page: .125 mm.; p. 183: .126 mm. *Location*: RLT.

Note one: Typographical evidence (e.g., the batter in 'him', p. 24, l. 35) indicates that this printing follows A1.1.j. The batter in 'him' is found in all subsequent printings. The advertisement for *The Yearling* (A3), published 1 April 1938, on the rear flap of the dust jacket suggests that the date of printing is 1938 or after. The statement on arrangements for royalties on the front flap of the dust jacket is different from A1.1.j.

Note two: All Grosset printings preceding A1.1.k are sewn in 8's. This and the following Grosset printings are sewn in 16's.

A 1.1.l
First American edition, twelfth printing [1940?]

New York: Grosset & Dunlap, n.d. [1940?]. *Binding*: Light green cloth. Sheet bulk: title page: .118 mm.; p. 183: .122 mm. *Location*: RLT.

Note: Typographical evidence (e.g., poor batter throughout) indicates that this printing follows A1.1.k. The advertisement on the rear flap of the dust jacket for *The Yearling* (A3), indicating that the novel has been awarded the Pulitzer Prize, and the advertisement on the back cover of the dust jacket for Richard Wright's *Native Son* (1940) suggest that the date of printing is 1940 or after. The statement on the arrangement for royalties on the front flap of the dust jacket is different from A1.1.k.

A 1.1.m
First American edition, thirteenth printing [194–?]

New York: Grosset & Dunlap, n.d. [194-?]. *Binding*: Olive cloth. Sheet bulk: title page: .156 mm.; p. 183: .146 mm. *Location*: RLT.

Note: The advertisement on the rear flap for *The Yearling* is the same as A1.1.k. The statement on arrangements for royalties on the front flap of the dust jacket states: 'Produced in full compliance with | wartime regulations'. There is a 'wartime conditions' statement on the title page.

A 1.1.n
First American edition, fourteenth printing [194–?]

New York: Grosset & Dunlap, n.d. [194–?]. *Binding*: Light green cloth. Sheet bulk: title page: .161 mm.; p. 183: .148 mm. *Location*: RLT.

Note: Typographical evidence (e.g., the batter in 'closer', p. 1, l. 3) indicates that this printing follows A1.1.m.

OTHER PRINTINGS WITHIN THE FIRST AMERICAN EDITION

A 1.1.o
First American edition, fifteenth printing (1977)

[rule frame, title in hollow font] SOUTH MOON | UNDER | By | Marjorie Kinnan Rawlings | [device] | NORMAN S. BERG, Publisher | "Sellanraa" | Dunwoody, Georgia | 1977

Facsimile of A1.1.b. 22.4 × 14.8 pp. *Binding*: Brown cloth. *Location*: RLT.

A 1.1.p
First American edition, sixteenth printing [1989?]

[Mattituck, New York: Amereon Ltd., n.d.]. *Binding*: Emerald cloth. *Location*: RLT.

Note: Unauthorized facsimile of A1.1.a. The Amereon catalogue (1989) claims that 365 copies have been reproduced on acid-free paper.

A 1.2
First British edition, only printing (1933)

SOUTH MOON UNDER

BY

MARJORIE KINNAN RAWLINGS

LONDON
FABER & FABER LIMITED
24 RUSSELL SQUARE

A 1.2: 18.8 × 12.5 cm.

> FIRST PUBLISHED IN SEPTEMBER MCMXXXIII
> BY FABER & FABER LIMITED
> 24 RUSSELL SQUARE LONDON W.C.I
> PRINTED IN GREAT BRITAIN
> BY BUTLER & TANNER LIMITED
> FROME AND LONDON
> ALL RIGHTS RESERVED

[1-4] 5-6 [7-8] 9-352

[A]^8 B-I^8 K-U^8 X-Y^8; 176 leaves.

Contents: p. 1: half title; p. 2: blank; p. 3: title page; p. 4: copyright page; pp. 5-6: 'PUBLISHERS'[sic] NOTE'; p. 7: 8-line description of the novel; p. 8: blank; pp. 9-352: text.

Typography and paper: (14.3) × 8.9 cm. Wove paper. No running heads.

Binding: Emerald calico-textured cloth. Front and back covers: blank; gold-stamped spine: 'SOUTH | MOON | UNDER | [device] | MARJORIE | KINNAN | RAWLINGS | FABER | AND FABER'. All edges trimmed.

Dust jacket: Front cover: '[on blue background in white] 'MARJORIE KIN-NAN | RAWLINGS | [on yellow circle background in red] SOUTH | MOON | UNDER | [on blue background in white] FABER AND FABER'; spine: on blue background: '[on yellow circle background in red] SOUTH | MOON | UNDER | [on blue background in white] FABER | & FABER'; back cover: '[on white background in red] THE FABER LIBRARY | A UNIFORM SERIES OF CON-TEMPORARY CLASSICS | EACH VOLUME | 3s. 6d. | net | [list of 19 works] | [star device] | FABER & FABER LIMITED | 24 RUSSELL SQUARE, LON-DON, W.C.1'; front flap: '[on white background in red] 'South Moon Under | *by* | MARJORIE KINNAN RAWLINGS | [28-line description of the novel] | [diago-nal dotted line in bottom right corner] 7s.6d. | net'; rear flap: on white back-ground in red: 9-line blurb for Faber & Faber.

Publication: 2,000 copies published on 14 September 1933. 7s.6d.

Printing: Butler and Tanner.

Locations: BL (deposit-stamped 14 September 1933), Bodleian (deposit-stamped 23 September 1933), FU (dj).

Note one: In a memo, 3 March 1933, to Maxwell Perkins, William G. Low outlined Faber's terms: £40 advance against a royalty of 10% to 2,000 copies, 12½% to 5,000, 15% to 10,000, and 20% thereafter. If 10,000 copies should be sold, the royalty on the next book would begin at 20%. Faber would receive options on the next two books by Rawlings. Brandt and Brandt, Rawlings's

Dust jacket for A1.2

18   A 1.3 *South Moon Under*

agents, agreed, even though Rawlings in a letter to Perkins, 3 March, complained about the options in particular and the handling of the foreign rights in general by Scribners (Scribners Archive).

Note three: British sales were disappointing. Just over 1,000 copies were sold before the book was remaindered in April 1936. Rawlings was offered remainder copies at 7d. (Faber and Faber Archives, Scribners Archives).

Note four: A Scribners memo, 10 October 1933, mentions sending, addressee not given, an "English paper bound copy of 'South Moon Under' " (that is, a bound set of Faber proofs). No such copy has been located.

A 1.3
Second American edition, only printing, "Armed Services Edition" [1945]

[title page enclosed in a decorated frame and divided by a vertical rule in the center]: [on left half of the page]: 'PUBLISHED BY ARRANGEMENT WITH | CHARLES SCRIBNER'S SONS, NEW YORK | *All rights reserved. No part of this book* | *may be reproduced in any form without* | *the permission of Charles Scribner's Sons* | COPYRIGHT, 1933, BY CHARLES SCRIBNER'S SONS | *Manufactured in the United States of America*'; [on right half of the page]: 'SOUTH MOON | UNDER | *by* | Marjorie Kinnan Rawlings | *Editions for the Armed Services, Inc.* | A NON-PROFIT ORGANIZATION ESTABLISHED BY | THE COUNCIL ON BOOKS IN WAR TIME, NEW YORK | [outside the frame at the bottom left] '724'.

11.4 × 16.7 cm.

[1–2] 3–318 [319–320]

Stapled; [1–10]^{16}; 160 leaves.

Contents: p. 1: title and copyright page; p. 2: author's summary; pp. 3–318: text; pp. 319–320: biographical notice: '*About the Author*'.

Binding: Multicolor wrappers. '724' printed in upper left corner of the front cover and at the bottom of the spine. All edges trimmed.

Locations: FU, PM, RLT.

Note: Armed Services Edition, no. 724, not for sale. The last publication date found in *A List of the First 534 Books Published for American Armed Services Overseas* (New York: Editions for Armed Services, Inc., [1945]) is January 1945. Although no precise dates are given in *Editions for the Armed Services, Inc.: A History* (New York: Editions for the Armed Forces, n.d.), p. 63, no. 724 is in the "V" series which was published late in 1945, approximately 125,000 copies.

Cover for A 1.3

Cover for A 1.4

OTHER EDITIONS

A 1.4
Third American edition, only printing [1945]

[rule, short rule, shorter rule] SOUTH MOON | UNDER | Marjorie Kinnan Rawlings | [publisher's device: rooster enclosed in a circle] | BANTAM BOOKS | NEW YORK | [three rules]

319 pp. Published November 1945. *Binding*: Wrappers. Edges stained in red. 'A BANTAM BOOK', no. 10. 25¢. *Location*: RLT (4).

Note: On 27 July 1951, Scribners gave permission to Bantam Books to do a British Empire Edition for distribution outside the United Kingdom (Scribners File-Cards). No copy of such a printing has been located.

A 1.6.a *South Moon Under*

Cover for A 1.6.a

A 1.5
Fourth American edition, only printing [1972]

New York: Charles Scribner's Sons, n.d. [1972]. vi + 270 pp. *Binding*: Wrappers. '*The Scribner Library*, CONTEMPORARY CLASSICS', no. SL387. 'A-8.72(C)'. $2.95. *Location*: RLT (2).

A 1.6.a
Fifth American edition, first printing [1974]

St. Simons Island, Georgia: Mockingbird Books, n.d. [1974]. vi + 249 pp. Published September 1974. *Binding*: Wrappers. 'A Mockingbird Book', no. 24199. $1.75. *Location*: RLT.

Note: 3,600 copies were printed in September 1974.

A 1.6.b
Fifth American edition, second printing [n.d.]

St. Simons Island, Georgia: Mockingbird Books, n.d. *Location*: From publisher's records, *not seen*.

Note: 6,400 copies printed.

A 1.6.c
Fifth American edition, third printing [1981]

St. Simons Island, Georgia: Mockingbird Books, n.d. [1981]. Published March 1981. *Binding*: Wrappers. 'A Mockingbird Book', no. 6020. $2.25. *Location*: RLT.

Note: 6,600 copies were printed in March 1981.

A 2.1.a *Golden Apples*

A 2 GOLDEN APPLES

A 2.1.a
First American edition, first printing (1935)

GOLDEN APPLES

By

Marjorie Kinnan Rawlings

Author of "South Moon Under"

NEW YORK
CHARLES SCRIBNER'S SONS
1935

A 2.1.a: 18.8 × 13.0 cm.

> COPYRIGHT, 1935, BY
> MARJORIE KINNAN RAWLINGS
>
> Printed in the United States of America
>
> *All rights reserved. No part of this book may be reproduced in any form without the permission of Charles Scribner's Sons*
>
> A
>
>

[i–viii] 1–352

[1–21]⁸ [22]⁴ [23]⁸; 180 leaves.

Contents: pp. i–ii: blank; p. iii: half title: 'GOLDEN APPLES'; p. iv: blank; p. v: title page; p. vi: copyright page; p. vii: section title: 'GOLDEN APPLES'; p. viii: blank; pp. 1–352: text.

Typography and paper: 15.5 (14.8) × 8.9 cm.; wove paper; 35 lines per page. Running heads: rectos: pp. 3–7, 11–15, 19–55, 59–89, 93–101, 105–107, 111–131, 135–175, 179–185, 189–203, 207–219, 223–279, 283–289, 293–303, 307–311, 315–317, 321–323, 327–351: 'GOLDEN APPLES'; pp. 2–22, 26–32, 36–48, 52–64, 68–70, 74–80, 84–96, 100–118, 122–126, 130–144, 148–162, 166–196, 200–224, 228–234, 238–246, 250–254, 258–260, 264–296, 300–330, 334–338, 342–346, 350–352: 'GOLDEN APPLES'.

Binding: Light orange calico-textured cloth. Front cover: goldstamped thick-thin-thin-thick vertical rule along spine top to bottom; '[at bottom third: goldstamped thin double rule] | [blackstamped, partly covering the rule] Golden | [goldstamped thin double rule] | [blackstamped, with the A overlapping the G of Golden] Apples | [goldstamped thin double rule, thin double rule] | [in black] MARJORIE KINNAN RAWLINGS | [goldstamped thin double rule]'; spine: '[goldstamped thin-thin double rule] | [blackstamped] Golden | [blackstamped] Apples | [goldstamped thin double, thin double rule] | [blackstamped] MARJORIE | [blackstamped] KINNAN | [blackstamped] RAWLINGS | [goldstamped thin double rule, then four sets of goldstamped thin double rule] | [blackstamped] SCRIBNERS | [goldstamped thin double rule]'; back cover: blank. Top edge trimmed and stained light green. Bottom edge trimmed. Fore-edge rough trimmed.

Dust jacket for A 2.1.a

Dust jacket: Front cover: on black background: illustration of orange tree (oranges in gold, leaves in shades of green, blossoms in white) at upper left extending onto spine; '[at left center in white] GOLDEN | APPLES | [gold rule extending from right margin to center] | [at bottom right in white] A NOVEL BY THE AUTHOR OF | [at bottom right in white] SOUTH MOON UNDER | [gold rule extending from right margin to center] | [at bottom in white] MARJO-RIE KINNAN RAWLINGS'; spine: on black background: continuation of orange tree illustration; [title in white] GOLDEN | APPLES | [gold rule] | author and publisher in white] MARJORIE | KINNAN | RAWLINGS | SCRIB-NERS'; back cover: on white background: '[at top center breaking a double rule frame in green] GOLDEN APPLES | [inside frame in black] by | Marjorie Kinnan Rawlings | Author of "South Moon Under" | [28-line description of the novel] | *Published by Charles Scribner's Sons*'; front flap: on white background in black except title in green: '[at upper right] $2.50 | GOLDEN APPLES | by | Marjorie Kinnan Rawlings | [file photo of Rawlings] | [20-line biography]'; rear flap: on white background in black except title in green: 'Marjorie Kinnan Rawlings' | · *first novel* | [in green] SOUTH MOON UNDER | *A Book-of-the-Month Club Selection and* | *acclaimed by leading critics.* | [30 lines consisting of four blurbs]'.

Publication: 10,150 copies published 1 October. Scribners File-Cards lists publication as 4 October. Listed in *Publishers' Weekly*, 128 (5 October 1935), 1301, and announced as 'Just Published' in the *New York Times Book Review* on 6 October. $2.50.

Printing: Printed and bound by the Scribner Press.

Locations: BL (deposit-stamped 29 October 1935), DLC (deposit-stamped 12 October 1935); FU (dj), InU (dj), PM (dj), RLT (dj), RM (dj).

Note one: 11,700 dust jackets were printed on 1 October 1935.

Note two: Scribners File-Cards indicates that two binding dummies were ordered on 23 November 1934 and were delivered on 15 January 1935.

Note three: A notation in Scribners Records reads: 'Plate correction to be | made—3/17/37/'. Since there were no Scribners printings after 1935, this correction was not made.

Note four: A notation in Scribners Records reads: 'Plates melted | 8/10/55'.

Note five: A Scribners Records entry for 7 August 1935 [1936?] notes that net sales were 15,240 copies, including 600 in wrappers. This number would account for the sales of the first two printings, including oversheets. No copies in wrappers have been located.

A 2.1.a *Golden Apples*

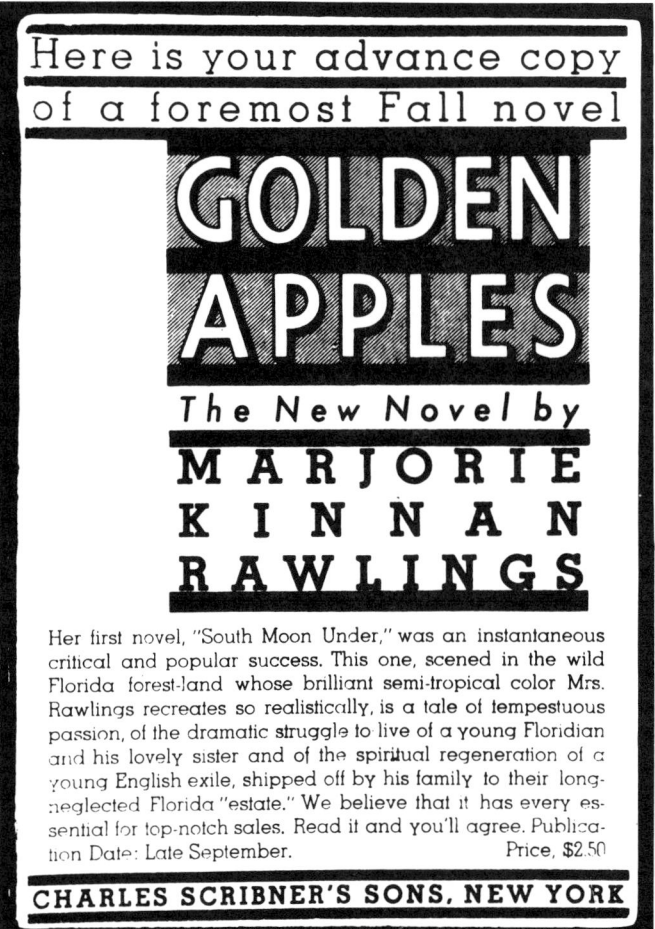

Cover of advance copy of A 2.1.a

Note six: Two advance copies have been seen:

18.8 × 13.2 cm.

[i–viii] 1–352.

[1–21]⁸ [22]⁴ [23]⁸; 180 leaves.

Contents: Same as A2.1.a.

Typography and paper: Same as A2.1.a.

Binding: Orange wrappers in black lettering: '[thick rule] | Here is your advance copy | [thick rule] | of a foremost Fall novel | [rule, thick in the middle] | [title in hollow font on diagonal rule background] GOLDEN [short thick rule] | APPLES | [short thick rule] | *The New Novel by* | [short thick rule] | MARJORIE | KINNAN | RAWLINGS | [short thick rule] | [10-line description of publication data] | [thick rule] | CHARLES SCRIBNER'S SONS, NEW YORK | [thick rule]'. The publication data projects: 'Publica- | tion Date: Late September. $2.50'.

Locations: RLT, RM.

A 2.1.b
First American edition, second printing (1935)

New York: Charles Scribner's Sons, 1935. 5,050 copies were ordered on 2 October 1935. The Scribners seal is retained, but the 'A' is removed from the copyright page. *Locations*: DLC, FU, PM.

Note one: 5,350 dust jackets were ordered on 22 October 1935.

Note two: The second printing was announced in the *New York Times Book Review* on 20 October 1935.

Note three: A presentation copy from Rawlings of this printing, which she marked up for serial publication in *Cosmopolitan* (C599), is at FU.

A 2.1.c
First American edition, third printing [1944]

[all enclosed in rule frame] | [title in hollow font] GOLDEN APPLES | By | Marjorie Kinnan Rawlings | Author of "South Moon Under" | [publisher's device enclosed in circle] | CLEVELAND AND NEW YORK | THE WORLD PUBLISHING COMPANY

vi + 352 pp. Copyright page: '*First Printing February 1944*'. 'Forum Books'. $1. *Binding*: Dark green cloth. Top edge stained reddish purple. *Location*: RLT.

Note: CBI lists a printing published by Grosset and Dunlap in 1937. This printing, if it exists, has not been located.

A 2.1.d
First American edition, fourth printing [1944]

Cleveland and New York: World Publishing Company, n.d. [1944]. Copyright page: '*Second Printing July 1944*'. *Binding*: Same as A2.1.c, except top edge stained green. *Location*: RLT.

Note: A copy has been seen with no staining on top edge (RLT).

A2.1.g *Golden Apples*

A2.1.e
First American edition, fifth printing [1946]

Cleveland and New York: World Publishing Company, n.d. [1946]. Copyright page: '*Third Printing April 1946*'. *Binding*: Blue cloth. Top edge stained same as A2.1.c. *Location*: RLT.

OTHER PRINTINGS WITHIN THE FIRST AMERICAN EDITION

A2.1.f
First American edition, sixth printing [1988]

Jacksonville, Florida: San Marco Book Store, n.d. [1988]. $19.95. *Location*: RLT.

Note: Facsimile reprint of A2.1.a, 1,100 copies. Binding and dust jacket imitate those of A1.1.a.

A2.1.g
First American edition, seventh printing [1989?]

[Mattituck, N.Y.: Amereon Ltd., n.d. (1989?)]. *Binding*: Black cloth. *Location*: RLT.

Note: This is an unauthorized facsimile reprint of A2.1.a.

A 2.2
First British edition, only printing [1939]

Marjorie Kinnan Rawlings

GOLDEN APPLES

William Heinemann Ltd
London :: Toronto

A 2.2: 19.0 × 12.5 cm.

A 2.2 *Golden Apples* 31

> PRINTED IN GREAT BRITAIN AT THE WINDMILL PRESS
> KINGSWOOD, SURREY

[i–vi] 1–346

[A]^8 B–I^8 K–U^8 W–X^8; 176 leaves.

Contents: p. i: half title: '*GOLDEN APPLES*'; p. ii: bibliograpy: '*Also by* | *MARJORIE KINNAN RAWLINGS* | [short rule] | THE YEARLING'; p. iii: title page; p. iv: copyright page; p. v: section title: '*GOLDEN APPLES*'; p. vi: blank; pp. 1–346: text.

Typography and paper: 15.3 (14.6) × 9.3 cm.; wove paper; 35 lines per page. Running heads: rectos: pp. 3–7, 11–21, 25–45, 49–61, 65–67, 71–77, 81–93, 97–115, 119–123, 127–141, 145–159, 163–193, 197–215, 219–291, 295–297, 301–305, 309–311, 315–317, 321–345: '*GOLDEN APPLES*'; versos: pp. 2–14, 18–30, 34–52, 56–86, 90–98, 102–104, 108–128, 132–172, 176–182, 186–200, 204–220, 224–230, 234–242, 246–250, 254–256, 260–274, 278–284, 288–324, 328–332, 336–340, 344–346: '*GOLDEN APPLES*'.

Binding: Light orange calico-textured cloth; front cover: blank; spine: gold-stamped on mauve (reddish purple) background: 'GOLDEN | APPLES | Marjorie | Kinnan | Rawlings | HEINEMANN'; back cover: blindstamped windmill device in lower right corner. Light brown endpapers. All edges trimmed.

Dust jacket: Front cover: green lettering on white background: '[title on orange designed background] Golden | Apples | A NOVEL BY THE AUTHOR OF | [title superimposed on an illustration in orange of a boy running with a fawn] THE YEARLING | MARJORIE KINNAN RAWLINGS'; spine: '[title and name in green on orange designed background continuous with front cover] Golden | Apples | *by* | MARJORIE | KINNAN | RAWLINGS | AUTHOR OF | The | Yearling | HEINEMANN'; back cover: enclosed in orange thick-thin-thick rule frame in green: 'THE YEARLING | by | Marjorie Kinnan Rawlings | *SOME PRESS OPINIONS* | [23 lines of blurbs] | 6th LARGE PRINTING. 8*s*. 6*d. net*'; front flap: on white background in green: 'GOLDEN APPLES | by | Marjorie Kinnan | Rawlings | [38-line description of the novel] | [price in lower right corner, clipped from RLT copy]'; rear flap: 'The success of | THE YEARLING | [32-line blurb on *The Yearling*] | *Now turn to the back of this | wrapper for other opinions about | this book.*'

Publication: 5,000 copies published on 31 July 1939. 7s.6d.

Printing: Windmill Press.

Locations: BL (deposit-stamped 31 July 1939), Bodleian (deposit-stamped 18 August 1939), RLT (dj).

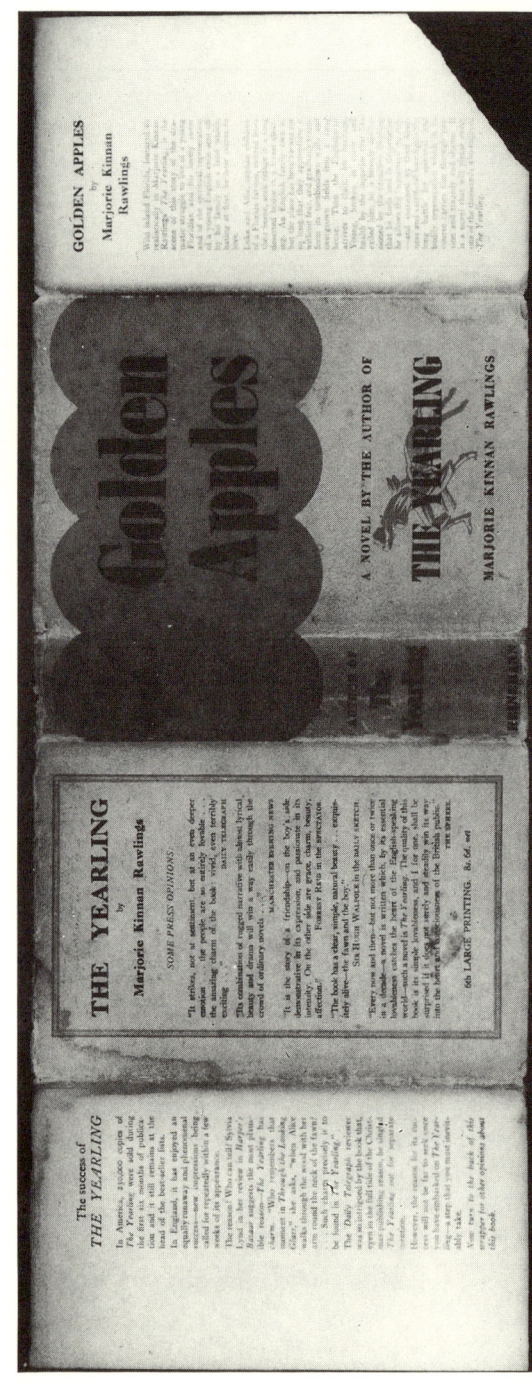

Dust jacket for A 2.2

A 2.3 *Golden Apples*

Cover for A 2.3

Note: Printed in braille. 6 vols. Victoria Park, Western Australia: Association for the Blind, n.d.

OTHER EDITION

A 2.3
Second English edition, only printing [1962]

Golden Apples | [french rule] | MARJORIE KINNAN RAWLINGS | WORLD DISTRIBUTORS LONDON

255 pp. Published 1962. 'CONSUL BOOKS', no. 1150. *Binding*: Multicolor wrappers. 3s.6d. *Locations*: BL (deposit-stamped 7 January 1962); RLT.

Note: An advertisement on p. 1, repeated on the back cover, erroneously describes *The Yearling* as 'that masterly story of a young girl and | her horse . . . which millions will remember as | a film—the film, incidentally, in which Miss | Elizabeth Taylor first achieved prominence as | a star'.

A3 THE YEARLING

A3.1.a
First American edition, first printing (1938)

> Marjorie Kinnan Rawlings
>
> # THE
> # YEARLING
>
>
>
> Decorations by
> Edward Shenton
>
> ─────────────────────
> CHARLES SCRIBNER'S SONS
> NEW YORK : 1938

A 3.1.a: 28.0 × 14.5 cm.

> COPYRIGHT, 1938, BY
> MARJORIE KINNAN RAWLINGS
>
> Printed in the United States of America
>
> *All rights reserved. No part of this book may be reproduced in any form without the permission of Charles Scribner's Sons*
>
> A
>
>

[i–viii] 1–428

[1–13]¹⁶ [14]¹⁰; 218 leaves.

Contents: p. i: blank; p. ii: 'BOOKS BY MARJORIE KINNAN RAWLINGS | [short rule] | *The Yearling* | *Golden Apples* | *South Moon Under* | [short rule] | CHARLES SCRIBNER'S SONS'; p. iii: half title: 'THE YEARLING'; p. iv: blank; p. v: title page; p. vi: copyright page; p. vii: section title: 'THE YEARLING'; p. viii: blank; pp. 1–428: text.

Typography and paper: 15.8 (15.3) × 10.2 cm.; wove paper; 34 lines per page. Running heads: rectos: pp. 3–27, 31–43, 47–51, 55–67, 71–95, 99–137, 141–157, 161–191, 195–237, 241–269, 273–277, 281–289, 293–327, 331–369, 373–389, 393–401, 405–409, 413–427: 'THE YEARLING'; versos: pp. 2–14, 18–20, 24–56, 58–72, 76–84, 88–120, 124–130, 134–176, 180–212, 216–218, 222–262, 266–310, 314–366, 370–376, 380–382, 386–428: 'THE YEARLING'.

Binding: Light grayish brown (beige) calico-textured cloth. Front cover: stamped in green: 'Marjorie Kinnan Rawlings | THE | YEARLING | [illustration of young boy holding a fawn]'; spine: stamped in green: 'Marjorie | Kinnan | Rawlings | [rule] | THE | YEARLING | SCRIBNERS'; back cover: blank. Light yellow endpapers. Top edge trimmed and stained green; fore-edge untrimmed; bottom edge trimmed.

Dust jacket: On a dark yellow background: '[white rule continuous with the spine] | [white-green-white-green-white-green-white rule continuous with the spine and broken in the middle by 'THE [in black] | YEARLING [in black] | [on a green background: illustration of a boy holding a fawn enclosed in a white

Dust jacket for A 3.1.a

box frame with a white rule at the top and bottom of the illustration] | [a grouping of egrets in white moving toward and continuous with the spine] | Marjorie Kinnan Rawlings [in black] | AUTHOR OF | [white-green-white-green-white-green-white rule continuous with the spine and broken in the middle] SOUTH MOON UNDER [in green on a white background] | [white rule continuous with the spine]'; spine: '[white rule continuous with the front cover] | [white-green-white-green-white-green-white rule continuous with the front cover] | THE [in black] | YEARLING [in black] | [white-green-white rule] | Marjorie [in black] | Kinnan [in black] | Rawlings [in black] | [illustration of an egret continuous with the spine] | [white-green rule] | SCRIBNERS [in black on a white background] | [green-white rule] | [white-green-white-green-white-green-white rule continuous with the front cover] | [white rule continuous with the front cover]'; rear cover: in black on a white background: 'THE YEARLING | *by* Marjorie Kinnan Rawlings | *author of "South Moon Under," etc.* | [27-line description of the novel] | *A Book-of-the-Month Club Selection*'; front flap: in black on a white background: '[upper right corner, in black] $2.50 | The Yearling | [photograph of Rawlings seated] | Marjorie Kinnan Rawlings | [19-line biography of Rawlings] | [rule] | *"The Yearling" is described on the back of this jacket*'; back flap: in black on a white background: 'Marjorie Kinnan | RAWLINGS | *has also written* | SOUTH MOON | UNDER | *A Book-of-the-Month Club Selection* | [2-line, 7-line blurbs of *South Moon Under*] | [asterisk-like device] | GOLDEN APPLES | [2-line, 4-line blurbs of *Golden Apples*]'.

Publication: 30,000 copies ordered on 1 April 1939. Announced in *Publishers' Weekly* 133 (29 January 1938), 605; advertised 133 (5 March 1938); and reviewed 133 (2 April 1938), 1499. Copyright #A117111.

Printing: Printed and bound by the Scribner Press.

Locations: DLC (deposit-stamped 13 April 1938), InU, PM (2, dj), RLT (3, dj), RM (2, dj).

Note one: Each chapter is headed by an illustration by Edward Shenton.

Note two: Two saleman's dummies were made up on 13 January 1938, one set of bound galleys on 24 February, and six advance copies on 22 March (Scribners File-Cards). No advance copies have been located. A salesman's dummy is owned by ViU.

Note three: The Scribners Records separates the accumulated sales of the trade edition from the Book-of-the-Month Club. For example, on 29 June 1938, 51,023 copies of the trade edition and 97,000 of the Book-of-the-Month Club had been sold; and by 16 November, 137,876 of the trade and 103,000 of the BOMC editions. By 28 May 1939, 187,833 copies of the trade and 108,000 of the BOMC edition had been sold. The sales of the original trade edition dropped sharply after 1940, no doubt because of competing editions like the

Pulitzer Prize Edition and the School Edition, as indicated by the total sales of 191,050 recorded by 1944.

Note four: The total sales of *The Yearling,* including this and all other editions through 1945, are detailed in the following memo (FU): No. 1 bestseller for twenty-three consecutive weeks from 29 May to 23 November 1938; it was a bestseller for ninety-three consecutive weeks from 17 April 1938 to 11 February 1940; it sold 60,000 copies in sixty days; 177,000 in six months; 240,000 in the first year; and 502,000 by July 1945. These figures are confirmed by Scribners advertisements. For example, in the *New York Times Book Review,* 11 December 1938, less than a year after publication, Scribners was claiming 250,000 sold. By the end of December, Scribners in the *Chicago Daily Tribune,* 31 December 1938, had raised the number to 260,000. One year after publication in its *Shoptalk* (April 1939), 1, and in the *New York Herald Tribune Books,* 2 April 1939, Scribners boasted 265,000 sales, claiming 1938 as " 'The Yearling's' year." In the MGM archives, Culver City, California, there is a telegram, 19 April 1946, from Olin Clark to W. S. Fadiman on sales to date: "700,000 including Trade 200,000, BOM [Book-of-the-Month Club] 108,000, and Armed Services 190,000."

Note five: A later dust jacket has been seen: front cover: left center: 'Awarded | Pulitzer | Prize | 1939'. Front flap same as the first issue; back flap contains an advertisement for Taylor Caldwell's *Dynasty of Death,* published 16 September 1938. *Location:* RM.

Note six: A manuscript, galleys, and various working notes of *The Yearling* are at the University of Florida.

Note seven: Printed in braille. 5 vols. Burwood, New South Wales: Royal Blind Society. n.d.

LATER PRINTINGS WITHIN THE FIRST AMERICAN EDITION

A 3.1.b
First American edition, second printing, for the Book-of-the-Month Club (1938)

New York: Charles Scribner's Sons, 1938. 82,000 copies. [3] April. *Locations:* PM, RLT (3), RM.

Note: The "A" on the copyright page and the price on the front flap of the dust jacket are removed on all Book-of-the-Month Club copies. No difference in text among BOMC printings has been noted. The publication date was announced in the *New York Herald Tribune Books* as 3 April 1938.

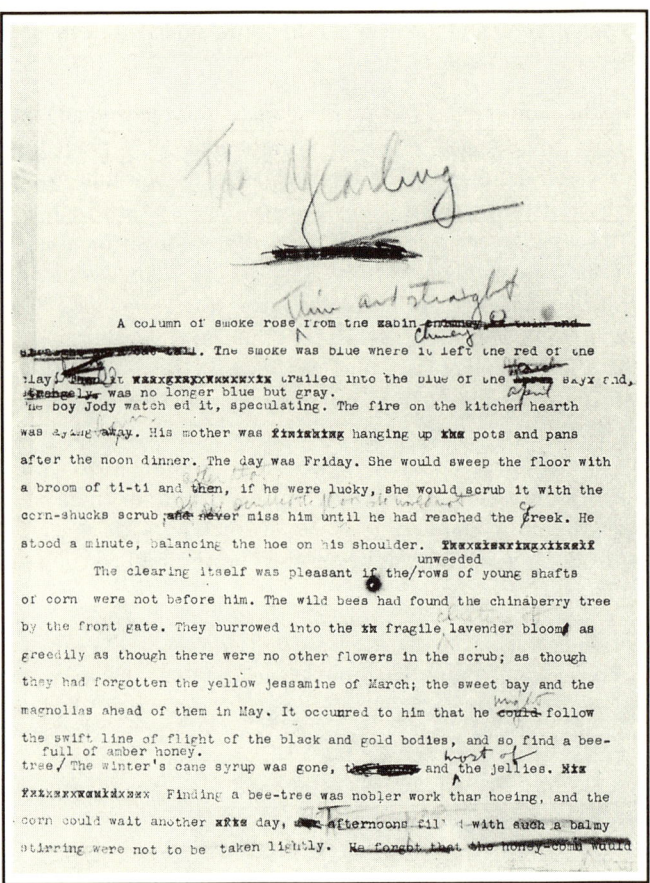

First manuscript page of A 3

A3.1.c
First American edition, third printing (1938)

New York: Charles Scribner's Sons, 1938. $2.50. 5,000 copies. 28 April. *Location*: From the copyright page of A3.1.aa, Scribners Records, *not seen*.

A3.1.d
First American edition, fourth printing, for the Book-of-the-Month Club (1938)

New York: Charles Scribner's Sons, 1938. 10,000 copies. [May] 1938. *Location*: From Scribners Records, *not seen*.

A3.1.f *The Yearling*

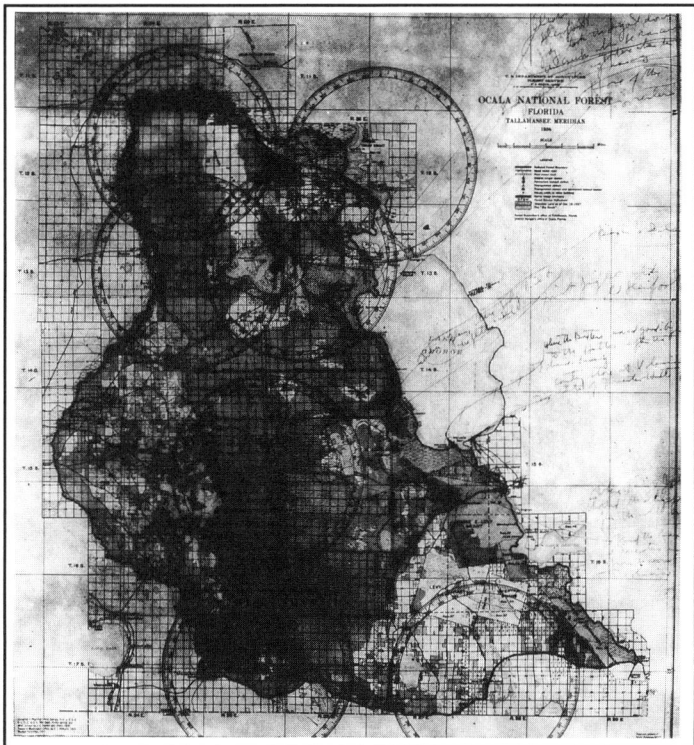

Map of *"The Yearling* country"

A3.1.e
First American edition, fifth printing, for the Book-of-the-Month Club (1938)

New York: Charles Scribner's Sons, 1938. 5,000 copies. [May] 1938. *Location*: From Scribners Records, *not seen*.

A3.1.f
First American edition, sixth printing (1938)

New York: Charles Scribner's Sons, 1938. $2.50. 5,150 copies. 26 May. *Locations*: From the copyright page of A3.1.aa, Scribners Records, *not seen*.

Note: A discrepancy between the number of copies ordered and the number published occurs infrequently in the Scribners Records. It is clear that on occasion Scribners chose to bind only a portion of the sheet stock, leaving the remainder for what they called "oversheets."

A3.1.g
First American edition, seventh printing (1938)

New York: Charles Scribner's Sons, 1938. $2.50. 10,000 copies. 17 June. *Location*: RLT.

A3.1.h
First American edition, eighth printing (1938)

New York: Charles Scribner's Sons, 1938. $2.50. 10,125 copies. 8 July. *Locations*: From the copyright page of A3.1.aa, Scribners Records, *not seen*.

A3.1.i
First American edition, ninth printing (1938)

New York: Charles Scribner's Sons, 1938. $2.50. 10,000 copies. 12 July. *Location*: RLT.

A3.1.j
First American edition, tenth printing (1938)

New York: Charles Scribner's Sons, 1938. $2.50. 10,150 copies. 28 July. *Location*: RLT.

A3.1.k
First American edition, eleventh printing (1938)

New York: Charles Scribner's Sons, 1938. $2.50. 10,200 copies. [August] 1938. *Location*: From copyright page of A3.1.aa, Scribners Records, *not seen*.

A3.1.l
First American edition, twelfth printing (1938)

New York: Charles Scribner's Sons, 1938. $2.50. 12,100 copies. [September] 1938. *Location*: RLT.

A3.1.m
First American edition, thirteenth printing (1938)

New York: Charles Scribner's Sons, 1938. $2.50. 10,250 copies. 21 September. *Location*: From copyright page of A3.1.aa, Scribners Records, *not seen*.

A3.1.n
First American edition, fourteenth printing (1938)

New York: Charles Scribner's Sons, 1938. $2.50. 11,000 copies. 25 October. *Locations*: From copyright page of A3.1.aa, Scribners Records, *not seen*.

A3.1.u *The Yearling* 43

A3.1.o
First American edition, fifteenth printing, for the Book-of-the-Month Club (1938)

New York: Charles Scribner's Sons, 1938. 6,000 copies. [October] 1938. *Locations*: From Scribners Records, *not seen*.

A3.1.p
First American edition, sixteenth printing (1938)

New York: Charles Scribner's Sons, 1938. $2.50. 11,000 copies. 2 November. *Locations*: From copyright page of A3.1.aa, Scribners Records, *not seen*.

A3.1.q
First American edition, seventeenth printing (1938)

New York: Charles Scribner's Sons, 1938. $2.50. 10,200 copies. 2 November. *Locations*: From copyright page of A3.1.aa, Scribners Records, *not seen*.

A3.1.r
First American edition, eighteenth printing (1938)

New York: Charles Scribner's Sons, 1938. $2.50. 10,350 copies. 20 December. *Location*: RLT.

A3.1.s
First American edition, nineteenth printing, for the Book-of-the-Month Club [1939]

New York: Charles Scribner's Sons, 1939. 5,000 copies. [December] 1938. *Locations*: From Scribners Records, *not seen*.

A3.1.t
First American edition, twentieth printing (1939)

New York: Charles Scribner's Sons, 1939. $2.50. 12,950 copies. 5 May. *Locations*: From copyright page of A3.1.aa, Scribners Records, *not seen*.

A3.1.u
First American edition, twenty-first printing (1939)

New York: Charles Scribner's Sons, 1939. $2.50. *Locations*: From the copyright page of A3.1.aa, Scribners Records, *not seen*.

Note: Scribners Records enters A3.1.t and A3.1.u as separate printings (Scribners printings no. 17–18), but lists the combined print total for the two as

44   A3.1.v *The Yearling*

12,900 copies. The copyright page of A3.1.aa lists them as separate printings (nos. 17–18), both produced in May.

A3.1.v
First American edition, twenty-second printing (1939)

New York: Charles Scribner's Sons, 1939. $2.50. 5,100 copies. 4 October. *Locations*: From copyright page of A3.1.aa, Scribners Records, *not seen*.

A3.1.w
First American edition, twenty-third printing (1939)

New York: Charles Scribner's Sons, 1939. $2.50. 5,300 copies. 14 December. *Locations*: From copyright page of A3.1.aa, Scribners Records, *not seen*.

A3.1.x
First American edition, twenty-fourth printing (1940)

New York: Charles Scribner's Sons, 1940. $2.50. 5,090 copies. 14 May. *Locations*: From copyright page of A3.1.aa, Scribners Records, *not seen*.

Note: Scribners Records lists the date of publication as 14 March, which is an entry error.

A3.1.y$_1$
First edition, "Popular Edition," twenty-fifth printing, American issue (1940)

THE | YEARLING | By | Marjorie Kinnan Rawlings | Author of «When the Whippoorwill—», «Golden Apples», | and «South Moon Under» | [illustration of boy holding a fawn] | Decorations by Edward Shenton | [rule] | CHARLES SCRIBNER'S SONS | NEW YORK : 1940

iv + 428 pp.

Contents: p. i: title page; p. ii: copyright page; p. iii: section title: 'THE YEARLING'; then same as A3.1.a.

Typography and paper: Same as A3.1.a.

Binding: Same as A3.1.a, except light bluish green calico-textured cloth. Blue coated endpapers on one side only. Top edge trimmed and stained blue. Fore-edge rough trimmed. Bottom edge trimmed.

Dust jacket: Front cover: background: blue sky at top and yellowish brown earth at the middle and bottom continuous with the spine: '[figure of a boy and a fawn running with a house and hammock scene in the background] | THE] | YEARLING [both in brown oriental-like lettering surrounded in white] | Marjorie Kinnan Rawlings [in blue on white background] | DECORATIONS by

A 3.1.y *The Yearling*

Front of dust jacket for A 3.1.y₁

EDWARD SHENTON [in brown] | POPULAR EDITION [in red on white rule background]'; spine: [title and name in white on blue background] THE | YEARLING | MARJORIE | KINNAN | RAWLINGS | SCRIBNER'S [blue on white rule background]'; back cover: in light purple on white background: '[photograph of Rawlings standing at a fence gate] | *Photo. by Mrs. Fred. E. Noble* | Marjorie Kinnan Rawlings | [3-line description of the photograph] | CHARLES SCRIBNER'S SONS · NEW YORK [in blue]'; front flap: on white background: '*Popular Edition $1.29* [in brown] | The Yearling [in blue] | *by* [in brown] | Marjorie Kinnan Rawlings [in brown] | *with jacket and chapter head-*

ings by [in orange] | *Edward Shenton* [in orange] | [22-line description of the novel in brown]'; rear flap: on white background: '[first two lines of a 17-line description in brown] | When the [in orange] | Whippoorwill [in orange] | *by* [in brown] | Marjorie Kinnan Rawlings [in blue] | [the rest of the 17-line description in brown]'.

Publication: 51,000 published 30 September 1940. Scribners Records lists date as 9 September. *Publishers' Weekly*, 138 (21 September 1940), 1,073, projects the publication date as '*September 9th*', then later lists the date as October. $1.29.

Location: RLT (2).

A3.1.y$_2$
First edition, "Popular Edition," twenty-fifth printing, Canadian issue (1940)

Toronto: Reginald Saunders, 1940.

The title leaf is a cancel. Pagination, collation, contents, and typography are the same as A3.1.y$_1$.

Binding: Three styles have been noted, priority undetermined:

Binding A: Same as A3.1.a, except 'SAUNDERS' substituted for 'SCRIBNERS' on the spine. Light blue coated endpapers, one side only. Top edge stained green.

Binding B: Same as A3.1.y$_1$, except 'SAUNDERS' is substituted for 'SCRIBNERS' on the spine.

Binding C: Same as A3.1.y$_1$, except light green calico-textured cloth, and 'SCRIBNERS' retained on the spine and no staining on top edge.

Dust jacket: Two styles have been noted, priority undetermined:

Jacket A: Same as A3.1.a, except: front cover: bottom middle, black on white background: *'AWARDED PULITZER PRIZE' is substituted for 'AUTHOR OF | SOUTH MOON UNDER'; spine: 'SAUNDERS' for 'SCRIBNERS'; back cover: black on white background:* ' "*A distinguished book .. As American as the Mississippi .. To | be read and read again.*" Atlantic Monthly | THE YEARLING | by Marjorie Kinnan Rawlings | *author of "South Moon Under,"* etc. | [20-line blurb]'; front flap: black on white background: [in bold] 'The Yearling | [file photo of Rawlings] | Marjorie Kinnan Rawlings | [19-line blurb] | [in an oblong circle] PRINTED | IN | U.S.A.'; rear flap: black on white background: "Our best writer's best book." | —*Vincent Sheean.* | [title through author in bold] For Whom The Bell Tolls | *by* | ERNEST HEMINGWAY | [25-line blurb]'.

A3.1.z *The Yearling* 47

Jacket B: Same as A3.1.y$_1$, except 'SAUNDERS' on the spine; 'REGINALD SAUNDERS · TORONTO' on the back cover; price removed from the front flap and 'LITHO IN U. S. A. [in blue]' added at the bottom.

Publication: 5,000 copies taken from the 51,000 sheets of the American printing on 10 July 1940, 500 on 28 November 1941, 500 on 21 January 1942, 500 on 25 May 1942, 500 on 13 August 1942, 500 on 22 October 1942, 500 on 23 November 1942, 500 on 27 April 1943, 500 on 24 June 1943, 1,000 on 27 January 1944. The final 1,000 depleted the stock of the first printing of 51,000.

Printing: p. ii: 'COPYRIGHT REGISTERED IN CANADA 1940 | BY REGINALD SAUNDERS | *All rights reserved. No part of this book may | be reproduced in any form without the permis- | sion of Charles Scribner's Sons, New York* | PRINTED IN THE UNITED STATES OF AMERICA | [Scribners seal]'.

Locations: Bindings A–C: RLT; jackets A–B: RLT.

Note: Jacket A is on binding A. The 'SCRIBNER'S' on the spine of binding B might suggest that copies in excess of 5,000 were sent to Canada from U.S. stock. There is no indication in Scribners Records of such a transaction.

A3.1.z
First American edition, "Popular Edition," twenty-sixth printing [1941]

New York: Charles Scribner's Sons, 1940. 25,200 copies ordered on 26 August 1941.

Location: RLT. This printing is not recorded on the copyright page of A3.1.aa.

Note one: Scribners Records indicates that the Popular Edition went out of print 10 September 1941.

Note two: It is apparent from the entries in Scribners Records that the Popular Edition did not sell well and that 18,200 sheets remained. These sheets, dated 1940, were used for the Palmetto Edition (1942):

New York: Charles Scribner's Sons, 1940 [1942]. Published September 1942.

Binding: Same as A3.1.y$_1$.

Dust jacket: Front cover: figure of a boy walking left to right through a hammock: 'THE PALMETTO EDITION' [at the top in blue on a white background] | THE YEARLING | [short rule] | MARJORIE KINNAN RAWLINGS [at the bottom in blue on white background]'; spine: continuous scene of the hammock: '[title, author, and publisher on white background] THE [in black] | YEARLING [in black] | [device in blue] | MARJORIE [in black] | KINNAN [in black] | RAWLINGS | [in black] | [device in

Front of dust jacket for A 3.1.z

blue] | SCRIBNERS [in blue]'; back cover: continuous scene with spine: figure of a fawn walking toward the boy; front flap: 'The Palmetto Edition [in blue script] | THE YEARLING [in black] | by [in blue script] | Marjorie Kinnan Rawlings | *Illustrated by Edward Shenton* [in blue] | [24-line blurb in black] | *The Jacket is a reproduction of* | *a painting made by N. C. Wyeth* | *in "The Yearling" country.* [in black] | THE PALMETTO EDITION at its [in blue] | special price will be available only [in blue] | until Christmas, 1942. [in blue]'; rear flap: 25-line blurb for *Cross Creek* and *Cross Creek Cookery*.

Location: RLT.

A3.1.dd *The Yearling* 49

A3.1.aa
First American edition, "Palmetto Edition," twenty-seventh printing (1942)

New York: Charles Scribner's Sons, 1942. 5,050 copies. 18 November 1942. $1.39. *Binding:* Same as A3.1.y$_1$. *Dust jacket: Not seen. Location:* RLT.

Note: This is the only printing of the Palmetto Edition; see A3.1.z, *Note two.*

A3.1.bb
First American edition, twenty-eighth printing (1944)

New York: Charles Scribner's Sons, 1944. $2.50. 3,020 copies. 4 January 1944. *Location:* From Scribners Records, *not seen.*

A3.1.cc
First American edition, twenty-ninth printing (1944)

New York Charles Scribner's Sons, 1944. $2.50. 3,200 copies. 1 July 1944. *Location:* From Scribners Records, *not seen.*

Note: A Scribners Records entry for 4 September 1947 indicates that 800 'oversheets' remain and that '800 covers [were] made and stamped 9-47'. It is possible that part of these oversheets are from the 1944 printing, but this does not seem likely, since the Records indicate that all 3,020 were sold. It is further possible that these 800 oversheets represent an accumulation from one or more previous printings. The publication of oversheets does not represent a new printing.

A3.1.dd
First American edition, thirtieth printing [1945]

Marjorie Kinnan Rawlings | THE | YEARLING | [illustration of a boy holding a fawn] | Decorations by | Edward Shenton | [thick-thin rule] | GROSSET & DUNLAP | PUBLISHERS NEW YORK | By arrangement with Charles Scribner's Sons.

viii + 428 pp. 20.6 × 14.0 cm. *Binding:* Same as A3.1.a, except light green cloth with blue stamping. Top edge trimmed and stained light green. *Dust jacket:* Cover and spine similar to A3.1.a, except at bottom center of the front cover: 'AWARDED PULITZER PRIZE', and at bottom of spine: 'GROSSET & DUNLAP'; back cover: same as A3.1.y$_2$; front flap: same as A3.1.a, except '149149' at the top and the wartime statement (same as copyright page) in green at the bottom; rear flap: advertisement for *South Moon Under.* On the copyright page the conditions of production are explained: '[decorated brace at left] | This book, while produced under | wartime conditions, in full com- | pliance with government regula- | tions for the conservation of paper | and other essential materials, is | COMPLETE AND UNABRIDGED | [decorated

COPYRIGHT, 1938, BY
MARJORIE KINNAN RAWLINGS

Printed in the United States of America

All rights reserved. No part of this book may be reproduced in any form without the permission of Charles Scribner's Sons

Published, April, 1938

First Printing,	April,	1938
Second Printing,	April,	1938
Third Printing,	May,	1938
Fourth Printing,	June,	1938
Fifth Printing,	June,	1938
Sixth Printing,	July,	1938
Seventh Printing,	July,	1938
Eighth Printing,	August,	1938
Ninth Printing,	August,	1938
Tenth Printing,	September,	1938
Eleventh Printing,	October,	1938
Twelfth Printing,	October,	1938
Thirteenth Printing,	October,	1938
Fourteenth Printing,	November,	1938
Fifteenth Printing,	December,	1938
Sixteenth Printing,	December,	1938
Seventeenth Printing,	May,	1939
Eighteenth Printing,	May,	1939
Nineteenth Printing,	September,	1939
Twentieth Printing,	December,	1939
Twenty-first Printing,	March,	1940

Pulitzer Prize Limited Edition 1939
Pulitzer Prize Edition 1939
Second Printing 1940
Popular Edition ...... September, 1940
Palmetto Edition...... September, 1942
Second Printing........November, 1942

Copyright page for A 3.1.aa

A3.1.hh *The Yearling* 51

brace at right]'. Paper bulk: title page: .125 mm; p. 151: .124 mm. 81,000 copies published. $1.49. *Location:* RLT (dj).

A3.1.ee
First American edition, thirty-first printing [1946]

New York: Grosset & Dunlap, n.d. [1946]. *Binding:* Light green cloth. Paper bulk: title page: .109 mm.; p. 151: .128 mm. 37,000 copies. *Location:* RLT.

Note: Smaller format (19.0 × 13.0 cm.).

A3.1.ff
First American edition, thirty-second printing [1946?]

New York: Grosset & Dunlap, n.d. [1946?]. *Binding:* Light green cloth. Paper bulk: title page: .107 mm.; p. 151: .112 mm. *Location:* RLT.

Note: Not listed in Grosset & Dunlap records.

A3.1.gg
First American edition, thirty-third printing [1946?]

New York: Grosset & Dunlap, n.d. [1946?]. *Binding:* Light green cloth. Paper bulk: .138 mm.; p. 151: .134 mm. *Location:* RLT.

Note: Not listed in Grosset & Dunlap records.

A3.1.hh
First American edition, thirty-fourth printing [1947]

New York: Grosset and Dunlap, n.d. [1947]. *Binding:* Same as A3.1.ee, except different stamping. Top edge trimmed and stained dark green. *Dust jacket:* Front cover: color illustration of Claude Jarman, Jr., holding a fawn, with an inset in the lower right of Jane Wyman and Gregory Peck; back cover: black and white studio photograph of Jarman, Peck (holding a fawn), and Wyman. Paper bulk: title page: .130 mm.; p. 151: .125 mm. 78,000 copies. *Location:* RLT.

Note one: There is no 'wartime conditions' statement on the copyright page.

Note two: This dust jacket was printed to take advantage of the MGM production of *The Yearling* in 1946. On the front flap at the lower right is a statement of condition: '[diagonal broken rule] | The | issuance of | this *complete and* | *unabridged new edition* | at a low price is made pos- | sible by the use of the same plates | made for the original edition and ac | ceptance by the author of a reduced royalty.'

A3.1.ii
First American edition, thirty-fifth printing [1948]

New York: Grosset & Dunlap, n.d. [1948]. *Binding:* Green cloth. Top edge trimmed and stained dark blue. Paper bulk: title page: .115 mm.; p. 151: .119 mm. 13,000 copies. *Location:* RLT.

A3.1.jj
First American edition, thirty-sixth printing [1948]

New York: Charles Scribner's Sons, n.d. [1948]. $3.50. *Location:* From Scribners Records, *not seen*.

Note one: In Scribners Records, 12 June 1952, 5,150 sheets are listed as 'ON HAND' and 3,000 are ordered to be bound which were published on 22 September; 1,000 more are bound on 29 April 1954, and 1,180 on 12 August 1954. The total for this printing is 5,080, which includes the binding of thirty oversheets. The Records entries at this point are ill-kept, and thus the above represents a reconstruction of the printing and binding sequence. At this point Scribners refers to the first edition as the 'Shenton Edition' or the 'Old Regular Edition'.

Note two: In Scribners Records there is a Scribners Office Memorandum, dated 1 September 1955: 'Ship the following materials to Vail-Ballou: | Text Plates | Binders dies (herewith).' In the Records is a note: '1 pckg. Orig. Cuts sent to Vail-Ballou on 18 January 1956.'

A3.1.kk
First American edition, thirty-seventh printing [1949]

New York: Grosset & Dunlap, n.d. [1949]. 7,500 copies. *Location:* From Grosset & Dunlap records, *not seen*.

A3.1.ll
First American edition, thirty-eighth printing [1950]

New York: Grosset & Dunlap, n.d. [1950]. 5,500 copies. *Location:* From Grosset & Dunlap records, *not seen*.

A3.1.mm
First American edition, thirty-ninth printing [n.d.]

New York: Charles Scribner's Sons, n.d. *Location: Not seen.*

Note: Scribners continued to order dust jackets, 6,400 on 30 September 1952 and 10,000 on 10 June 1955, which suggests that there were further printings, even though there is no indication of further printings in Scribners Records.

A3.1.uu *The Yearling* 53

A3.1.nn
First American edition, fortieth printing [1962]

New York: Charles Scribner's Sons, n.d. [1962]. 'b-4.62[MC]'. $1.65. *Binding:* Green-gray glossy wrappers. 'The Scribner Library SL40'. *Location:* RLT.

A3.1.oo
First American edition, forty-first printing [1963]

New York: Charles Scribner's Sons, n.d. [1963]. 'D-1.63[MCol]'. *Binding:* Same as A3.1.nn, except no price. *Location:* RLT.

A3.1.pp
First American edition, forty-second printing [1964]

New York: Charles Scribner's Sons, n.d. [1964]. 'F-4.64[MCOL]'. $1.65. *Binding:* Same as A3.1.nn. *Location:* RLT.

A3.1.qq
First American edition, forty-third printing [1965]

New York: Charles Scribner's Sons, n.d. [1965]. 'H-12.65[MCOL]'. $1.65. *Binding:* Same as A3.1.nn. *Location:* RLT.

A3.1.rr
First American edition, forty-fourth printing [1967]

New York: Charles Scribner's Sons, n.d. [1967]. 'I-2.67[MCol]'. $1.65. *Binding:* Same as A3.1.nn. *Locations:* ISNU, RLT.

A3.1.ss
First American edition, forty-fifth printing [1968]

New York: Charles Scribner's Sons, n.d. [1968]. 'K-12.68[MCol]'. *Binding:* Same as A3.1.nn. *Location:* RLT.

A3.1.tt
First American edition, forty-sixth printing [1970]

New York: Charles Scribner's Sons, n.d. [1970]. 'M-3.70[MC]'. $2.45. *Bindings:* (A) Brown-gray glossy wrappers; (B) brown cloth. *Locations:* Binding A: RLT, RM; binding B: RM.

A3.1.uu
First American edition, forty-seventh printing [1973]

New York: Charles Scribner's Sons, n.d. [1970]. 'P-5.73[C]'. $3.95. *Binding:* Same as A3.1.nn.

A3.1.vv
First American edition, forty-eighth printing [1982]

New York: Charles Scribner's Sons, n.d. [1982]. $6.95. *Binding:* Same as A3.1.nn, except different spine. *Location:* RLT.

A3.1.ww
First American edition, forty-ninth printing [1984]

New York: Charles Scribner's Sons, n.d. [1984]. *Binding:* 'Perma-Bound' glassine boards. *Location:* RM.

Note: Cloth copy listed on the copyright page, *not seen.*

A3.1.xx
First American edition, fiftieth printing [1986]

New York: Collier Macmillan, n.d. [1986]. $4.95. *Binding:* Brown glossy wrappers. *Location:* RLT.

Note one: Cloth copy listed on the copyright page, *not seen.*

Note two: Reprinted in 1988 as '50th ANNIVERSARY EDITION'.

A3.1.yy
First American edition, fifty-first printing [1988]

New York: Trumpet Club [Dell Publishing Co.], n.d. [1988]. *Location:* InWinG.

Note: '50th ANNIVERSARY EDITION . . . TRUMPET CLUB SPECIAL EDITION'.

A3.1.zz
First American edition, fifty-second printing [1989]

New York: Charles Scribner's Sons, n.d. [1989]. $3.95. *Binding:* Multicolor glossy wrappers. *Location:* RLT.

Note: 'Scribner Classics in Rack-Size Editions'.

A3.1.aaa
First American edition, fifty-third printing [1992]

Facsimile reprinting. New York: Charles Scribner's Sons, 1938 [1992]. 'THE FIRST EDITION LIBRARY'. *Locations:* PM, RLT, RM.

A 3.1.aaa *The Yearling*

Note: The binding and dust jacket are also facsimiles. Copies are in a gray calico-textured box, with a reproduction of the front of the dust jacket on the front and a reproduction of the rear cover on the back. A card discussing provenance is enclosed.

A 3.2.a
First British edition, first printing (1938)

Marjorie Kinnan Rawlings
THE
YEARLING

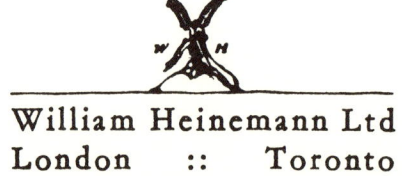

William Heinemann Ltd
London :: Toronto

A 3.2.a: 19.7 × 13.0 cm.

A 3.2.a *The Yearling* 57

```
PRINTED IN GREAT BRITAIN AT THE WINDMILL PRESS
              KINGSWOOD, SURREY
```

[i–vi] 1–410

[A]⁸ B–I⁸ K–U⁸ W–Z⁸ AA–BB⁸; 208 leaves.

Contents: p. i: half title: '*THE YEARLING*'; p. ii: blank; p. iii: title page; p. iv: copyright notice + printer's imprint; p. v: section title: '*THE YEARLING*'; p. vi: blank; pp. 1–410: text.

Typography and paper: 15.8 (15.3) × 9.3 cm.; wove paper; 36 lines per page. Running heads: rectos: pp. 3–13, 17–39, 43–51, 55–67, 71–89, 93–113, 117–123, 127–129, 133–149, 153–167, 171–203, 207–209, 213–227, 231–251, 255–257, 261–265, 269–277, 281–355, 359–361, 365–367, 371–385, 389–409: '*THE YEARLING*'; versos: pp. 2–18, 22–24, 28–46, 52–62, 66–78, 82–182, 186–298, 302–314, 318–352, 356–374, 378–392, 396–410: '*THE YEARLING*'.

Binding: Light blue calico-textured cloth. Front cover: illustration of a boy holding a fawn; spine: goldstamped on boxed dark blue background: 'THE | YEARLING | Marjorie | Kinnan | Rawlings | HEINEMANN'. Light bluish gray endpapers. All edges trimmed.

Dust jacket: Front cover: '[all on white background] *The* | *Yearling* | [illustration in black and brownish red of a boy sitting on a wooden fence, with a barn in the background, looking at a fawn] | a novel | by | MARJORIE KINNAN RAWLINGS'; spine: 'THE | YEARLING | by | MARJORIE | KINNAN | RAWLINGS | [Heinemann logo in brownish red of a windmill with 'W' on one side and 'H' on the other] | HEINEMANN'; back cover: 'MORE NOVELS FROM AMERICA | [rule] | [advertisement for four novels]'; front flap: '*The Yearling* | by MARJORIE KINNAN RAWLINGS | 34–line blurb on the novel] | [star device, then 3-line blurb on the novel] | [in lower right corner] 8s.6d. | NET'; rear flap: '*Man's Courage* | by JOSEPH VOGEL | [39-line blurb on Vogel's novel'.

Publication: 2,600 copies published on 24 October 1938. 8s.6d.

Printing: Windmill Press.

Locations: BL (deposit-stamped 24 October 1938); Bodleian (deposit-stamped 31 October 1938); FU (dj).

Note one: The contract with Heinemann was signed on 1 April 1938.

Note two: Printed in braille. 1 vol., abridged for children. Millswood, South Australia: Braille Writing Association, n.d.

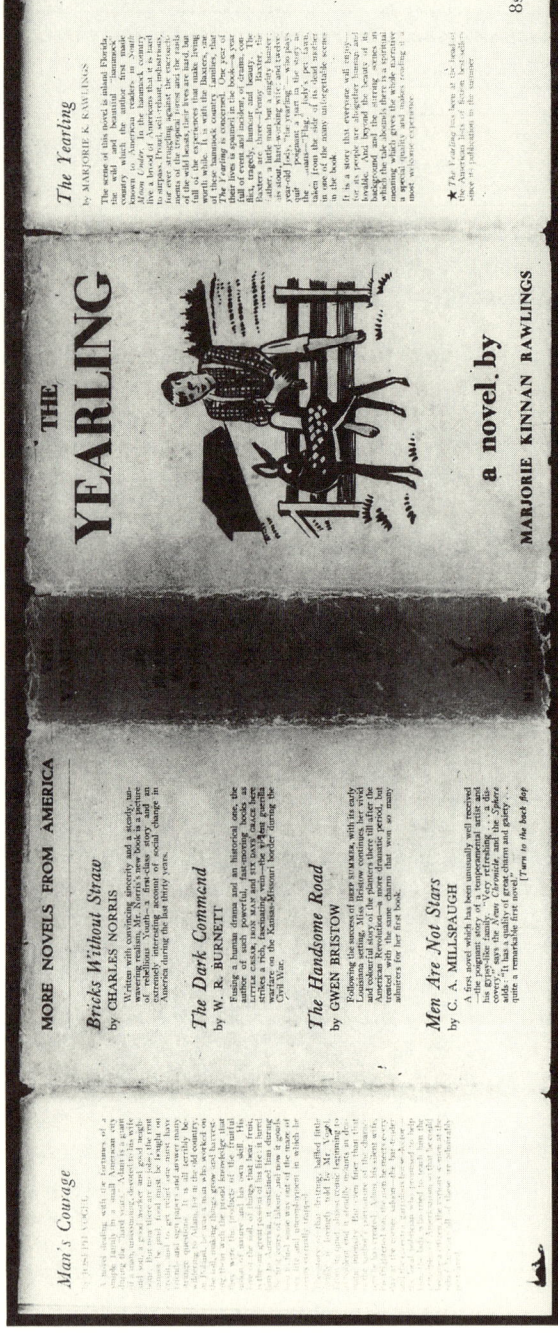

Dust jacket for A 3.2.a

A3.2.h *The Yearling* 59

OTHER PRINTINGS WITHIN THE FIRST BRITISH EDITION

A3.2.b
First British edition, second printing [1938]

London: William Heinemann, n.d. [1938]. Produced in October. *Location:* From copyright page A3.2.d, *not seen.*

A3.2.c
First British edition, third printing [1938]

London: William Heinemann, n.d. [1938]. *Binding:* Blue cloth. Produced in November. *Location:* RLT.

A3.2.d
First British edition, fourth printing [1938]

London: William Heinemann, n.d. [1938]. *Binding:* Blue cloth. Produced in November. *Location:* RLT.

A3.2.e
First British edition, fifth printing [1938]

London: William Heinemann, n.d. [1938]. Produced in December. *Location:* From copyright page A3.2.h, *not seen.*

A3.2.f
First British edition, sixth printing [1938]

London: William Heinemann, n.d. [1938]. Produced in December. *Location:* From copyright page A3.2.h, *not seen.*

A3.2.g
First British edition, seventh printing [1938]

London: William Heinemann, n.d. [1938]. *Binding:* Blue cloth. Produced in December. *Location:* RLT.

Note: Advertisement on the front flap of the dust jacket reports 230,000 copies sold of the Scribners printing.

A3.2.h
First British edition, eighth printing [1940]

THE | YEARLING | by | Marjorie Kinnan Rawlings | WORLD BOOKS | 20 HEADFORT PLACE SW 1 | LONDON

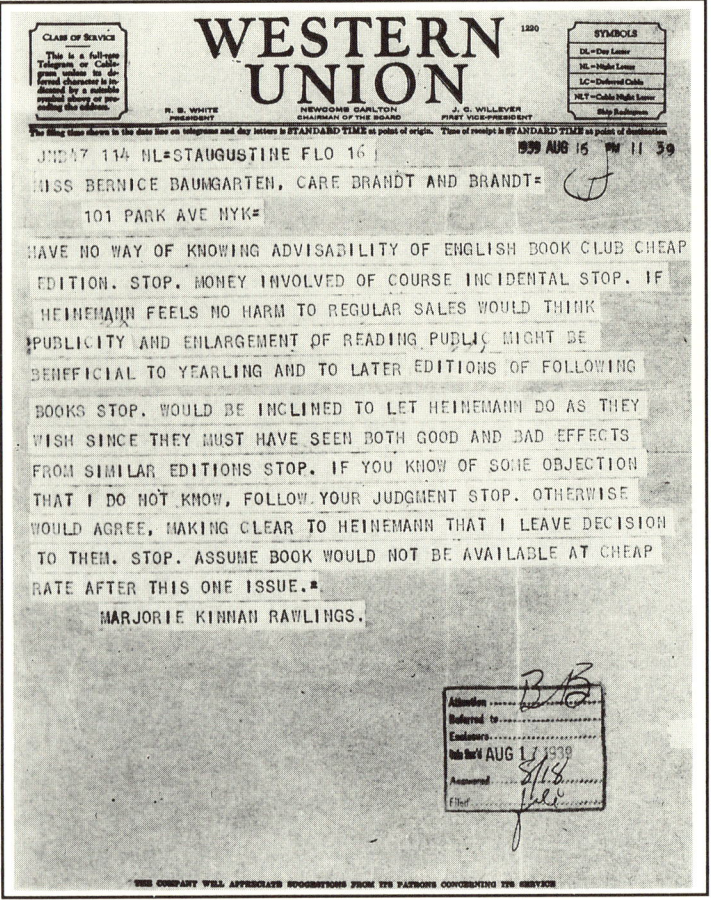

Telegraph authorization for A 3.2.h

vi + 410 pp. *Binding:* Light brown over lighter brown calico-textured cloth. Copyright: 'PUBLISHED BY WORLD BOOKS 1940 | BY ARRANGEMENT WITH | WILLIAM HEINEMANN LTD'. 2s.6d. 'WORLD BOOKS EDITION'. Thick stock: .157 mm. Top edge trimmed and stained green. Printed in January. *Location:* RLT.

Note: Publication information on the front flap of dust jacket: 'In | the United States it sold | 250,000 copies during the first | six months of publication; | and in England six editions | were for within three | months.'

A 3.2.i
First British edition, ninth printing [1940?]

A 3.2.n *The Yearling* 61

London: World Books, n.d. [1940?]. *Binding:* Brown cloth. Thin stock: .150 mm. Top edge trimmed and stained dark green. *Location:* RLT.

A 3.2.j
First British edition, tenth printing [1940]

THE | YEARLING | by | Marjorie Kinnan Rawlings | THE REPRINT SOCIETY | LONDON

vi + 410 pp. *Binding:* Light green calico-textured cloth, leather label on spine, top edge stained light purple. Copyright: 'PUBLISHED BY THE REPRINT SOCIETY LTD 1940 | BY ARRANGEMENT WITH | WILLIAM HEINEMANN LTD'. 3s.6d. *Location:* RLT.

A 3.2.k
First British edition, eleventh printing [1941]

London: William Heinemann, n.d. [1941]. Produced in March. *Location:* From copyright page of A3.8.d, *not seen.*

A A3.2.l
First British edition, twelfth printing [1941]

London: William Heinemann, n.d. [1941]. Produced in December. *Location:* From copyright page of A3.8.d, *not seen.*

A 3.2.m
First British edition, thirteenth printing [1942]

London: William Heinemann, n.d. [1942]. Produced in October. *Location:* From copyright page of A3.8.d, *not seen.*

A 3.2.n
First British edition, fourteenth printing [1943]

London: William Heinemann, n.d. [1943]. Produced in March. *Location:* From copyright page of A3.8.d, *not seen.*

A 3.3.a
Second American edition, "Pulitzer Prize Limited Edition," limited printing on laid paper (1939)

THE YEARLING

by

Marjorie Kinnan Rawlings

With Illustrations by
N. C. WYETH

New York
CHARLES SCRIBNER'S SONS
1939

A 3.3.a: 23.2 × 17.8 cm.

A 3.3.a *The Yearling* 63

Contents: pp. a–b: blank; p. i: blank; p. ii: limitation notice and inscriptions; p. iii: half title; p. iv: blank; p. v: title page; p. vi: printer's imprint + printer's device; pp. vii–viii: list of illustrations; pp. ix–xii (recto only): facsimile of Wyeth letter, dated 'Ocala—Fla. | Feb. 4 1939', on visit to Rawlings' Florida; p. xiii: section title; p. xiv: blank; pp. 1–6; color illustration on recto of 'JODY AND THE FLUTTER-MILL' inserted after p. 6; 7–34: color illustration on recto of 'THE FIGHT WITH OLD SLEWFOOT' inserted after p. 34; 35–44; gray on light brown tone illustration on recto of 'Fodder-wing' inserted after p. 44; 45–54; color illustration on recto of 'PENNY TELLS THE STORY OF THE BEAR FIGHT' inserted after p. 54; 55–88; color illustration on recto of 'THE DANCE OF THE WHOOPING CRANES' inserted after p. 88; 89–120; color illustration on recto of 'THE FIGHT AT VOLUSIA' inserted after p. 120; 121–144; color illustration on recto of 'THE VIGIL' inserted after p. 144; 145–158; color illustration on recto of 'JODY FINDS THE FAWN' inserted after p. 158; 159–184; gray on light brown tone illustration on recto of 'Pa and Ma Forrester' inserted after p. 184; 185–196; color illustration on recto of 'THE BURIAL OF FODDER-WING' inserted after p. 196; 197–218; color illustration on recto of 'THE STORM' inserted after p. 218; 219–258; color illustration on recto of 'PENNY TEACHES JODY HIS SUMS' inserted after p. 258; 259–288; color illustration on recto of 'THE FORRESTERS GO TO TOWN' inserted after p. 288; 289–330; color illustration on recto of 'THE DEATH OF OLD SLEWFOOT' inserted after p. 330; 331–352; color illustration on recto of 'JODY AND FLAG' inserted after p. 352; 353–390; color illustration on recto of 'JODY LOST' inserted after p. 390; 391–400: text.

Typography and paper: 17.6 (16.7) × 10.6 cm.; laid paper (vertical chain lines: 3.2 cm.), watermarked: 'Utopia' [in script], with device of scales in balance enclosed in a hanging circle; 36 lines per page. Running heads: recto: pp. 3–13, 17–39, 43–51, 55–67, 71–111, 115–145, 149–163, 167–177, 181–197, 201–203, 207–221, 225–245, 249–251, 255–259, 263–347, 351–375, 379–399: 'The Yearling'; verso: p. viii: 'Illustrations'; pp. 2–18, 22–24, 28–46, 50–62, 66–78, 82–88, 92–120, 124–126, 130–270, 274–290, 294–306, 310–344, 348–364, 368–382, 386–400: same as recto.

Binding: Two styles have been noted, priority determined:

Binding A: Yellowish green (emerald) fine linen-grain cloth. Goldstamped in center of the front cover: '[circle] | [inside the circle a sunburst with the head of a fawn]'; goldstamped spine: '[rule | *THE* | *YEARLING* | [device] | MARJO-RIE | KINNAN | RAWLINGS | [device] | *SCRIBNERS* | [rule]'. Decorated endpapers, not coated, of a boy walking a fawn. No flyleaves. Top edge in gold. Fore-edge and bottom edge untrimmed. Enclosed in a light gray fold inside a cardboard box (24.8 × 19.2 cm.) covered with light gray paper.

Front covers for Bindings A and B, A 3.3.a

A 3.3.a *The Yearling*

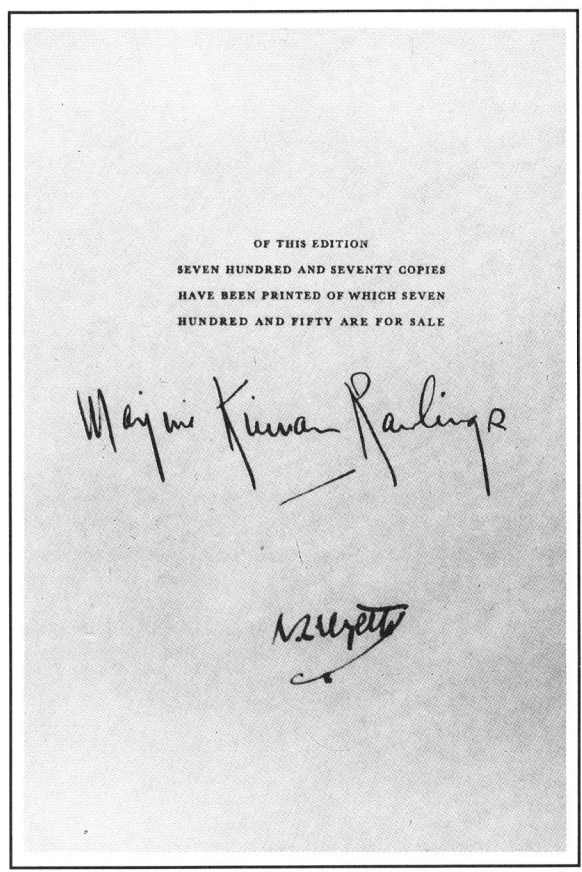

Certificate of limitation for A 3.3.a

Goldstamped black label on the spine of the fold: 'THE | YEARLING | [ornament] | MARJORIE | KINNAN | RAWLINGS | [ornament]'.

Binding B: Blue calico-textured cloth. Front cover: goldstamped head of a fawn in the upper third; goldstamped: 'THE | YEARLING' in lower third; goldstamped spine: 'THE | YEARLING | MARJORIE | KINNAN | RAWLINGS | SCRIBNERS'. Decorated color endpapers, not coated, of a boy walking a fawn. No flyleaves. Top and bottom edges trimmed. Fore-edge rough trimmed. In cardboard box (24.5 × 19.3 cm.) covered with grayish blue paper; white paper label (12.9 × 4.7 cm.) on spine, in grayish blue: 'THE | YEARLING | [illustration of the head of a fawn] | MARJORIE | KINNAN | RAWLINGS | SCRIBNERS'.

Publication: Limitation notice, p. ii: 'OF THIS EDITION | SEVEN HUNDRED AND SEVENTY COPIES | HAVE BEEN PRINTED OF WHICH

The Yearling

for his hips and shoulders. He stretched out one arm and laid his head on it. A shaft of sunlight, warm and thin like a light patchwork quilt, lay across his body. He watched the flutter-mill indolently, sunk in the sand and the sunlight. The movement was hypnotic. His eyelids fluttered with the palm-leaf paddles. Drops of silver slipping from the wheel blurred together like the tail of a shooting star. The water made a sound like kittens lapping. A rain frog sang a moment and then was still. There was an instant when the boy hung at the edge of a high bank made of the soft fluff of broom-sage, and the rain frog and the starry dripping of the flutter-mill hung with him. Instead of falling over the edge, he sank into the softness. The blue, white-tufted sky closed over him. He slept.

When he awakened, he thought he was in a place other than the branch bed. He was in another world, so that for an instant he thought he might still be dreaming. The sun was gone, and all the light and shadow. There were no black bolts of live oaks, no glossy green of magnolia leaves, no pattern of gold face where the sun had sifted through the branches of the wild cherry. The world was all a gentle gray, and he lay in a mist as fine as spray from a waterfall. The mist tickled his skin. It was scarcely wet. He rolled over on his back and it was as though he looked up into the soft gray breast of a mourning dove.

He lay, absorbing the fine-dropped rain like a young plant. When his face was damp at last and his shirt was moist to the touch, he left his nest. He stopped short. A deer had come to the spring while he was sleeping. The fresh tracks came down the east bank and stopped at the water's edge. They were sharp and pointed, the tracks of a doe. They sank deeply into the sand, so that he knew the doe was an old one and a large. Perhaps she was heavy with fawn. She had come down and drunk deeply from the spring, not seeing him where he slept. Then she had scented him. There

6

JODY AND THE FLUTTER MILL

Illustration for A 3.3.a

A 3.3.a *The Yearling* 67

SEVEN | HUNDRED AND FIFTY ARE FOR SALE'. Underneath notice, signed in black ink: 'Marjorie Kinnan Rawlings'; underneath Rawlings's signature, signed in blue ink: 'N. C. Wyeth'. 770 copies published 30 October 1939. $10.00 Copyright #A135257.

Printing: Printed and bound by the Scribner Press.

Locations: Binding and box A: PM, RLT, RM; binding and box B: PM, RLT.

Note one: Scribners Records indicates that 850 copies of the special letter and the limitation notice were printed, and 770 copies of the two special illustrations.

Slipcase and box for A 3.3.a, Binding A; spine and box for A 3.3.a, Binding B

Boxes for A 3.3.a, Bindings A and B

Note two: Scribners Records indicates that 520 copies were in "bound stock" in 1939, and that 280 more copies were bound in August 1952, no doubt from the remaining sheets. 323 new gray slipcases (boxes) were ordered on 31 July 1952. These new bindings may in fact be the cheaper binding (B) listed above. The Records further notes that the original $10.00 price was reduced to $7.50 for the 1952.

Note three: It has not been established that all 770 copies were signed. There is one unique signing, reported by Norton S. Baskin, not located. Rawlings signed one sheet 'Lolly Pop Twitters', and Wyeth signed below it, 'I All New She Did [sic]'.

Note four: The facsimile of the Wyeth letter (pp. ix–xii) is on 'Caslon Bond' paper.

Note five: The facsimile of the letter on pp. ix–xii, and the illustrations inserted after p. 44 and p. 184 are special to this edition.

Note six: Copyright page has an 'A' and a Scribners seal.

A 3.3.b

Second American edition, "Pulitzer Prize Edition," first trade printing, first printing (1939)

A 3.3.b: 28.0 × 15.0 cm.

400 pp.; 28.0 × 15.0 cm.

Contents: pp. a–b: blank; p. i: blank; p. ii: 'BOOKS BY MARJORIE KINNAN RAWLINGS | [rule] | *The Yearling* | *Golden Apples* | *South Moon Under* | [rule] | CHARLES SCRIBNER'S SONS'; p. iii: half title: '*PULITZER PRIZE EDITION* [underlined] | The Yearling'; p. iv: blank; p. v: title page; p. vi: copyright page; pp. vii–viii: list of illustrations; p. ix: section title: 'The Yearling'; p. x: blank; pp. 1–400: text and illustrations same as the Pulitzer Prize Limited Edition; pp. 401–404: blank.

Typography and paper: 17.5 (16.6) × 10.5 cm.; wove paper; 36 lines per page. Running heads: same as Pulitzer Prize Limited Edition.

Binding: White over light brown coarse linen-textured cloth. Front cover stamped in dark brown, with the lettering in hollow font: 'The Yearling | Marjorie | Kinnan | Rawlings | [an illustration of a palmetto near water's edge runs up the left side of the cover]'; spine stamped in dark brown: 'The | Yearling | [figure of a fawn's head] | Marjorie | Kinnan | Rawlings | Scribners'; back cover: blank. Endpapers: same as the Pulitzer Prize Limited Edition. Top edge trimmed and stained in green; fore-edge untrimmed; bottom edge trimmed.

Dust jacket: Two styles have been noted:

Jacket A: Front cover: pictorial scene (continuous from front cover to spine to back cover) on a light brown background with black lettering: 'PULITZER PRIZE EDITION | The Yearling | Marjorie Kinnan Rawlings | [scene of boy petting a fawn with father looking on] | *With pictures by* | N. C. Wyeth'; spine: 'The | Yearling | Marjorie | Kinnan | Rawlings | Scribner'; back cover: '[mother with three dogs below her looking at son and father]'; front flap: light brown background with black lettering: 'PULITZER PRIZE EDITION | *The Yearling* | by | Marjorie Kinnan | Rawlings | With *14 full-color illustrations* | *by* N. C. Wyeth | [25-line description of the novel] | [*Continued on back flap*]'; rear flap: '[*Continued from front flap*] | [38-line description of the novel] | Charles Scribner's Sons, New York'.

Jacket B: Same as A, except in black at the top of the front cover: 'THE | YEARLING | MARJORIE KINNAN RAWLINGS | *With pictures by* | N. C. Wyeth'; spine: 'THE | YEARLING | Marjorie | Kinnan | Rawlings'. Front and rear flaps blank.

Publication: 12,400 copies published 30 October 1939. *Publishers' Weekly*, 138 (28 September 1940), 1317, lists the publication date as 'October 21st'. Scribners Records notes the date as 1 November 1939. $3.50.

A 3.3.c *The Yearling*

Front of dust jacket B for A 3.3.b

Printing: Printed and bound by the Scribner Press.

Locations: Dust jacket A: RLT (2); dust jacket B: PM.

Note: Copyright page has an 'A' and a Scribners seal.

A 3.3.c
Second American edition, third printing (1939)

New York: Charles Scribner's Sons, 1939. 10,350 copies. 6 December 1939.
Location: RLT.

Note: Scribners ordered 25,000 dust jackets on 1 November 1939.

OTHER PRINTINGS, SCRIBNERS "ILLUSTRATED CLASSIC"

A3.3.d
Second American edition, fourth printing (1940)

New York: Charles Scribner's, 1940. *Location:* RLT.

Note one: Scribners Records does not list this printing.

Note two: Three bindings have been seen. *Binding A:* Same as A3.4.b; *binding B:* Light orange calico-textured cloth; *binding C:* Black calico-textured cloth. Boxed: light grayish green: front: 'THE | YEARLING | MARJORIE KINNAN | RAWLINGS | *Illustrated by* | N. C. WYETH | [pasted on at the bottom of the box in black lettering on a white background] 'The Yearling | $2.50'. *Locations:* Binding A: RLT; binding B: RLT; binding C: PM.

Note three: This is the first printing of the 'Illustrated Classic'. The 'A' is dropped and the Scribners seal is retained on the copyright page.

A3.3.e
Second American edition, fifth printing (1942)

New York: Charles Scribner's Sons, 1942. *Location:* InU.

Note: This printing is not listed in Scribners Records.

A3.3.f
Second American edition, sixth printing (1945)

New York: Charles Scribner's Sons, 1945, 1,750 copies. 30 October 1944. *Location:* GU.

A3.3.g
Second American edition, seventh printing (1946)

New York: Charles Scribner's Sons, 1946. *Location:* MKRH, RLT.

Note: This printing is not listed in Scribners Records.

A3.3.h
Second American edition, eighth printing (1954)

New York: Charles Scribner's Sons, 1954. *Location:* RLT.

A 3.3.o *The Yearling* 73

A 3.3.i
Second American edition, ninth printing (1957)

New York: Charles Scribner's Sons, 1957. *Location:* RLT.

A 3.3.j
Second American edition, tenth printing (1960)

New York: Charles Scribner's Sons, 1960. *Location:* ISNU.

A 3.3.k
Second American edition, eleventh printing (1961)

New York: Charles Scribner's Sons, 1961. x + 405 pp. *Location:* RLT.

Note: On the copyright page: '*Reset August 1961*'.

A 3.3.l
Second American edition, twelfth printing (1966)

New York: Charles Scribner's Sons, 1966. *Location:* RLT.

A 3.3.m
Second American edition, thirteenth printing [1967]

New York: Charles Scribner's Sons, n.d. [1967]. *Location:* NjR.

Note: Copyright renewed 1967.

A 3.3.n
Second American edition, fourteenth printing (1970)

New York: Charles Scribner's Sons, 1970. *Location:* RLT.

A 3.3.o
Second American edition, "Deluxe Edition," fifteenth printing [1985]

New York: Charles Scribner's, n.d. [1985]. xii + 402 pp. $24.95. Limited Edition, p. i: 'Three hundred and fifty copies of this edition of *The Yearling* | have been specially bound and numbered, | of which this is number _____'.
Binding: Light olive fine linen-grain cloth: front cover: stamped frame, with coated illustration attached inside the frame (18.6 × 13.7 cm.) of a boy, looking into a fireplace, holding a fawn; at the top of the illustration, black on a yellow background: 'THE | YEARLING | [three diamonds] | *by* MARJORIE KINNAN RAWLINGS'; goldstamped spine: '[floral rule device] | THE | YEARLING | [rule] | MARJORIE | KINNAN | RAWLINGS | [three diamonds] | ILLUS-TRATED BY | N. C. WYETH | [floral devices, side by side, extending to the

bottom] | SCRIBNERS | [rule] | [fifteen diamonds]'; back cover: goldstamped ISBN: '0-684-18508-3'. Cardboard box covered with same material as the binding, with ISBN in gold on the lower left of the left side, and the blindstamped initials, 'MKR', on the lower right of the right side. Top edge in gold. Gold colored reader's ribbon. Fore-edge untrimmed; bottom edge trimmed. *Locations:* PM, RLT, RM.

A 3.3.p
Second American edition, trade edition, sixteenth printing (1985)

New York: Charles Scribner's Sons, 1985. xii + 402. *Price* (front flap): '$19.95 | until 12/31/85 | [diagonal broken line] | $22.95'. *Binding:* Same cloth as A3.4.o. *Location:* RLT.

Note: This and A3.4.o are printed on thick stock using 'Linotype Baskerville'. The text (pp. 1–400) is from the plates of A3.3.a; a leaf (pp. 401–402) explaining the provenance of this printing is added.

LATER EDITIONS

A 3.4
First German edition, only printing, in English [1939]

[Enclosed in a triple box, decorated box, double box frame] THE YEARLING | BY | MARJORIE | KINNAN RAWLINGS | LEIPZIG | BERNHARD TAUCHNITZ

330 pp.; 18.0 × 11.5 cm.

Note one: 'COPYRIGHT JULY 1939'. *Tauchnitz Edition,* no. 5,360, 'Extra Number'. *Binding:* Glossy wrappers. *Location:* FU.

Note two: See William B. Todd and Ann Bowden, *Tauchnitz International Editions in English 1841–1955* (New York: Bibliographical Society of America, 1988), 768, 1008, who point out that there were subsequent printings through December 1943, when the Tauchnitz premises were destroyed.

A 3.5.a
Third American edition, "School Edition," first printing [1941]

THE | YEARLING | By | Marjorie Kinnan Rawlings | *Decorations by* | EDWARD SHENTON | *CHARLES SCRIBNER'S SONS · NEW YORK | CHICAGO · BOSTON · ATLANTA · SAN FRANCISCO · DALLAS*

xvi + 428 pp.

Cover for A 3.5.a

Contents: Color illustration inserted before p. i; p. i: title page; p ii: copyright page; p. iii: half title: 'THE YEARLING'; pp. iv–v: map of Florida with inset on p. iv of the '*General area covered by scenes | of |* THE YEARLING'; p. vi: blank; pp. vii–viii: 'Mrs. Rawlings' Introduction'; black and white glossy photograph on recto of Rawlings with two hunting dogs; ix–xiii: 'INTRODUCTION' completed; p. xiv: blank; p. xv: section title: 'THE YEARLING'; p. xvi: blank; then same as A3.1.a.

Bindings: Priority not determined:

Binding A: Orange calico-textured cloth, not embossed; front cover: '[in orange on a green background in a half circle] THE YEARLING | [in green in quarter circle] SCHOOL EDITION | [illustration in black of boy holding a fawn] | [in green] Marjorie Kinnan Rawlings'; spine in black: 'THE | YEAR-

LING | MARJORIE | KINNAN | RAWLINGS | [in green leaf and in the middle of the leaf] SCHOOL EDITION | SCRIBNERS'. All edges trimmed.

Binding B: Same as A, except beige cloth.

Publication: 20,500 copies published on 1 October 1941. $1.00.

Locations: Binding A: PM, RLT; binding B: PC.

Note one: Text from the plates of A3.1.a.

Note two: Scribners Records indicates that 22,400 inserts and 20,500 frontispieces were printed on 1 October.

Note three: Rawlings's introduction, exclusive to the "School Edition," is dated 'June, 1941'.

A 3.5.b
Third American edition, second printing [1943]

New York: Charles Scribner's Sons, n.d. [1943]. 10,150 copies. 1 March 1943. $1.00. *Location:* From Scribners Records, *not seen.*

A 3.5.c
Third American edition, third printing [1944]

New York: Charles Scribner's, n.d. [1944]. 10,000 copies. 30 June 1944. $1.00. *Location:* PC.

Note: On copyright page: 'C'.

A 3.5.d
Third American edition, fourth printing [1945]

New York: Charles Scribner's Sons, n.d. [1945]. 5,500 copies. 30 August 1945. $1.00. *Location:* From Scribners Records, *not seen.*

A 3.5.e
Third American edition, fifth printing [1946]

New York: Charles Scribner's Sons, n.d. [1946]. 5,150 copies. 14 May 1946. $1.00. *Location:* RLT.

Note: On copyright page: 'E'.

A 3.5.f
First American edition, sixth printing [1947]

A3.5.k *The Yearling* 77

New York: Charles Scribner's Sons, n.d. [1947]. 10,500 copies. 7 January 1947. $1.00. *Locations:* RLT, RM.

Note one: On copyright page: 'F'.

Note two: The following plate alterations were made in the 1947 School Edition.

31.19	big as a barrel] like a Georgia nigger
34.18	dogs] nigger-dogs
51.23	baby's] nigger baby's
343.24–25	(*expression removed*)] nigger-fash/ion
351.6	black] nigger

These alterations are found in all subsequent printings of the School and the Regular (A3.1) Editions. The authority for these alterations is not known.

Note three: Printed in braille. 4 vols. Louisville: American Printing House for the Blind, 1979. A second recording is narrated by Neal Mullins.

A3.5.g
Third American edition, seventh printing [1947]

New York: Charles Scribner's Sons, n.d. [1947]. 10,250 copies. 24 November 1947. $1.00. *Location:* From Scribners Records, *not seen.*

A3.5.h
Third American edition, eighth printing [1949]

New York: Charles Scribner's Sons, n.d. [1949]. 10,300 copies. 28 February 1949. $1.56. *Location:* From Scribners Records, *not seen.*

A3.5.i
Third American edition, ninth printing [1950]

New York: Charles Scribner's Sons, n.d. [1950]. 10,250 copies. 24 February 1950. $1.80. *Location:* From Scribners Records, *not seen.*

A3.5.j
Third American edition, tenth printing [1951]

New York: Charles Scribner's Sons, n.d. [1951]. 5,150 copies. 1 August 1951. $2.00. *Location:* From Scribners Records, *not seen.*

A3.5.k
Third American edition, eleventh printing [1952]

New York: Charles Scribner's Sons, n.d. [1952]. 5,175 copies. 1 February 1952. $1.80. *Location:* From Scribners Records, *not seen.*

A3.5.l
Third American edition, twelfth printing [1953]

New York: Charles Scribner's Sons, n.d. [1953]. 5,150 copies. 30 September 1953. $2.20. *Location:* From Scribners Records, *not seen.*

A3.5.m
Third American edition, thirteenth printing [1954]

New York: Charles Scribner's, n.d. [1954]. 7,500 copies. 10 February 1954. $2.40. *Location:* From Scribners Records, *not seen.*

A3.5.n
Third American edition, fourteenth printing [1955]

New York: Charles Scribner's Sons, n.d. [1955]. 7,500 copies. 28 February 1955. $2.60. *Location:* From Scribners Records, *not seen.*

A3.5.o
Third American edition, fifteenth printing [1959?]

New York: Charles Scribner's Sons, n.d. [1959?]. *Location:* RM.

Note: This and the following printings are not noted in Scribners Records.

A3.5.p
Third American edition, sixteenth printing [1960?]

New York: Charles Scribner's Sons, n.d. [1960?]. *Location:* RLT.

A3.6.a
Fourth American edition, "Armed Services Edition," first printing [1943]

[all enclosed in a double frame, split in the center by a single vertical line]: '[at left of vertical line] PUBLISHED BY ARRANGEMENT WITH | CHARLES SCRIBNER'S SONS, NEW YORK | *All rights reserved. No part of this book | may be reproduced in any form without | the permission of Charles Scribner's Sons.* | COPYRIGHT, 1938, BY MARJORIE KINNAN RAWLINGS'; '[right of vertical line] THE | YEARLING | *By* | MARJORIE KINNAN RAWLINGS | *Armed Services Editions* | COUNCIL ON BOOKS IN WARTIME, INC. | NEW YORK

[i–ii] 1–413 [414]; 11.0 × 16.8 cm.

Stapled; [1–13]^{16}; 208 leaves.

Contents: p. i: copyright and title page; p. ii: printer's imprint; pp. 1–413: text; p. 414: blank.

A 3.6.b *The Yearling*

Covers for A 3.6.a-b

Binding: Multicolor wrappers. 'B-55' on upper left cover; 'B | 55' at bottom of spine.

Location: RLT.

Note: A List of the First 534 Books Published for the American Armed Forces Overseas (New York: Editions for the Armed Services, Inc., [1945], p. 3, lists the date of publication as October 1943. *Editions for the Armed Services, Inc.: A History* (New York: Editions for the Armed Services, Inc., n.d.), p. 37, estimates that approximately 50,000 copies were published.

A 3.6.b
Fourth American edition, "Armed Services Edition," second printing [1945]

New York: Armed Services Editions, n.d. [1945].

80   A3.7.a *The Yearling*

Pagination, signatures, and contents the same as A3.6.a, except 'S-33' and 'S | 33' are substituted for 'B-55' and 'B | 55'; and the conditions of publication statement on the front cover is different.

Locations: FU, PM, RLT, RM.

Note: Editions for the Armed Services, Inc.: A History, p. 58, lists S33 as a '*(Reprint)*', published in late 1945, approximately 125,000 copies.

A3.7.a
Fifth American edition, first printing [1946]

THE | YEARLING | *by* | MARJORIE | KINNAN | RAWLINGS | [figure carrying a torch] | [rule] | THE MODERN LIBRARY · NEW YORK | [rule]

v + 400 pp. *Binding:* Green calico-textured cloth. All edges trimmed; top edge stained charcoal. Decorated endpapers. Published by Random House. $1.45. *Location:* RLT.

A3.7.b
Fifth American edition, second printing [1947?]

New York: Modern Library, n.d. [1947]. *Location:* RLT.

Note: On copyright page: 'FIRST *Modern Library* EDITION, 1946'.

A3.8.a
Second British edition, first printing [1947]

THE YEARLING | BY | MARJORIE KINNAN RAWLINGS | *Reprinted by* | ARTHUR BAKER LTD. | 30 MUSEUM STREET, LONDON W.C.1 | *in association with* | WILLIAM HEINEMANN LTD.

320 pp. Published in 1947. *Binding:* Light orange calico-textured cloth. 10s.6d. *Location:* RLT.

A3.8.b
Second British edition, second printing [1953?]

London: William Heinemann, n.d. [1953?]. *Location:* Listed in CBI, *not seen.*

Note: Printed in braille. 5 vols. North Rocks, New South Wales: Royal Institute for Deaf and Blind Children, 1979.

A3.8.c
Second British edition, third printing [1955]

A3.10.a *The Yearling* 81

London: William Heinemann, n.d. [1955]. *Binding:* Blue cloth. 6s. *Location:* RLT. 'CHEAP EDITION'.

Note: An ad for *The Sojourner* (1953) is on the rear flap.

A3.8.d
Second British edition, fourth printing [1955]

London: William Heinemann, n.d. [1955]. *Binding:* Light blue cloth. *Location:* RLT. 'CHEAP EDITION'. Produced in April.

A3.8.e
Second British edition, fifth printing [1955?]

London: William Heinemann, n.d. [1955?]. *Binding:* Multicolor wrappers. *Location:* RLT.

A3.8.f
Second British edition, sixth printing [1958]

London: Landsborough Publications Ltd., n.d. [1958]. *Binding:* Multicolor wrappers. *Location:* BL. 'A FOUR SQUARE BOOK'.

A3.8.g
Second British edition, seventh printing [1970]

London: Arthur Barker, n.d. [1970]. *Location:* Barry University, *not seen.*

A3.9.a
Third British edition, first printing [1953]

Ill. Vera Jarman. London: William Heinemann, n.d. [1953]. 202 pp. *Binding:* Light blue calico-textured cloth. *Location:* RLT. 'THE NEW WINDMILL SERIES'.

Note: Abridged with glossary.

A3.9.b
Third British edition, second printing [1992]

London: Mammoth, n.d. [1992]. 200 pp. *Binding:* Multicolor wrappers. *Location:* RLT.

Note: The glossary (pp. 201–202) is removed.

A3.10.a
Sixth American edition, first printing [1962]

[illustration of a boy holding a fawn with the title at right] | THE | YEARLING | BY MARJORIE KINNAN RAWLINGS | *Decorations by* EDWARD SHENTON | *With a Study Guide by* | MARY LOUISE FAGG | *Jacksonville, Florida | and* | EDITH COWLES | *Robert E. Lee High School | Jacksonville, Florida* | CHARLES SCRIBNER'S SONS | 597 *Fifth Avenue, New York 17, New York*

464 pp. Published 1962. $4.20. *Binding:* Light yellow calico-textured cloth. *Location:* FU.

Note: The text is from the plates of A3.1.a, and the Study Guide is on pp. 431–464.

A3.10.b
Sixth American edition, second printing [1963]

New York: Charles Scribner's Sons, n.d. [1963]. June 1963. *Location:* FU.

A3.10.c
Sixth American edition, third printing [1970]

New York: Charles Scribner's Sons, 1970. December 1970. *Location:* PC.

A3.11
Fourth British edition, only printing [1963]

Harmondsworth, England: Penguin Books. 300 pp. *Binding:* Multicolor wrappers. *Location:* BL. 'Penguin Books   A Peacock Book, PK 22'.

Note: 'This abridged edition first published in Peacock Book 1963'.

A3.12
Seventh American edition, only printing [1964]

Marjorie Kinnan Rawlings | THE | YEARLING | [illustration of boy holding a fawn] | Decorations by | Edward Shenton | Large Type Edition | [thick-thin rule] | [logo of an eye with the figure of a 'J' dropping out of it] | A KEITH JENNISON BOOK | *Franklin Watts, Inc., Publishers* | *A Division of Grolier Club Incorporated* | 575 *Lexington Ave. New York, New York* 10022

428 pp. *Copyright page:* 'G-12.64 [MCOL]'. $6.95. *Binding:* Light green calico-textured cloth. *Locations:* MKRH, RLT.

Note: 'The text of this large type edition | is complete and unabridged.'

A3.13
Eighth American edition, only printing (1966)

A3.17.a *The Yearling* 83

New York: Charles Scribner's, 1966. v + 469 pp. *Binding:* Light brown patterned sand cloth. *Location:* RLT.

A3.14.a
Fifth British edition, first printing [1966]

London: William Heinemann, n.d. [1966]. 428 pp. 30s. *Locations:* From copyright page of A3.14.c, CBI, *not seen.*

A3.14.b
Fifth British edition, second printing [1969]

London: William Heinemann, n.d. [1969]. *Location:* INSU.

A3.14.c
Fifth British edition, third printing [1974]

London: William Heinemann, n.d. [1974]. *Locations:* RLT, RM.

A3.15
Sixth British edition, only printing [1976]

London: Pan Books, n.d. [1976]. 335 pp. Illus. Julie Stiles. *Binding:* Multicolor wrappers. 'A Piccolo Book'. *Locations:* MKRH, RLT.

A3.16
Ninth American edition, only printing [1977]

New York: Charles Scribner's Sons, n.d. [1977]. viii + 431 pp.. Illus. N. C. Wyeth. *Binding:* Dark green leather gilt, all edges in gold. Franklin Library 'Limited Edition'. *Location:* RM.

Note one: The title page lists Scribners as the publisher, even though the publisher was Franklin Library.

Note two: The text, together with the decorated endpapers and illustrations, is a resetting in Linotype Baskerville of the Wyeth Limited Edition.

A3.17.a
Tenth American edition, first printing [1983]

[Enclosed in a reddish brown thin-thick frame] MARJORIE KINNAN RAWLINGS | THE | YEARLING | [ornament] | Illustrated by Thomas B. Allen | THE FRANKLIN LIBRARY | FRANKLIN CENTER, PENNSYLVANIA

vi + 380 pp. *Binding:* Brown leather gilt, all edges gold. *Locations:* RLT, RM.

84   A3.17.b *The Yearling*

Note: 22,477 copies were published as part of the Franklin Mint Pulitzer Prize series which began publication in 1975. *The Yearling* is no. 18 of 53 volumes.

A3.17.b
Tenth American edition, second printing [1984]

Franklin Center, Pennsylvania: Franklin Library, 1984.

Binding: Red leather gilt, all edges gold. *Locations:* RLT, RM.

A3.18
Eleventh American edition, only printing [1984]

The | YEARLING | [illustration] | *by Marjorie Kinnan Rawlings* | WITH PICTURES BY N. C. WYETH | [in script surrounded by a scroll design] The | Southern Classics | Library | TM

401 pp. Published in 1984. *Binding:* Brown leather, faux marbled endpapers. *Location:* FU.

Note one: On p. 401: 'This special edition . . . is privately published by *Southern Living Gallery* for members of *Southern Classics Library* . . . from the 1945 edition. . . . New Type composed in Bulmer and Baskerville. Text printed on 60-pound Olde Style paper. . . .'

Note two: Published with the book is a 22-page commentary on laid paper: pp. 3–4: editor's note; pp. 5–21: an essay on Rawlings by Celestine Sibley.

A3.19
Twelfth American edition, only printing [1992]

The Yearling. Norwalk, Connecticut: Easton Press, n.d. [1992]. $46.00. *Binding:* Green leather gilt, all edges in gold. *Location:* From publisher's records, not seen.

A3.20
Thirteenth American edition, only printing [1993]

[rule] | [title and name in script] THE | YEARLING | *MARJORIE KINNAN* | *RAWLINGS* | *Illustrations by* | EDWARD SHENTON | *Afterword by* | THOMAS DePIETRO | [illustration of a fawn] | THE WORLD'S BEST READING | [rule] | The Reader's Digest Association, Inc. | Pleasantville, N.Y. · Montreal | [rule]

362 pp. *On copyright page:* 'This Reader's Digest edition contains the complete

A 3.22 *The Yearling*   85

text . . . | Copyright © 1993'. *Binding:* Dark green leather spine on boards. *Location:* RM.

Note: The afterword appears on pp. 355–362.

UNDATED EDITIONS

A 3.21
First Chinese edition, in English [n.d.]

Shanghai: Modern Book Co., n.d. vi + 410 pp. $7.50. *Binding:* Black straight morocco-grain cloth. *Location:* FU.

A 3.22
THE | YEARLING | Marjorie Kinnan Rawlings | INTERNATIONAL COLLECTORS LIBRARY | *Garden City, New York*

v + 373 pp. *Binding:* Dark blue faux leather with gold stamping. Laid paper, all edges trimmed, with reader's ribbon. *Locations:* RLT, RM.

A4 WHEN THE WHIPPOORWILL

A4.1.a
First American edition, first printing (1940)

> # When the Whippoorwill—
>
>
>
> ## Marjorie Kinnan Rawlings
>
> ### CHARLES SCRIBNER'S SONS
> ### NEW YORK : 1940

A 4.1.a: 21.9 × 14.4 cm.; illustration in black surrounded by gold.

A 4.1.a *When the Whippoorwill*

> COPYRIGHT, 1931, 1932, 1933, 1934, 1936, 1939, 1940, BY
> MARJORIE KINNAN RAWLINGS
>
> Printed in the United States of America
>
> *All rights reserved. No part of this book may be reproduced in any form without the permission of Charles Scribner's Sons*
>
> A
>
>

[i–x] 1–275 [276–280]

[1⁸(1₄+ χ1) 2–18⁸]; 145 leaves.

Contents: p. i: blank; p. ii: 'BOOKS BY MARJORIE KINNAN RAWLINGS | [rule] | *The Yearling* | *Golden Apples* | *South Moon Under* | [rule] | CHARLES SCRIBNER'S SONS'; p. iii: half title: 'When the Whippoorwill—'; p. iv: blank; p. v: title page; p. vi: copyright page; p. vii: contents; p. viii: blank; p. ix: section title: 'When the Whippoorwill—'; p. x: quotation; pp. 1—19: 'A Crop of Beans'; pp. 20–40: 'Benny and the Bird Dogs'; pp. 41–118: 'Jacob's Ladder'; pp. 119–129: 'The Pardon'; pp. 130–155: 'Varmints'; pp. 156–174: 'The Enemy'; pp. 175–216: 'Gal Young Un'; pp. 217–232: 'Alligators'; pp. 233–240: 'A Plumb Clare Conscience'; pp. 241–250: 'A Mother in Mannville'; pp. 251–275: 'Cocks Must Crow'; pp. 276–280: blank.

Typography and paper: 16.4 (15.7) × 10.2 cm.; laid paper (vertical chain lines: 2.2 cm.); 34 lines per page. Running heads: rectos: pp. 3–19: *'A CROP OF BEANS'*; 21–39: *'BENNY AND THE BIRD DOGS'*; 43–117: *'JACOB'S LADDER'*; 121–129: *'THE PARDON'*; 131–155: *'VARMINTS'*; 157–173: *'THE ENEMY'*; 177–215: *'GAL YOUNG UN'*; 219–231: *'ALLIGATORS'*; 235–239: *'A PLUMB CLARE CONSCIENCE'*; 243–249: *'A MOTHER IN MANNVILLE'*; 253–275: *'COCKS MUST CROW'*; versos: pp. 2–18, 22–128, 132–154, 158–274: *'WHEN THE WHIPPOORWILL—'*.

Binding: Light bluish green calico-textured cloth. Front cover: '[goldstamped thick-thin-thin-thick vertical rule along the spine from top to bottom] | [at bottom third: goldstamped thin-thin rule | [in black, partly covering the rule] When the | [goldstamped thin-thin rule] | [in black, partly covering the rule]

Whippoorwill— | [goldstamped thin-thin, thin-thin rule] | [in black] MARJO-RIE KINNAN RAWLINGS | [goldstamped thin-thin rule]'; spine: '[goldstamped thin-thin rule] | [title in black] When the | Whippoorwill | [goldstamped thin-thin, thin-thin rule] | [in black] RAWLINGS | [goldstamped thin-thin rule, then four sets of thin-thin rule continuous with the rule on the front cover] | [in black] SCRIBNERS | [goldstamped thin-thin rule]'; back cover: blank. Light brown coated endpapers (verso front and recto back not coated). Top and bottom edges trimmed. Fore-edge rough trimmed.

Dust jacket: Front cover: on green background: '[gold rule at top] | [title in white] WHEN THE | WHIPPOORWILL— | [black and white ink sketch in oval, partly outlined in white, centered over a thick gold rule] | [in white] *By the Author of* THE YEARLING | [in black] MARJORIE KINNAN | [in white] RAWLINGS | [gold rule at bottom and in black script at right corner] Neely'; spine: on black background: '[gold rule continuous with the front] | [title in white] WHEN THE | WHIPPOORWILL— | [thin-thick-thicker-thickest quadruple gold rule] | [author in black on thick rule continuous with the front] MARJORIE | KINNAN | RAWLINGS | [thickest-thicker-thick-thin quadruple gold rule] | [in white] SCRIBNERS | [gold rule at bottom continuous with the front]'; back cover: on white background: '[black and white file photo of Rawlings sitting against a tree holding a dog in her lap] | [all printing in black] Marjorie Kinnan Rawlings | *author of the Pulitzer Prize winning novel* | The Yearling | [11-line blurb] | [in rule frame at the left] Regular Edition | *Illustrated with 34 decorations by* | *Edward Shenton* [in rule frame at the right] Pulitzer Prize Edition | *With 14 illustrations in full color* | *by N. C. Wyeth* | CHARLES SCRIBNER'S SONS · NEW YORK'; front flap: '[black lettering on white background] $2.50 [at top right] | WHEN THE | WHIPPOORWILL— | *by* | Marjorie Kinnan Rawlings | *author of* "The Yearling" | [35-line description of the stories]'; rear flap: black lettering on white background: 'Marjorie Kinnan | Rawlings | *has lived for more than a decade* | *in inland Florida among the people* | *about whom she writes in* | When the | Whippoorwill— | [26-line quotation]'.

Publication: 8,150 copies published on 2 April 1940. Scribners File-Cards and Copyright Office record publication as 29 April. Advertised in the *New York Herald Tribune Book Review* (28 April 1940). $2.50. Copyright A140361.

Locations: DLC (deposit-stamped 10 April 1940), PM (dj), RLT (2, dj), RM (2, dj).

Printing: Printed and bound by the Scribner Press.

Note one: 10,250 copies of the dust jacket printed on 5 April 1940.

Dust jacket for A 4.1.a

Note two: The section title (χ^1) is pasted in. In all subsequent printings, the front matter is rearranged to avoid this single leaf.

Note three: A presentation copy with light yellow endpapers has been seen (FU): 'For Norton [Baskin] | with love | Marjorie [underlined]'.

A4.1.b
First American edition, second printing (1940)

New York: Charles Scribner's Sons, 1940. 5,600 copies. 27 April 1940. *Locations*: FU, RLT.

Note one: The 'A' is removed and the Scribners seal is retained on the copyright page in this and all subsequent printings.

Note two: The front matter is rearranged: p. i: half title; p. ii: bibliography; p. iii: title page; p. iv: copyright; p. v: contents; p. vi: blank; p. vii: section title; p. viii: quotation; then same as first printing.

Note three: Second and third printings are not differentiated on the copyright page.

Note four: 5,250 dust jackets printed on 1 May 1940.

A4.1.c
First American edition, third printing (1940)

New York: Charles Scribner's Sons, 1940. 5,080 copies. 30 May 1940. *Location*: From Scribners Records, *not seen.*

Note: 5,150 dust jackets printed on 5 June 1940.

A4.1.d
First American edition, fourth printing (1943)

New York: Charles Scribner's Sons, 1943. 1,000 copies. 11 November 1943. *Location*: CoU.

A4.1.e
First American edition, fifth printing [1945]

New York: Charles Scribner's Sons, n.d. [1945]. 1,000 copies. 5 October 1945. *Binding*: Gray calico-textured cloth. *Location*: State Library of Florida, Tallahassee.

Note one: 1,650 dust jackets printed on 17 October 1945.

Note two: A Scribners Records entry indicates that the price of the book was

A4.1.i *When the Whippoorwill*

raised to $3.00 on 26 January 1949, even though the last printing recorded was in 1945.

Note three: In Scribners Records is an entry: '1/56—5 boxes text plates to Haddon'.

OTHER PRINTINGS WITHIN THE FIRST EDITION

A4.1.f
First American edition, sixth printing [1973]

Dunwoody, Georgia: Norman S. Berg, n.d. [1973].

Facsimile of A4.1.a. *Binding*: Light green cloth. Light green endpapers. Top edge trimmed and stained gold. *Location*: RLT.

Note one: Front and rear flaps of the dust jacket are facsimiles of A4.1.a.

Note two: On the front cover and the spine of the dust jacket 'Whippoorwill' is misspelled 'Whipoorwill'.

A4.1.g
First American edition, seventh printing [1988]

Jacksonville, Florida: San Marco Book Store, n.d. [1988].

Facsimile of A4.1.b., or a later printing. *Binding and dust jacket*: Facsimiles of A4.1.a. 808 copies. $19.95. *Location*: RLT.

A4.1.h
First American edition, eighth printing [1988]

Jacksonville, Florida: San Marco Book Store, n.d. [1988].

Note: Facsimile of 1,000 copies. This printing was ordered after the stock of the seventh printing was sold. The copyright pages of the seventh and eighth printings are not differentiated.

A4.1.i
First American edition, ninth printing [1989?]

[Mattituck, New York: Æonian Press, n.d. (1989?)].

Facsimile reprint of A1.1.b, or later printing. *Binding*: Black cloth. No dust jacket issued. Light purple endpapers. $18.95. *Location*: RLT.

Note: This is an unauthorized reprint, said to be 'limited to 300 copies' (p. iv).

A 4.2
First British edition, only printing [1940]

WHEN THE WHIPPOORWILL—

BY

MARJORIE KINNAN RAWLINGS

WILLIAM HEINEMANN LTD
LONDON :: TORONTO

A 4.2: 19.1 × 12.5 cm.

A 4.2 *When the Whippoorwill*

> FIRST PUBLISHED 1940
>
> PRINTED IN GREAT BRITAIN AT THE WINDMILL PRESS,
> KINGSWOOD, SURREY.

[i–vi] 1–266

[A]⁸ B-I⁸ K-R⁸; 136 leaves.

Contents: p. i: half title; p. ii: '*By the same author* | [rule] | THE YEARLING | GOLDEN APPLES | SOUTH MOON UNDER'; p. iii: title page; p. iv: copyright page: 'FIRST PUBLISHED 1940 | PRINTED IN GREAT BRITAIN AT THE WINDMILL PRESS, | KINGSWOOD, SURREY'; p. v: '*Contents*'; p. vi: 'When the Whippoorwill calls, it's time | for the corn to be in the ground'; pp. 1–19: 'A Crop of Beans'; pp. 20–39: 'Benny and the Bird Dogs' pp. 40–115: 'Jacob's Ladder'; pp. 116–126: 'The Pardon'; pp. 127–151: 'Varmints'; pp. 152–170: 'The Enemy'; pp. 171–210: 'Gal Young Un'; pp. 211–225: 'Alligators'; pp. 226–233: 'A Plumb Clare Conscience'; pp. 234–242: 'A Mother in Mannville'; pp. 243–266: 'Cocks Must Crow'.

Typography and paper: 15.6 (14.9) × 9.2 cm.; wove paper; 39 lines per page. Running heads: versos: pp. 2–18, 22–38, 42–114, 118–126, 128–150, 154–224, 228–232, 236–266: 'WHEN THE WHIPPOORWILL'; rectos: pp. 3–19: 'A CROP OF BEANS'; pp. 21–39: 'BENNY AND THE BIRD DOGS'; pp. 41–115: 'JACOB'S LADDER'; pp. 117–125: 'THE PARDON'; pp. 129–151: 'VARMINTS'; pp. 153–169: 'THE ENEMY'; pp. 173–209: 'GAL YOUNG UN'; pp. 213–225: 'ALLIGATORS'; pp. 227–233: 'A PLUMB CLARE CONSCIENCE'; pp. 235–241: 'A MOTHER IN MANNVILLE'; pp. 245–265: 'COCKS MUST CROW'.

Binding: Bluish green calico-textured cloth. Silverstamped spine: 'When the | Whippoorwill — | Marjorie | Kinnan | Rawlings. | HEINEMANN.'

Dust jacket: Not seen. Presence of dust jacket not confirmed.

Publication: 2,000 copies published on 23 September 1940. 8s.

Printing: Windmill Press.

Locations: BL (deposit-stamped 30 September 1940), Bodleian (deposit-stamped 18 November 1940).

OTHER EDITIONS

A 4.3.a
Second American edition, first printing [1975]

New York: Ballantine Books, n.d. [1975].

v + 249 pp. *Binding*: Multicolor wrappers. 20,100 copies. May 1975. 'A Mockingbird Book'. $1.75. *Location*: RLT.

A 4.3.b
Second American edition, second printing [1980]

St. Simons Island, Georgia: Mockingbird Books, 1980. *Binding*: Multicolor wrappers. 6,300 copies. *Location*: RM.

A 4.3.c
Second American edition, third printing [n.d.]

St. Simons Island, Georgia: Mockingbird Books, n.d. *Binding*: Multicolor wrappers. 7,300 copies. *Location*: From publisher's records, *not seen.*

A5 CROSS CREEK

A5.1.a
First American edition, first printing (1942)

CROSS CREEK

By

Marjorie Kinnan Rawlings

Decorations by
EDWARD SHENTON

New York
CHARLES SCRIBNER'S SONS
1942

A 5.1.a: 20.8 × 14.0 cm.

> COPYRIGHT 1942, BY
> MARJORIE KINNAN RAWLINGS
>
> COPYRIGHT 1933 BY SCRIBNER'S MAGAZINE
> COPYRIGHT 1942 BY THE ATLANTIC MONTHLY
>
> Printed in the United States of America
>
> *All rights reserved. No part of this book may be reproduced in any form without the permission of Charles Scribner's Sons*
>
> A

[i–viii] 1–368

[1–10]¹⁶ [11]¹² [12]¹⁶; 188 leaves.

Contents: p. i: blank; p. ii: 'BOOKS BY MARJORIE KINNAN RAWLINGS | [rule] | [list of five books] | [rule] | CHARLES SCRIBNER'S SONS'; p. iii: half title: 'CROSS CREEK | [illustration of a hummingbird eating from a hand]'; p. iv: blank; p. v: title page; p. vi: copyright page; p. vii: section title: 'CROSS CREEK'; p. viii: blank; pp. 1–368: text.

Typography and paper: 16.3 (15.6) × 10.2 cm.; wove paper; 34 lines per page. Running heads: rectos: pp. 3–5: 'Cross Creek'; 7–17: 'For This Is An Enchanted Island'; 19–27: 'Taking Up the Slack'; 29–39: 'The Magnolia Tree'; 41–47: 'The Pound Party'; 49–55: 'The Census'; 57–63: 'The Evolution of Comfort'; 65–67: 'Antses in Tim's Breakfast'; 71–75: 'The Widow Slater'; 79–81: 'Catching One Young'; 83–95: '"Geechee"'; 99–107: 'A Pig Is Paid For'; 109–121: 'My Friend Moe'; 123–143: 'Residue'; 145–165: 'Toady-frogs, Lizards, Antses, and Varmints'; 167–179: 'The Ancient Enmity'; 181–203: 'Black Shadows'; 207–241: 'Our Daily Bread'; 245–267: 'Spring at the Creek'; 269–297: 'Summer'; 299–309: 'Fall'; 313–341: 'Winter'; 343–357: 'Hyacinth Drift'; 361–367: 'Who Owns Cross Creek?'; versos: pp. 2–16, 20–26, 30–38, 42–46, 50–54, 58–62, 66–80, 84–106, 110–120, 124–142, 146–164, 168–178, 182–266, 270–296, 300–340, 344–368: 'Cross Creek'. Paper bulk: title page: .157 cm.; p. 151: .157 cm.

Binding: Light green calico-textured cloth; front cover: stamped in silver an illustration of an egret in a swamp; silverstamped spine: '[thick rule] | [in silver box with lettering in light green] CROSS | CREEK | [short rule] | Marjorie | Kinnan | Rawlings | [thick silver rule below the box] | [thick silver rule with lettering in light green 'SCRIBNERS' | [thick silver rule]'; back cover: blank. Front and rear pastedown and free endpapers: in green and white: continuous

A 5.1.a *Cross Creek* 97

illustration of orange grove. Top and bottom edge untrimmed. Fore-edge rough trimmed.

Dust jacket: Upper two-thirds of the front cover, spine, and rear cover: in color a continuous scene; front cover: upper two-thirds, two houses along a creek with a boat pulled along the bank, bottom third: black on yellow background: 'CROSS CREEK | *by* | Marjorie Kinnan Rawlings | *Author of "The Yearling"* | [green rule at bottom]'; spine: upper two-thirds scene continuous with front and rear covers, bottom third: black on yellow background: 'CROSS | CREEK | [short rule] | Marjorie | Kinnan | Rawlings | [short rule] | SCRIBNERS | [green rule at bottom]'; back cover: upper two-thirds scene continuous with rear cover, bottom third: black on yellow background: 'CROSS CREEK | *The Story of the Yearling Country* | *and its People* | [green rule at bottom]'; front flap: '[upper right corner in red] $2.50 | [in blue] Cross Creek | [in black] *by* | [in black] *Marjorie Kinnan Rawlings* | [in blue] With drawings done on the scene by | [in blue] *Edward Shenton who also illustrated* | [in blue] *"The Yearling"* | [38-line description in black of the book] | [in red] *Jacket drawing by Robert Camp, Jr.*'; rear flap: '[photograph of Rawlings sitting at her desk] | [in blue] *Marjorie Kinnan Rawlings* | [in blue] *outside her home at Cross Creek*'.

Publication: 7,500 copies published on 16 March 1942. Copyright A169035. Listed in *Publishers' Weekly*, 141 (31 January 1942), 456. Advertised in the *New York Times Book Review*, 8 March 1942. $2.50.

Printing: Printed and bound by the Scribner Press.

Locations: FU (dj), DLC (deposit-stamped 27 February 1942), InU (dj), MKRH (dj), PM (3, dj), RLT (dj), RM (3, dj).

Note one: 8,000 dust jackets and 7,500 bindings were ordered on 10 March.

Note two: Scribners Records entries for *Cross Creek* are incomplete. The distinction among printings is different from the usual. 'A' copies were printed first; copies without the 'A' or the Scribners seal next; copies with the 'A' and the Scribners seal next; and copies with only the seal next. The determination that 'A' is the first printing is based upon three advance copies in the PM Collection. Copy one is a presentation copy: 'For Aunt Ida . . . March 1942'; copy two: 'For Cliff & Gladys [Lyons] . . . March 17, 1942'; and copy three: 'For my good friend | Phil May — | March 1942'. Each was sent to Rawlings in advance of the official publication date of 16 March. Rawlings characteristically presented the first advance to her Aunt Ida, as stated in the advance of *When the Whippoorwill*—: 'For Aunt Ida— | the first copy, as usual— | with love——Marjorie [name underlined]'. These advance copies of *Cross Creek* all have $2.50 on the front flap of the dust jacket. Further, the DLC deposit copy,

Dust jacket for A 5.1.a

A 5.1.a *Cross Creek*   99

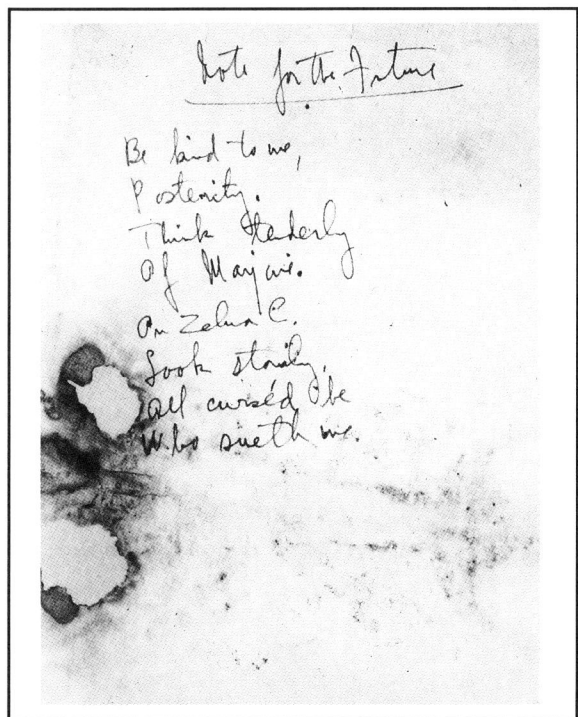

Manuscript of poem on the "Cross Creek" trial, A 5

normally the first printing, is an 'A' copy. Finally, an examination of the progressive deterioration of the type and of the differences in paper bulk confirms the distinction among printings.

Note three: In advertisements in the *New York Times Book Review*, 15 March 1942, and the *New York Herald Tribune Book Review*, 22 March 1942, Scribners claimed a 'First Printing, 275,000 copies,' which includes the Book-of-the-Month Club. An advertisement in the *New York Times Book Review*, 12 April 1942, and again on 19 April 1942, reported Scribners '*Now in its 400th Thousand*', which includes the Book-of-the-Month Club. In the *New York Times Book Review*, 26 April 1942, '*455th Thousand*' had been printed. In the *New York Times Book Review*, 14 June 1942, *Cross Creek* is declared 'America's No. 1 best selling book of non-fiction'.

Note four: Scribners File-Cards indicates that on 2 March 1942, two salesman's dummies were delivered.

Note five: Three advance copies have been seen:

    21.0 × 14.2 cm.

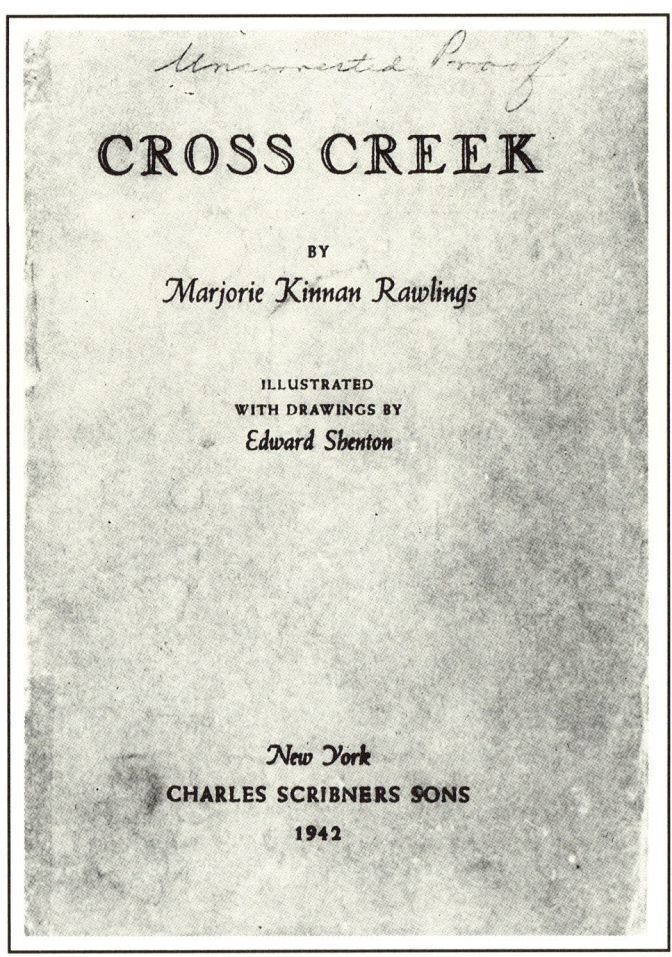

Cover of proof copy for a 5.1.a

[i–ii] 1–368 [369–370].

[1–22]⁸ [23]¹⁰; 186 leaves.

Contents: Same as A5.1.a.

Typography and paper: Same as A5.1.a.

Binding: Light green wrappers; front cover: 'Cross Creek [in hollow font] | BY | *Marjorie Kinnan Rawlings* | ILLUSTRATED | WITH DRAWINGS BY | *Edward Shenton* | *New York* | CHARLES SCRIBNERS SONS | 1942'. Spine and back cover: blank. No flyleaves. Top and bottom edges untrimmed. Fore-edge rough trimmed.

A5.1.c *Cross Creek* 101

Locations: PM, RLT, RM.

Note: The font is uneven on the following page numbers: '4^5', '2^{5}1', 3^{5}2'. It is corrected in A5.1.a.

Note six: A condensed form of *Cross Creek* was published in *Reader's Digest*, 41, no. 244 (August 1942), 149–176.

A5.1.b
First American edition, second printing, for the Book-of-the-Month Club (1942)

New York: Charles Scribner's Sons, 1942. *Binding and dust jacket*: Same as A5.1.a, except there is a crimp in the bottom left corner of the back cover, and the '$2.50' has been removed from the front flap. Paper bulk: title page: .156 mm.; p. 151: .148 mm. *Locations*: PM, RLT.

Note one: 'A' but no Scribners seal on the copyright page.

Note two: 225,000 copies ordered on 13 February 1942, published in March.

Note three: The crimp on the bottom left edge of the back cover indentifies first printing BOMC copies.

Note four: There is a fold (4 pp.) containing a 3-page blurb by Henry Seidel Canby, reprinted from the *Book-of-the-Month Club News*, laid in some BOMC copies.

A5.1.c
First American edition, third printing (1942)

New York: Charles Scribner's Sons, 1942. *Binding and dust jacket*: Same as A5.1.a, except '$2.50' has been removed from the front flap. Sheet bulk: title page: .151 mm.; p. 151: .154 mm. *Location*: RLT.

Note one: 'A' but no Scribners seal on the copyright page.

Note two: 2,000 copies published on 27 March 1942.

Note three: The third printing exhibits the same batter as the first two printings, although the damaged 'i' in 'jail' and the damaged 'i' in 'Sissie', p. 199, l. 16, are less visible.

A 5.1.d
Canadian issue, only printing, from the American plates, fourth printing (1942)

CROSS CREEK

By

Marjorie Kinnan Rawlings

Decorations by
EDWARD SHENTON

REGINALD SAUNDERS
TORONTO : 1942

A 5.1.d: 20.9 × 14.5 cm.

> COPYRIGHT REGISTERED IN CANADA 1942
>
> BY REGINALD SAUNDERS
>
> *All rights reserved. No part of this book may be reproduced in any form without the permission of Charles Scribner's Sons, New York*
>
> PRINTED IN THE UNITED STATES OF AMERICA

Pagination is the same as A5.1.a.

Contents: Same as A5.1.a.

Typography and paper: Same as A5.1.a, except sheet bulk: title page: .157 cm.; p. 151: .164 cm.

Binding: Same as A5.1.a, except on the bottom of the spine there are no rules, and 'SAUNDERS' is substituted for 'SCRIBNERS'. Top edge stained yellow. Fore-edge rough trimmed. Bottom edge trimmed.

Dust jacket: Same as A5.1.a, except on the spine 'SAUNDERS' is substituted for 'SCRIBNERS'; and on the front flap '$3.00' is printed in the upper right corner and '*Litho in U. S. A.*' in the bottom left corner.

Publication: Unknown number of copies printed. Published [April] 1942. $3.00.

Printing: 'PRINTED IN THE UNITED STATES OF AMERICA'.

Location: RLT (dj).

Note: The Canadian issue is a separate printing from the American plates, in sequence the fourth printing from the American plates. The Canadian issue exhibits distinct differences in the batter from the first three printings. In the first three printings, for example, the 'g' in 'young' on p. 39, l. 5, and the 'M' in 'Mama', p. 47, l.2, are defective. The title leaf is reset.

LATER PRINTINGS WITHIN THE FIRST EDITION

A5.1.e
First American edition, fifth printing (1942)

New York: Charles Scribner's Sons, 1942. *Binding and dust jacket*: Same as A5.1.c. Sheet bulk: title page: .155 mm.; p. 151: .145 mm. *Location*: RLT.

Note one: 'A' is dropped from the copyright page.

Note two: 2,500 copies published on 2 April 1942.

A 5.1.f
First American edition, sixth printing, for the Book-of-the-Month Club (1942)

New York: Charles Scribner's Sons, 1942. *Binding and dust jacket*: Same as A5.1.b. Sheet bulk: title page: .153 mm.; p. 151: .155 mm. *Location*: RLT.

Note one: 'A' is dropped from the copyright page.

Note two: 100,000 copies ordered on 1 April 1942, published in April.

A 5.1.g
First American edition, seventh printing (1942)

New York: Charles Scribner's Sons, 1942. *Binding and dust jacket*: Same as A5.1.c, except the top edge is stained yellow. Sheet bulk: title page: .157 mm.; p. 151: .156 mm. *Location*: RLT.

Note one: 'A' is dropped from the copyright page.

Note two: 15,000 copies ordered on 16 April, published in April.

A 5.1.h
First American edition, eighth printing, for the Book-of-the-Month Club (1942)

New York: Charles Scribner's Sons, 1942. *Binding and dust jacket*: Same as A5.1.b. Sheet bulk: title page: .142 mm.; p. 151: .162 mm. *Location*: RLT.

Note one: 'A' is dropped from the copyright page.

Note two: 16,900 copies ordered on 16 April 1942, published in April.

A 5.1.i
First American edition, ninth printing (1942)

New York: Charles Scribner's Sons. 1942. *Binding and dust jacket*: Same as A5.1.c, except the top edge is stained yellow. Sheet bulk: title page: .147 mm.; p. 151: .157 mm. *Location*: RLT.

Note one: 'A' and seal on the copyright page.

Note two: There is a BOMC *News* laid in this copy, but there is no crimp in the binding. The presence of the *News* and the lack of a crimp are not determinative. However, the order for 100,000 linings (see *Note three*) would suggest that there was at least one more printing for BOMC.

A5.1.m *Cross Creek* 105

Note three: Scribners Records does not document this or the subsequent printings, although it is certain, from Scribners own newspaper advertisements, that there were other printings in 1942 and 1943. On 19 April 1942, for example, Scribners advertised that 455,000 copies had been published. An entry in the Records for 3 August 1942 notes an order for 100,000 linings (endpapers).

A5.1.j
First American edition, tenth printing (1942)

New York: Charles Scribner's Sons, 1942. *Binding and dust jacket*: Same as A5.1.c, except the top edge is stained yellow. Sheet bulk: title page: .153 mm.; p. 151: .147 mm. *Location*: RLT.

Note: 'A' and Scribners seal on the copyright page.

A5.1.k
First American edition, eleventh printing (1944)

New York: Charles Scribner's Sons, 1944. *Binding and dust jacket*: Same as A5.1.c. Sheet bulk: title page: .149 mm.; p. 151: .155 mm. *Location*: RLT.

Note one: Scribners seal on the copyright page.

Note two: The similar batter (e.g., the 't' in 'to' on p. 89, l. 2) indicate that this printing follows A5.1.i–j.

A5.1.l
First American edition, twelfth printing [1946]

CROSS CREEK | By | Marjorie Kinnan Rawlings | Decorations by | EDWARD SHENTON | [illustration] | New York | GROSSET & DUNLAP, *Publishers* | *By arrangement with Charles Scribner's Sons*

From the plates of A5.1.a. Published January 1946. *Binding*: Same as A5.1.a, except goldstamped spine: '[thick rule] | [title and name in green on goldstamped background] CROSS | CREEK | [short rule] | Marjorie | Kinnan | Rawlings | [thick rule] | GROSSET | & DUNLAP | [thick rule]'. Top edge stained yellow. $1.49. *Location*: RLT.

A5.1.m
First American edition, thirteenth printing [1954]

New York: Grosset & Dunlap, n.d. [1954].

Location: Listed in *Publishers' Weekly*, 166 (10 July 1954), 139, *not seen*.

A5.1.n
First American edition, fourteenth printing [1960]

New York: Charles Scribner's Sons, n.d. [1960]. 'G-11.60[H]'. $4.50. *Location*: RLT.

A5.1.o
First American edition, fifteenth printing [1962]

New York: Charles Scribner's Sons, n.d. [1962]. *Binding A*: Coated color-printed wrappers; binding B: Cloth. 'A-8.62[C]'. $1.65. *Location*: RLT.

A5.1.p
First American edition, sixteenth printing (1975)

CROSS CREEK | By | Marjorie Kinnan Rawlings | *Decorations by* | EDWARD SHENTON | [illustration] | Norman S. Berg, Publisher | "Sellanraa," | Dunwoody, Georgia. | 1975

Facsimile of A5.1.a. On thick stock paper. *Binding*: Olive calico-textured cloth, with a black continuous spine. *Dust jacket*: Multicolor. *Location*: RLT.

A5.1.q
First American edition, seventeenth printing [1980]

New York: Charles Scribner's Sons, n.d. [1980.] $7.95. *Location*: Listed in CBI and BIP (1984), *not seen.*

A5.1.r
First American edition, eighteenth printing [1987]

CROSS CREEK | By | Marjorie Kinnan Rawlings | *Decorations by* | Edward Shenton | [illustration] | Collier Books | *Macmillan Publishing Company* | *New York*

$4.95. *Binding*: Multicolor wrappers. *Location*: RLT.

A 5.2.a
First British edition, first printing [1942]

CROSS CREEK

BY

MARJORIE KINNAN RAWLINGS

Decorations by
EDWARD SHENTON

WILLIAM HEINEMANN LTD
LONDON   ::   TORONTO

A 5.2.a: 19.6 × 13.0 cm.

> FIRST PUBLISHED 1942
>
> WAR ECONOMY
>
> THIS BOOK IS PRODUCED IN COMPLETE
> CONFORMITY WITH THE AUTHORISED
> ECONOMY STANDARDS
>
> PRINTED IN GREAT BRITAIN AT THE WINDMILL PRESS
> KINGSWOOD, SURREY

TWO STATES HAVE BEEN NOTED, PRIORITY UNDETERMINED

1st state: i–iv 1–310

[A]⁸ B–I⁸ K–T⁸(T₈+'U'1) [V]⁴; 157 leaves.

Contents: p. i: half title: 'CROSS CREEK' + illustration of a bird feeding from a hand; p. ii: '*Also by* | MARJORIE KINNAN RAWLINGS | [short rule] | WHEN THE WHIPPOORWILL— | THE YEARLING'; p. iii: title page; p. iv: copyright page; pp. 1–310: text.

2nd state: i–iv 1–310 [311–312]

[A]⁸ B–I⁸ K–T⁸ U⁶; 158 leaves.

Contents: Same as first state, except pp. 311–312 are blank.

Typography and paper: 15.7 (15.1) × 10.1 cm.; wove paper; 39 lines per page. Running heads: rectos: pp. 3–5: 'Cross Creek'; pp. 7–13: 'For This Is An Enchanted Island'; pp. 15–21: 'Taking Up the Slack'; pp. 23–31: 'The Magnolia Tree'; pp. 33–39: 'The Pound Party'; pp. 41–45: 'The Census'; pp. 47–51: 'The Evolution of Comfort'; pp. 53–55: 'Antses in Tim's Breakfast'; pp. 57–61: 'The Widow Slater'; pp. 63–67: 'Catching One Young'; pp. 69–79: ''Geechee'; pp. 81–87: 'A Pig Is Paid For'; pp. 89–99: 'My Friend Moe'; pp. 101–117: 'Residue'; pp. 119–137: 'Toady-frogs, Lizards, Antses, and Varmints'; pp. 139–149: 'The Ancient Enmity'; pp. 151–169: 'Black Shadows'; pp. 171–203: 'Our Daily Bread'; pp. 205–223: 'Spring at the Creek'; pp. 225–249: 'Summer'; pp. 251–261: 'Autumn'; pp. 263–287: 'Winter'; pp. 289–301: 'Hyacinth Drift'; pp. 303–309: 'Who Owns Cross Creek'; versos: pp. 2–4, 8–310: 'Cross Creek'.

Binding: Two styles have been noted:

> *1st state:* Light green calico-textured cloth; front cover in center: blindstamped illustration of a palm; spine: graystamped: 'CROSS CREEK | [circular rule] | Marjorie | Kinnan | Rawlings | HEINEMANN'; back cover: lower

A 5.2.c *Cross Creek*

right: blindstamped illustration of a windmill. Light brownish gray uncoated endpapers. All edges trimmed.

2nd state: Same as first state, except light bluish green cloth. Light brown uncoated endpapers.

Dust jacket: Front cover: on white background: '[in green] CROSS | [in green] CREEK | [in white in diagonal on diagonal red background] by the author of | The Yearling | [in green] MARJORIE KINNAN | RAWLINGS'; spine: on white background: '[all in green] CROSS | CREEK | *by* | Marjorie | Kinnan | Rawlings | HEINEMANN'; back cover: on white background: '[illustration of Rawlings holding a dog in her lap] | MARJORIE KINNAN RAWLINGS | Author of the Pulitzer Prize Winning Novel. | THE YEARLING | [17-line blurb on *The Yearling*]'; front flap: on white background: '[all in green]: '[39-line blurb on *Cross Creek*] | [in lower right corner] 9s.6d. | NET'; rear flap: on white background: 'Also by | MARJORIE KINNAN | RAWLINGS | [title in bold] When the | Whippoorwill— | [18-line blurb]'.

Publication: 7,500 copies published on 30 November 1942. 9s.6d.

Printing: Windmill Press.

Locations: 1st state: RLT (dj); 2nd state: BL (deposit-stamped 30 November 1942), RLT (dj).

Note one: In 1st state, the signed leaf 'U' (pp. 301–302) is a disjunctive leaf and is pasted to leaf T_8 (pp. 299–300). In 2nd state, the signed leaf 'U' is conjugate with U_6 (pp. 311–312), a blank leaf. The content of each leaf 'U' is identical.

Note two: Printed on the verso of the dust jacket is a complete cover for Marie C. Oemler's *The Butterfly Man*.

Note three: Scribners File-Cards, 1 September 1942, indicates that Heinemann paid £30 for the use of the Shenton illustrations.

A 5.2.b
First British edition, second printing [1942]

London: William Heinemann, n.d. [1942]. *Binding:* Same as A5.2.a. *Location:* RLT.

Note: Produced in December; unknown number of copies printed.

A 5.2.c
First British edition, third printing [1943]

Dust jacket for A 5.2.a

A 5.3 *Cross Creek*

Cover for A 5.3

London: William Heinemann, n.d. [1943]. *Binding*: Same as A5.2.a, except olive green. *Location*: RLT.

Note one: Produced in January 1943; unknown number of copies printed.

Note two: Printed in braille. 9 vols. Brisbane, Australia: Queensland Braille Writing Association, n.d. [1990].

A 5.2.d
First British edition, fourth printing [1943]

London: William Heinemann, n.d. [1943]. *Binding*: Same as A5.2.a, except light bluish green. *Location*: RLT.

Note: Produced in April 1943; unknown number of copies printed.

OTHER EDITIONS

A 5.3
Second American edition, "Armed Services Edition," only printing [1943]

[enclosed in a double rule frame, split in the center with a single vertical rule]: '[left of vertical rule] PUBLISHED BY ARRANGEMENT WITH | CHARLES SCRIBNER'S SONS, NEW YORK | *Manufactured in the United States of*

America'; '[right of vertical rule] CROSS CREEK | *By* | Marjorie Kinnan Rawlings | *Armed Services Editions* | COUNCIL ON BOOKS IN WARTIME, INC. | NEW YORK

[i–ii] [1–2] 3–347 [348–350]; double-column format. 11.5 × 16.6 cm.

Stapled; 1–11^{16}; 176 leaves.

Binding: Multicolor wrappers.

Locations: FU, PM.

Note: A List of the First 534 Books Published for American Armed Forces Overseas (New York: Editions for the Armed Services, Inc., [1945]), p. 4, lists the date of publication as December 1943. *Editions for the Armed Services, Inc.: A History* (New York: Editions for the Armed Services, Inc., n.d.), p. 39, estimates that 50,000 copies were published.

A 5.4
Second British edition, only printing [1944]

CROSS CREEK | *by* | MARJORIE KINNAN RAWLINGS | *Decorations by* | EDWARD SHENTON | THE BOOK CLUB | 121 CHARING CROSS ROAD | LONDON W.C.2

iv + 312 pp. *Binding*: Rose calico-textured cloth. *Dust jacket*: Multicolor with young black girl on the front cover. 2s.6d. *Location*: RLT (3).

Note: Published in 1944 on thin stock: 'WAR ECONOMY | [rule] | THIS BOOK IS PRODUCED IN COMPLETE | CONFORMITY WITH THE AUTHO-RIZED | ECONOMY STANDARDS'.

A 5.5
Third American edition, only printing [1966]

CROSS | *Marjorie Kinnan Rawlings* | CREEK | *With a new introduction by Shirley Ann Grau* | *Decorations by Edward Shenton* | [publisher's device at lower right] | *Time Reading Program special edition* | TIME INCORPORATED · NEW YORK

xxiii + 383 pp. Published in 1966. *Binding*: Multicolor wrappers. *Location*: RLT.

Note: The Editor's Preface occupies pp. ix–xiv; Grau's introduction, pp. xv–xxi.

A 5.6.a–j
Fourth American edition, first-ninth printings [1974–1985]

Covers for A 5.6.b and A 5.6.j

CROSS CREEK | Marjorie Kinnan Rawlings | BALLANTINE BOOKS · NEW YORK

vi + 279 pp. *Binding*: Multicolor wrappers. *Location*: RLT.

Note: 'A Mockingbird Book'. The second and following printings are published by Mockingbird Books. The copyright page for A5.6.j and the publisher's records indicate that there were nine printings of this edition, the ninth in March 1985. The first (March 1974), the fourth (March 1980), the fifth (April 1982), the seventh (August 1983), and the ninth (March 1985) have been seen (RLT). The number of copies printed is as follows: 28,600, 7,000, 10,600, 6,700, 5,400, 6,300, 6,200, 20,700, 10,200.

A5.7
Third British edition, only printing [1984]

[London]: Fontana, n.d. [1984]. 312 pp. *Binding*: Wrappers. *Location*: Listed in the World Catalogue, *not seen*.

A5.8.a$_1$
Fifth American edition, "Limited Edition of the 50th Anniversary Edition," only printing, first issue, (1992)

CROSS CREEK | BY | Marjorie Kinnan Rawlings | *Introduction by* | Carol Anita Tarr | and | Rodger L. Tarr | *Decorations by* | EDWARD SHENTON | [illustration] | SOUTH MOON BOOKS | Jacksonville, Florida | 1992

Limited to 1,000 copies. a–b, i–xx, 1–368 pp.

Contents: p. a: limitation notice, signed by Philip S. May, Jr.; p. b: blank; p. i: half title: 'CROSS CREEK | [illustration]'; p. ii: blank; inserted between p. ii and p. iii a color illustration on the verso; p. iii: title page; p. iv: copyright page; pp. v–vi: 'Preface'; pp. vii–xvii: 'Introduction'; p. xviii: blank; p. xix: section title: 'CROSS CREEK'; p. xx: blank; pp. 1–368: text.

Binding and dust jacket: Same as A5.1.a, except 'SOUTH MOON' substituted for 'SCRIBNERS' on the spine and the price removed from the front flap.

Note one: Promotional fold: 'Special 50th Anniversary Edition | ... | Limited to 26 lettered copies | and 200 numbered copies, | each of which is signed by | Norton Baskin ... | Dessie Smith Prescott ... | Idella Parker ... | Jake Glisson ...'. Lettered copies ($300 prepublication) $400; numbered copies ($125 prepublication) $150. Lettered copies in special slipcase; numbered copies in slipcase. There is also a 'Special Limited Edition' of 1,000 copies ($30), signed by Philip May, Jr.

Note two: The text is reset, but to conform to A5.1.a.

A5.8.a *Cross Creek* 115

A5.8.a$_2$
Fifth American edition, "Numbered Edition of the 50th Anniversary Edition," only printing, second issue, 1992

Jacksonville, Florida: South Moon Books, 1992. Limited to 200 copies.

Contents: p. a: limitation notice; p. b: blank; p. c.: 'This is copy _____ | of the | Special 50th Anniversary Edition | of | *Cross Creek* | [followed by the signatures of Norton Baskin, Dessie Smith Prescott, Idella Parker, and Jake Glisson]'; p. d: blank; p. i: half title; p. ii: blank; a color illustration is inserted between p. ii and p. iii; then same as the first issue.

Binding and dust jacket: Same as the first issue. In green cloth box.

A5.8.a$_3$
Fifth American edition, "Lettered Edition of the 50th Anniversary Edition," only printing, third issue, 1992

Jacksonville, Florida: South Moon Books, 1992. Limited to 26 copies.

Contents: p. a: limitation notice; p. b: four photographs: top left: Norton Baskin; top right: Dessie Smith Prescott; bottom left: Idella Parker; bottom right: Jake Glisson; p. c: same as the second issue, except numbered 'A [–Z]'; p. d: blank; p. i: half title; p. ii: blank; inserted between p. ii and p. iii a photograph of Rawlings; then same as the first issue.

Binding: White coarse linen grain cloth; spine: goldstamped green leather label: 'CROSS | CREEK | [short rule] | Marjorie | Kinnan | Rawlings'. Top edge in gold. Fore-edge and bottom edge trimmed. Box, same as second issue, except glued on left side, in a blindstamped frame, is an illustration (14.5 × 13.3 cm.) of Cross Creek.

A6 CROSS CREEK COOKERY

A6.1.a
First American edition, first printing (1942)

Cross Creek Cookery

by

Marjorie Kinnan Rawlings

with drawings by
Robert Camp

NEW YORK
CHARLES SCRIBNER'S SONS
1942

A 6.1.a: 21.0 × 14.0 cm.

A 6.1.a *Cross Creek Cookery*

```
COPYRIGHT, 1942, BY
MARJORIE KINNAN RAWLINGS
———
Printed in the United States of America

All rights reserved. No part of this book
may be reproduced in any form without
the permission of Charles Scribner's Sons
A
```

[a–b] [i–iv] v–xiii [xiv] xv–xii [xxiii–xxiv] 1–47 [48] 49–69 [70–71] 72–79 [80–81] 82–93 [94–95] 96–103 [104–105] 106–208 [209] 210–218 [219–220] 221–230

[1–16]^8; 128 leaves.

Contents: p. a: half title: '*Cross Creek | Cookery |* [illustration]'; p. b: blank; p. i: blank; p. ii: illustration; p. iii: title page; p. iv: copyright page; pp. v–xiii: '*Contents*'; p. xiv: blank; pp. xv–xxii: '*Cross Creek Menus*'; p. xxiii: section title: '*Cross Creek | Cookery |* [illustration]'; p. xxiv: blank; pp. 1–218: recipes; p. 219: section title: '*Index*'; p. 220: blank; pp. 221–230: index.

Typography and paper: 15.5 (14.8) × 10.1 cm.; thick wove paper; 30 lines per page. Running heads: versos: pp. vi–xii: 'CONTENTS'; xvi–xxii: 'CROSS CREEK MENUS'; pp. 2–4: 'TO OUR BODIES' GOOD'; pp. 6–16: 'SOUPS'; pp. 20–36: 'HOT BREADS'; pp. 40–46: 'LUNCHEON DISHES'; pp. 50–64: 'VEGETABLES'; pp. 68, 72–76: 'POTATOES, RICE, AND GRITS'; pp. 78, 82–92, 96–98: 'FLORIDA SEA FOODS'; pp. 102, 106–136: 'GAME AND MEATS'; pp. 138–146: 'SALADS'; pp. 150–206: 'DESSERTS'; pp. 208–214: 'PRESERVES, JELLIES, AND MARMALADES'; p. 218: ' "BETTER A DINNER OF HERBS" '; pp. 222–230: 'INDEX'; rectos: pp. vii–xiii: 'CONTENTS'; pp. xvii–xxi: 'CROSS CREEK MENUS'; p. 3: 'TO OUR BODIES' GOOD'; pp. 7–17: 'SOUPS'; pp. 19–37: 'HOT BREADS'; pp. 39–47: 'LUNCHEON DISHES'; pp. 51–65: 'VEGETABLES'; pp. 67–69, 73–75: 'POTATOES, RICE, AND GRITS'; pp. 79, 83–93, 97–99: 'FLORIDA SEA FOODS'; pp. 101–103, 107–135: 'GAME AND MEATS'; pp. 139–147: 'SALADS'; pp. 149–205: 'DESSERTS'; pp. 207, 211–215: 'PRESERVES, JELLIES, AND MARMALADES'; p. 217: ' "BETTER A DINNER OF HERBS" '; pp. 223–229: 'INDEX'. Sheet bulk: title page: .158 mm.; p. 50: .153 mm.

Binding: Multicolored calico-textured cloth. Front cover, spine, and back cover: continuous scene of fisherpeople in a Florida setting; front cover: '[title and author in orange with white outline] Cross Creek | Cookery | Marjorie Kinnan Rawlings'; spine: '[in black] MARJORIE | KINNAN | RAWLINGS |

Dust jacket for A 6.1.a

A6.1.c *Cross Creek Cookery*

CROSS | CREEK | COOKERY | SCRIBNERS'. Front and rear pastedowns and endpapers: black and white illustration of swamp scene. All edges trimmed.

Dust jacket: Front cover, spine, and back cover: same as the binding; front flap: black on white background: '[upper right corner] $2.50 | *Cross Creek | Cookery* | by | Marjorie Kinnan Rawlings | *Author of "Cross Creek," "The Yearling," etc.* | [33–line description of the book] | [*Continued on Back Flap*]'; rear flap: black on white background: '[*Continued from Front Flap*] | [11-line description] | [three stars] | [25-line biography of Rawlings] | [three stars] | [5-line biography of the illustrator Robert Camp]'.

Publication: Unknown number of copies printed. Published 16 November 1942. $2.50. Copyright A169035.

Printing: Printed and bound by the Scribner Press.

Locations: InU (dj), PM (dj), RLT (2, dj), RM (dj).

Note one: The first edition, first printing, has an 'A' but no Scribners seal on the copyright page.

Note two: Interspersed among the recipes are Rawlings's comments on the local history of the recipes in question, as well as a number of illustrations by Robert Camp.

Note three: The DLC deposit copy has not been located. The priority of the first and second printings is inferred.

A6.1.b
First American edition, second printing (1942)

New York: Charles Scribner's Sons, 1942. *Binding and dust jacket*: Same as A6.1.a. Sheet bulk: title page: .152; p. 50: .153. *Location*: RLT.

Note one: Copyright page same as A6.1.a.

Note two: A copy has been seen where the price on the dust jacket has been clipped and '$3.00' in blue has been stamped below the clip. *Location*: RLT.

A6.1.c
First American edition, third printing (1942)

New York: Charles Scribner's Sons, 1942. *Binding and dust jacket*: Same as A6.1.a, except white endpapers with no decoration. Sheet bulk: title page: .109 mm.; p. 50: .114 mm. *Location*: RLT.

Note: Copyright page same as A6.1.a.

A6.1.d
First American edition, fourth printing (1942)

New York: Charles Scribner's Sons, 1942. *Binding and dust jacket*: Same as A6.1.a, except white endpapers with no decoration. Sheet bulk: title page: .101 mm.; p. 50: .108 mm. *Location*: RLT.

Note: Copyright page same as A6.1.a.

A6.1.e
First American edition, fifth printing (1942)

New York: Charles Scribner's Sons, 1942. *Binding*: Light brown cloth, white endpapers with no decoration. *Dust jacket*: Same as A6.1.a. Sheet bulk: title page: .097 mm.; p. 50: .111 mm. *Location*: RLT.

Note: Copyright page same as A6.1.a.

A6.1.f
First American edition, sixth printing [1960]

New York: Charles Scribner's Sons, n.d. [1960]. *Binding*: Same as A6.1.e. *Dust jacket*: Same as A6.1.a, except '$3.95' is printed in the upper left corner of the front flap. Sheet bulk: title page: .134 mm.; p. 50: .131 mm. 'C-3.60[MH]'. *Location*: RLT.

A6.1.g
First American edition, seventh printing [1962]

New York: Charles Scribner's Sons, n.d. [1962]. *Binding*: Same as A6.1.e. *Dust jacket*: Same as A6.1.a. 'H-9.62[MH]'. *Location*: FU.

A6.1.h
First American edition, eighth printing [1966]

New York: Charles Scribner's Sons, n.d. *Binding*: Same as A6.1.e. *Dust jacket*: Same as A6.1.e, except '$4.50' is printed in the upper right corner of the front flap, and everything after the first star device is dropped on the rear flap. 'J-10.66[MH]'. *Location*: RLT.

A6.1.i
First American edition, ninth printing [1969]

New York, Charles Scribner's Sons, n.d. [1969]. *Binding*: Same as A6.1.e. *Dust jacket*: Same as A6.1.a, except '$6.95' is printed on the upper center of the front flap. 'L-10.69[MH]'. *Location*: FU.

A6.1.l *Cross Creek Cookery*

A6.1.k
First American edition, tenth printing [1971]

New York: Charles Scribner's Sons, n.d. [1971]. *Binding A*: Same as A6.1.e. *Dust jacket*: Same as A6.1.i. SBN 684-104873. *Binding B*: Multicolor wrappers. 'A-1.71[C]'. *Locations*: Binding A: RLT; binding B: PC.

A6.1.l
First American edition, eleventh printing [n.d.]

New York: Charles Scribner's Sons, n.d. *Binding A*: Light green buckram; *binding B*: Multicolor wrappers. $7.95. *Locations*: Bindings A–B: RLT.

A6.2
First British edition, only printing [1960]

The
Marjorie Kinnan Rawlings
Cookbook

Cross Creek Cookery

LONDON
HAMMOND, HAMMOND & COMPANY

A 6.2: 20.0 × 13.0

A6.2 *Cross Creek Cookery* 123

> First published in Great Britain 1960
>
> © *Copyright 1942 by Marjorie Kinnan Rawlings*
> *Printed in Great Britain by*
> *Cox & Wyman, Ltd., London, Fakenham and Reading*
> *for Hammond, Hammond & Co. Ltd.,*
> *87, Gower Street, W.C.1*
> 860

[1–5] 6–14 [15] 16–18 [19] 20–28 [29] 30–45 [46] 47–53 [54] 55–66 [67] 68–72 [73] 74–88 [89] 90–118 [119] 120–126 [127] 128–173 [174] 175–179 [180] 181–182 [183] 184–192

[A]^8 B–I^8 K–M^8; 96 leaves.

Contents: p. 1: half title: 'The | Marjorie Kinnan Rawlings | Cookbook'; p. 2: 'Other Books by | Marjorie Kinnan Rawlings' + list of six books; p. 3: title page; p. 4: copyright page; pp. 5–14: 'CONTENTS'; 'ERRATUM' inserted after p. 14; pp. 15–182: recipes; pp. 183–192: 'Index'.

Typography and paper: 15.1 (14.2) × 9.2 cm.; wove paper; 34 lines per page. Running heads: versos: pp. 6–14: 'CONTENTS'; pp. 16–18: 'TO OUR BODIES' GOOD'; pp. 20–28: 'SOUPS'; pp. 30–44: 'HOT BREADS'; pp. 48–52: 'LUNCHEON DISHES OR, THE EMBROIDERY CLUB'; pp. 56–66: 'VEGETABLES'; pp. 68–72: 'POTATOES, RICE AND GRITS'; pp. 74–88: 'FLORIDA SEA FOODS'; pp. 90–118: 'GAME AND MEATS'; pp. 120–126: 'SALADS'; pp. 128–172: 'DESSERTS'; pp. 176–178: 'PRESERVES, JELLIES AND MARMALADES'; pp. p. 182: "BETTER A DINNER OF HERBS"; pp. 184–192: 'INDEX'; rectos: pp. 7–13: 'CONTENTS'; p. 17: 'TO OUR BODIES' GOOD'; pp. 21–27: 'SOUPS'; pp. 31–45: 'HOT BREADS'; pp. 47–53: 'LUNCHEON DISHES OR, THE EMBROIDERY CLUB'; pp. 55–65: 'VEGETABLES'; pp. 69–71: 'POTATOES, RICE AND GRITS'; pp. 75–87: 'FLORIDA SEA FOODS'; pp. 91–117: 'GAME AND MEATS'; pp. 121–125: 'SALADS'; pp. 129–173: 'DESSERTS'; PP. 175–179: 'PRESERVES, JELLIES AND MARMALADES'; p. 181: "BETTER A DINNER OF HERBS"; pp. 185–191: 'INDEX'.

Binding: Light green calico-textured cloth. Front cover: blank; blackstamped spine: '[in script] The | MARJORIE | KINNAN | RAWLINGS | COOKBOOK | [publisher's device] | HAMMOND | HAMMOND'. All edges trimmed.

Dust jacket: Multicolored front cover and spine: a continuous scene looking out over a lake from under a canopy and across a restaurant table; front cover: '[lettering in black over top one-third] The [in script] | MARJORIE KINNAN | RAWLINGS | COOKBOOK [brown leaf decorations interspersed among the

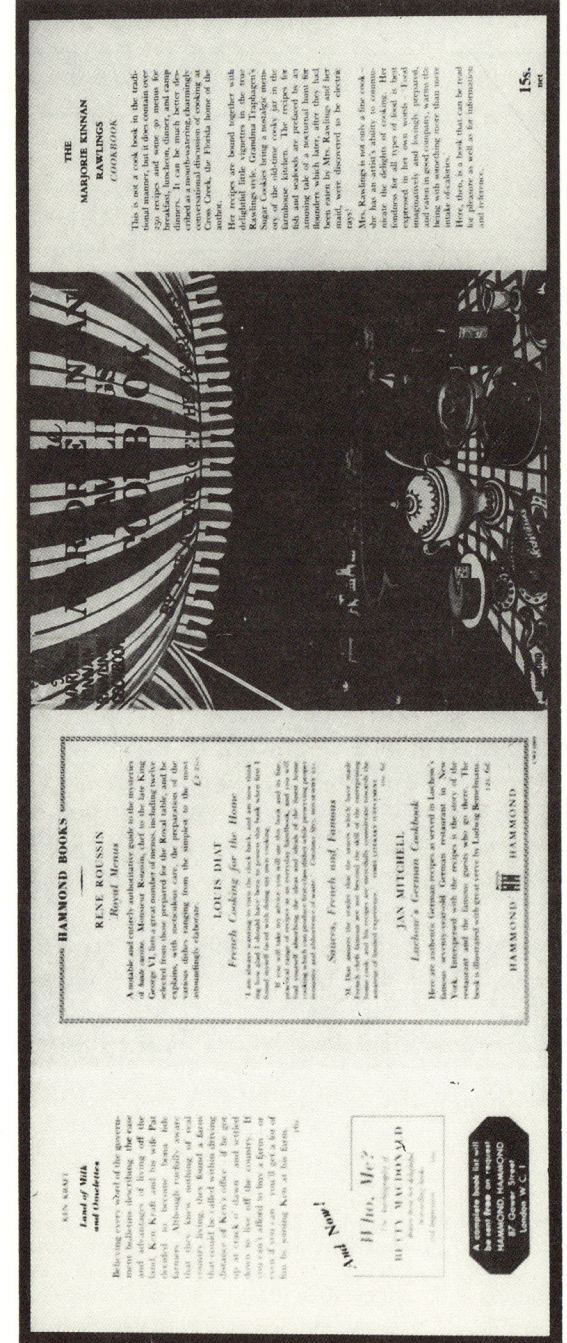

Dust jacket for A 6.27

A 6.2 *Cross Creek Cookery*

letters] | [in circular format] BY THE AUTHOR OF: "THE YEARLING" '; spine: '[lettering in black] The [in script] | MARJORIE | KINNAN | RAWLINGS | COOKBOOK | [publisher's device] | HAMMOND | HAMMOND'; back cover on cream background: enclosed in a red decorated frame: '[in black inside the top line of the frame] HAMMOND BOOKS | [in black french rule] | [31-line blurb for four books] | [in black] HAMMOND [in red publisher's device] [in black] HAMMOND | [outside frame at bottom right in black] CWF 1060'; front flap: in black on a white background: 'THE | MARJORIE KINNAN | RAWLINGS | [in red] COOKBOOK | 33-line description of the book] | [in right bottom corner a diagonal broken line] 15s. | net'; rear flap: in black on a white background] '[19-line blurb] | [7 line blub in red and blue in a red frame] | [white on a blue background clipped at the corners] A complete book list will | be sent free [free in bold] on request | HAMMOND, HAMMOND | 87 Gower Street | London W.C. 1'.

Publication: Unknown number of copies printed. Published October 1960. 15s.

Printing: Cox and Wyman.

Locations: Bodleian Library (deposit-stamped 16 March 1962), PM (dj), RLT (dj), RM (dj)

Note: The erratum slip (5.6 × 10.2), inserted after p. 14, is as follows:

'[centered in bold] ERRATUM | [centered in bold] *The Marjorie Kinnan Rawlings Cookbook* | The Publishers regret that a printer's error has | occurred on page 51, where the sub-title | [centered] IDELLA'S CHEESE SOUFFLÉ | has been wrongly inserted. This sub-title should | be dropped three lines, so that the paragraph at | present immediately below it becomes the con- | cluding paragraph of the recipe above it.'

A 7 JACOB'S LADDER

A 7
Only edition, only printing (1950)

A 7: 20.2 × 12.5 cm.

A7 *Jacob's Ladder*

> Copyright 1931, 1940, 1950 by
> Marjorie Kinnan Rawlings
> Manufactured by
> H. Wolff Book Manufacturing Co., New York
>
> DESIGNED BY MARSHALL LEE

[i–viii] [1–2] 3–118 [119–120]

[1–4]¹⁶; 64 leaves.

Contents: p. i: ladder design on a green background; p. ii: blank; p. iii: half title: 'JACOB'S LADDER'; pp. iv–v: continuous title page; p. vi: copyright page; p. vii: ladder design; p. viii: double ladder design, black over light green; p. 1: section title: light green ladder design; section title in black: 'JACOB'S LADDER'; p. 2: blank; pp. 3–118: text; pp. 119–120: blank.

Typography and paper: (13.2) × 8.9 cm.; wove paper; 27 lines per page. Running heads: versos: 4–60, 64–78, 82–88, 92–118: 'Jacob's Ladder'.

Binding: Light green calico-textured cloth. Front cover: stamped alligator-hide design; spine (vertical, top to bottom): '[in black at the top] MARJORIE KINNAN RAWLINGS [in light green at the middle] Jacob's Ladder | [in light green at the bottom] UNIVERSITY OF MIAMI PRESS'. Black endpapers. Top edge trimmed and stained salmon. Fore-edge and bottom edge trimmed.

Dust jacket: Front cover: shades of greenish blue on a white background: '[in black] JACOB'S | LADDER | [rural scene with a mother holding a baby in her lap on the front porch of a cracker shack] | DRAWINGS BY JESSIE AYERS | MARJORIE KINNAN RAWLINGS'; spine: '*Marjorie | Kinnan | Rawlings* | [title vertical in script] JACOB'S LADDER | *The | University | of | Miami | Press*'; back cover: on white background: '*Recent publications of the* | University of Miami Press | [10-line ad for a book] | [french rule] | [14-line ad for a book] | *University of Miami Press* | *Coral Gables, Florida* | *Distributed by* FARRAR, STRAUS AND COMPANY, INC., N. Y., N. Y.'; front flap: on white background: '[upper right corner] $2.75 | *Jacob's Ladder* | *by* | Marjorie Kinnan Rawlings | [32-line blurb] | *(Continued on back flap)*'; rear flap: '[photograph of Rawlings] | *(Continued from front flap)* | 14-line blurb] | *With eight illustrations* | *by Jessie Ayers* | THE UNIVERSITY OF MIAMI PRESS | Coral Gables, Florida | *Distributed by* | FARRAR, STRAUS AND COMPANY, INC. | New York, N. Y.'

Publication: Unknown number of copies printed. Published 4 December 1950. $2.75. Copyright A57961. Announced for publication on 4 December in *Publishers' Weekly*, 158 (28 October 1950), 2,007; listed in *Publishers' Weekly*, 158 (16 December 1950), 2,529.

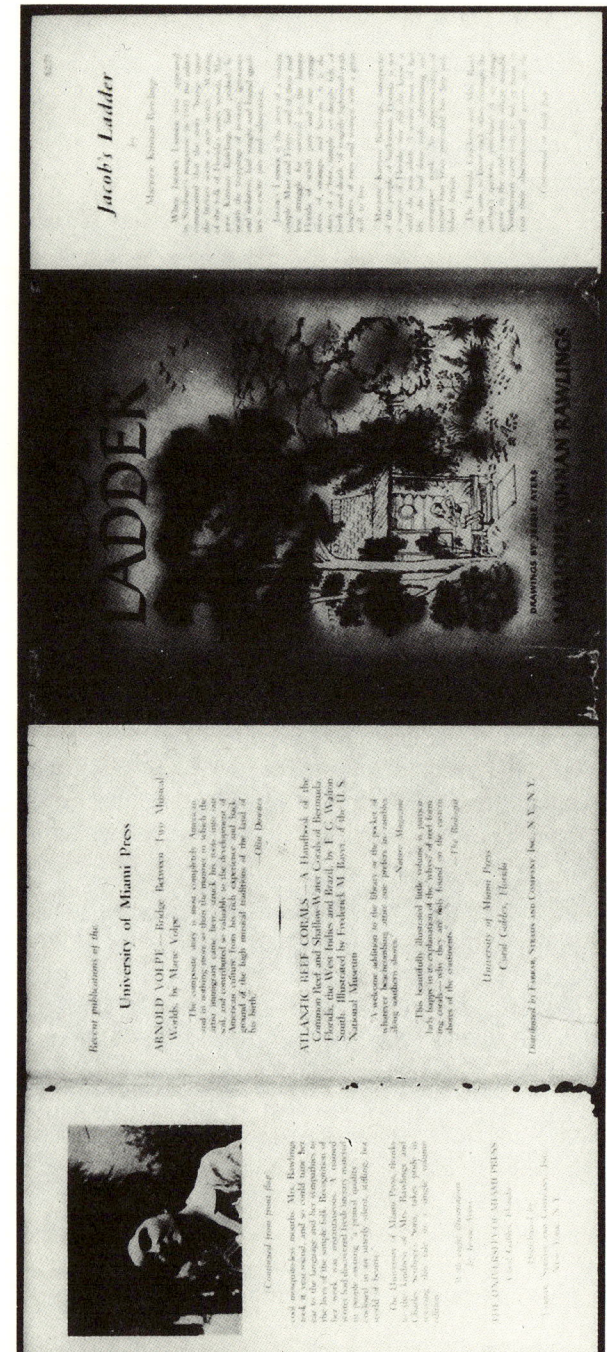

Dust jacket for A7

A 7 *Jacob's Ladder* 129

Printing: H. Wolff Book Manufacturing Co.

Locations: DLC (deposit-stamped 27 July 1951), FU (dj), InU (dj), PM (dj), RLT (dj), RM (dj).

Note: See C590.

A8 THE SOJOURNER

A8.1.a₁
First American edition, "Presentation Edition," first printing, first issue (1953)

THE SOJOURNER

Marjorie Kinnan Rawlings

New York   CHARLES SCRIBNER'S SONS   1953

A 8.1.a₁: 21.0 × 14.0 cm.

A8.1.a *The Sojourner*

> COPYRIGHT, 1953, BY
> MARJORIE KINNAN RAWLINGS
>
> Printed in the United States of America
>
> *All rights reserved. No part of this book*
> *may be reproduced in any form without*
> *the permission of Charles Scribner's Sons*
>
> A

[a–b] [i–viii] 1–327 [328]

[χ]¹ [1–10]¹⁶ [11]⁸; 169 leaves.

Contents: p. a: presentation leaf: '[decorated rule] | PRESENTATION | EDITION | NUMBER ——— | [short decorated rule] | [Rawlings's signature in black ink]'; p. b: blank; p. i: half title: 'THE SOJOURNER'; p. ii: 'BOOKS BY MARJORIE KINNAN RAWLINGS | [list of seven books] | CHARLES SCRIBNER'S SONS'; p. iii: title page; p. iv: copyright page; p. v: 3-line quotation from '1 Chronicles 29:15'; p. vi: blank; p. vii: section title: 'THE SOJOURNER'; p. viii: blank; pp. 1–327: text; p. 328: blank.

Typography and paper: (15.8) × 10.0 cm.; wove paper; 38 lines per page. No running heads.

Binding: Light gray, with brown highlights, calico-textured cloth. Front cover: blank; blackstamped spine (vertical, top to bottom): '[bottom left] RAWLINGS [horizontal rule] [top right] THE SOJOURNER [bottom left] Scribners'; back cover: blank. All edges trimmed.

Dust jacket: Front cover and spine continuous: on dark blue background: '[in light yellow] *Marjorie Kinnan Rawlings* | [title in white] THE | SOJOURNER | [multicolor figure of a man extending to the bottom, looking down upon a town] | [to the right of the figure, in pinkish purple] *a novel* | [in light yellow] *by the author of* | [in light yellow] THE YEARLING | [town with clouds extending over it at bottom right]'; spine (vertical, top to bottom) in very light yellow: '*Rawlings* [on top] THE [on bottom] SOJOURNER [horizontal, in pinkish purple, at the bottom] Scribners'; back cover: black on white background: '[on the outside top right of a photograph illustration of Rawlings] *Erich Hartmann*

Dust jacket for A 8.1.a₁

A 8.1.a *The Sojourner* 133

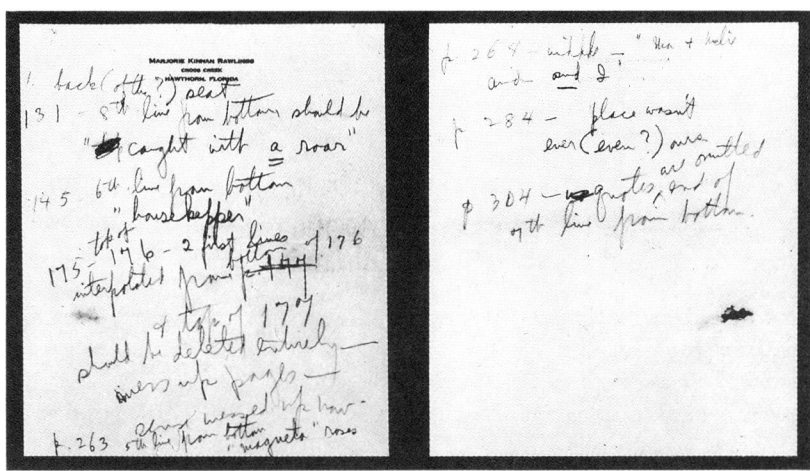

Corrections to the first printing of A 8.1.a₁

| [the illustration] | *Marjorie Kinnan Rawlings* | Published by | CHARLES SCRIBNER'S SONS | *New York*'; front flap: black on a white background: '[in upper right corner] $3.50 | THE | SOJOURNER | *by* | Marjorie Kinnan Rawlings | Pulitzer Prize Winner | author of *Cross Creek, The Yearling*, etc. | [18-line description of the novel] | *(continued on back flap)* | Jacket design by George W. Thompson'; rear flap: black on white background: '*(continued from front flap)* | [32-line description]'.

Publication: In the Scribners Records for 28 November 1952 is the note: '600 Ltd. Spec[ial]'. Published on 5 January 1953. $3.50. Copyright A75434. Listed in *Publishers' Weekly*, 163 (10 January 1953), 148.

Printing: Printed and bound by the Scribner Press.

Locations: PM (dj), RLT (dj), RM (dj).

A 8.1.a₂
First American edition, first printing, second issue, for the trade (1953)

New York: Charles Scribner's Sons, 1953. 26,000 copies published 5 January 1953. $3.50. Copyright A75434. Listed in *Publishers' Weekly*, 163 (10 January 1953), 148. Paper bulk: title page: .133 mm.; p. 151: .143 mm. *Locations*: InU (dj), PM (dj), RLT (dj), RM (2, dj).

Note one: Same as the first issue, except lacks presentation leaf.

Note two: Scribners Records indicates that 30,000 dust jackets were printed by the Graphic Offset Company on 31 December 1952. A separate order number indicates that 10,000 more were printed on the same day. Another order was placed for 5,000 on 31 March 1953.

Note three: Written in Scribners Records for 17 June 1955 is the note: 'Destroy all | printing material'.

Note four: A list of corrections in Rawlings's hand to the second issue has been seen: p. 1, l. 18: 'back (of the?) seat': not corrected in subsequent printings; p. 131, l. 31: 'caught with a roar': not corrected in subsequent printings; p. 145, l. 33: 'housekepper': corrected in the Book-of-the-Month Club printing; p. 176: the first two lines are improperly inserted; the first line appears properly at the bottom of p. 176, and the second line appears properly at the top of p. 177: corrected in the Book-of-the-Month Club printing; p. 263, l. 35: 'magneta roses' changed to 'magenta roses' in the Book-of-the-Month Club printing; p. 264, l. 23: 'Ma and 'Melie and and I': corrected in the Book-of-the-Month Club printing; p. 284, l. 25, 'ever' not corrected in subsequent printings; and p. 304, l. 32, quotation marks omitted at the end of the line: not corrected in subsequent printings.

Note five: A sound recording for the American Foundation for the Blind was made in 1982. The narrator is Joel Crothers.

Note six: An advance presentation copy has been seen (FU): 'For my very dear friends, | the Robertsons, | this advance copy, | with my love, | Marjorie Kinnan Rawlings [underlined] | December 1952 [date underlined]'.

Note seven: The DLC deposit copy has no deposit date, but has both an 'A' and a Scribners seal on the copyright page.

OTHER PRINTINGS WITHIN THE FIRST AMERICAN EDITION

A 8.1.b
First American edition, second printing (1953)

New York: Charles Scribner's Sons, 1953. *Binding*: Same as A8.1.a$_1$. 10,200 copies. 31 December 1952. Paper bulk: title page: .136 mm.; p. 151: .126 mm. *Location*: RLT.

Note: 'A' and Scribners seal on the copyright page.

A 8.1.c
First American edition, third printing (1953)

A8.1.e *The Sojourner*

New York: Charles Scribner's Sons, 1953. *Binding*: Same as A8.1.a₁. 5,150 copies. 31 December 1952. Paper bulk: title page: .128 mm.; p. 151: .125 mm. *Location*: RLT.

Note: Scribners seal on the copyright page.

A8.1.d
First American edition, fourth printing (1953)

New York: Charles Scribner's Sons, 1953. *Binding*: Same as A8.1.a₁. 3,875 copies. 1 February 1953. *Location*: From Scribners Records, *not seen*.

Note one: Scribners Records indicates that 5,000 wrappers were printed by Graphic Offset Company on 31 March 1953.

Note two: The distinction between the third and fourth printings has not been determined.

A8.1.e
First American edition, fifth printing, for the Book-of-the-Month Club [1953]

[in light blue] THE SOJOURNER | Marjorie Kinnan Rawlings | CHARLES SCRIBNER'S SONS | *New York*

[i–vi] 1–313 [314]

No sewing, gatherings glued to spine.

Contents: p. i: half title; p. ii: blank; p. iii: title page; p. iv: copyright page; p. v: quotation from *1 Chronicles* 29:15; p. vi: blank; pp. 1–313: text; p. 314: blank.

Typography and paper: (16.9) × 9.9 cm.; wove paper; 40 lines per page. No running heads. Paper bulk: title page: .121 mm.; p. 151: .114 mm.

Binding: Blue calico-textured cloth. Front cover: blank; yellowstamped spine (vertical, top to bottom): '[lower left] RAWLINGS [horizontal rule] [top right] THE [center] SOJOURNER [under the 'er' of 'SOJOURNER'] Scribners'; back cover: blank. Top edge stained yellow. Fore-edge rough trimmed. Bottom edge trimmed.

Dust jacket: Same as A8.1.a₁, except on the back cover 'Published by | CHARLES SCRIBNER'S SONS | *New York*' is removed; on the front flap the price is removed and at the bottom right is added: '[in red] BOOK CLUB | EDITION'; and at the bottom of the rear flap: 'PRINTED IN THE U.S.A.' is added.

Publication: Unknown number of copies published. Price to Club Members $1.89. The Book-of-the-Month Club *Family Reading Club News* indicates: 'THE FEBRUARY 1953 SELECTION'.

Location: PM (dj), RLT (3, dj), RM (dj).

Note one: From the plates of A8.1.a_1, but the type is rearranged to shorten the number of pages. Page numbers and chapter headings have been reset.

Note two: Scribners Records does not mention the Book-of-the-Month Club printings.

A8.1.f
First American edition, sixth printing, for the Book-of-the-Month Club [1953]

New York: Charles Scribner's Sons, n.d. [1953]. *Binding and dust jacket*: Same as A8.1.e. Paper bulk: title page: .119 mm.; p. 151: .123 mm. *Location*: RLT (dj).

Note: The priority of A8.1.e and A8.1.f has not been determined.

A8.1.g
First American edition, seventh printing, for the Book-of-the-Month Club [1953]

New York: Charles Scribner's Sons, n.d. [1953]. *Binding and dust jacket*: Same as A8.1.e. Paper bulk: title page: .117 mm.; p. 151: .116 mm. *Location*: RLT.

Note: Chapter headings are reset in light blue.

A8.1.h
First American edition, eighth printing, for the Peoples Book Club [1953]

THE SOJOURNER | Marjorie Kinnan Rawlings | PEOPLES BOOK CLUB | CHICAGO

Binding: Black linen-textured cloth. Multicolor pastedown and free endpapers depicting a dance. *Dust jacket*: Multicolor front cover depicting a man leaning on a fence; spine lists title, author, and publisher; and back cover has a black-and-white illustration of Rawlings, followed by a blurb. *Publication*: 1953. Number of copies published unknown. Paper bulk: title page: .133 mm.; p. 151: .134 mm. *Locations*: RLT (3, dj), RM (dj).

Note: Copyright, p. iv: 'This is a special edition published | exclusively for the members of the | PEOPLES BOOK CLUB. P. O. Box 6570A, | Chicago 80, Illinois. It was originally | published by Charles Scribner's Sons.'

A8.1.1 *The Sojourner*

A8.1.i
First American edition, ninth printing, for the Peoples Book Club [1953]

Chicago: Peoples Book Club, n.d. [1953]. *Binding and dust jacket*: Same as A8.1.h. Paper bulk: title page: .130 mm.; p. 151: .125 mm. *Location*: RLT.

Note: The priority of A8.1.h and A8.1.i has not been determined.

A8.1.j
First American edition, tenth printing (1977)

THE SOJOURNER | Marjorie Kinnan Rawlings | NORMAN S. BERG, Publisher | "Sellanraa" | Dunwoody, Georgia | 1977

Facsimile of A8.1.a$_2$. *Binding*: Dark blue calico-textured cloth. *Dust jacket*: Blue lettering on white background. Printed on thin stock (title page: .094 mm.; p. 101: .096 mm.). *Publication*: Unknown number of copies printed. *Locations*: PM, RLT.

Note: Copyright page, p. iv: 'By arrangement with | Charles Scribner's, Sons | ISBN 910220-82-4'.

A8.1.k$_1$
First American edition, eleventh printing, first issue (1977)

Dunwoody, Georgia: Norman S. Berg, 1977.

Facsimile of A8.1.a$_2$. *Binding*: Blue linen-grain cloth. *Dust jacket*: This is a library binding, and therefore it is possible that no dust jacket was printed. Printed on thick stock (title page: .142 mm.; p. 101: .138 mm.). *Location*: RLT.

Note: The priority of A8.1.j and A8.1.k has not been determined.

A8.1.k$_2$
First American edition, eleventh printing, second issue (1991)

Atlanta, Georgia: Cherokee Publishing Co., 1991. *Binding*: Gray calico-textured cloth. *Location*: RLT.

Note: The second issue is made up of the remainder sheets of the first issue.

A8.1.l
First American edition, twelfth printing [1989]

[Mattituck, N.Y.: Amereon Ltd., n.d. (1989)]. *Binding*: Red calico-textured cloth. *Location*: RLT.

Note: This is an unauthorized facsimile from the Book-of-the-Month Club printing. All references to Charles Scribner's Sons in the frontmatter have been removed.

A 8.2.a
First British edition, first printing [1953]

THE SOJOURNER

by

MARJORIE KINNAN RAWLINGS

WILLIAM HEINEMANN LTD
MELBOURNE :: LONDON :: TORONTO

A 8.2.a: 19.6 × 12.8 cm.

A8.2.a *The Sojourner* 139

> FIRST PUBLISHED 1953
>
> PRINTED IN GREAT BRITAIN
> AT THE WINDMILL PRESS
> KINGSWOOD, SURREY

[i–vi] 1–337 [338]

[1]¹⁶ 2–10¹⁶ 11¹²; 172 leaves.

Contents: p. i: half title: 'THE SOJOURNER'; p. ii: '*Books by Marjorie Kinnan Rawlings* | [list of seven books]'; p. iii: title page; p. iv: copyright page; p. v: 3-line quotation from *1 Chronicles* 29:15; p. vi: blank; pp. 1–337: text; p. 338: blank.

Typography and paper: (15.8) × 9.7 cm.; wove paper; 37 lines per page. No running heads. Paper bulk: title page: .136 mm.; p. 101: .131 mm.

Binding: Dark blue calico-textured cloth. Front cover: blank; goldstamped spine: 'The | Sojourner | [star device] | MARJORIE | KINNAN | RAWLINGS | HEINEMANN'; back cover: blindstamped windmill device in lower right corner. All edges trimmed.

Dust jacket: Front cover, spine, and back cover continuous background: upper two-thirds light purple (lavender) with white stars, and bottom third black separated by red line. Front cover: '[in white] MARJORIE KINNAN | RAWLINGS | [figure of man standing at left center] | [center and right in white] The Sojourner | [in white] author of The Yearling | [illustration of farm buildings at lower right]'; spine: '[in white] MARJORIE | KINNAN | RAWLINGS | The | Sojourner | [windmill device] | Heinemann'; back cover: '[all lettering in white] The new novel | by the author of | The Yearling'; front flap: black lettering on white background: 'THE | SOJOURNER | *by* | *Marjorie Kinnan* | *Rawlings* | author of *The Yearling* | [23–line description] | (*Continued on the back flap*) | [in lower right] 12s 6d | NET'; rear flap: black lettering on white background: '(*Continued from the front flap*) | [22-line description] | HEINEMANN'.

Publication: 20,000 copies published on 23 February 1953. 12s.6d.

Printing: Windmill Press.

Locations: BL (deposit-stamped 30 January 1953), Bodleian (deposit-stamped 12 March 1953), RLT (dj).

Note one: On the left edge of the first leaf of some gatherings is, for example: '[bottom to top] SOJOURNER 8', meaning the eighth gathering of *The Sojourner*.

Note two: Scribners File-Cards indicates that a set of galleys was mailed to

Dust jacket for A 8.2

A8.4 *The Sojourner*

Heinemann on 4 June 1952 and that Heinemann made an offer to publish on 8 July 1952.

Note three: Printed in braille. 6 vols. Annerley, Australia: Queensland Braille Writing Association, n.d.

A8.2.b
First British edition, second printing [1953]

London: William Heinemann, n.d. [1953]. *Binding:* Same as A8.2.a. Paper stock: title page: .124 mm.; p. 101: .122 mm. *Location:* RLT.

Note: A second printing is not listed in Heinemann records. The priority of A8.2.a and A8.2.b has not been determined.

OTHER EDITIONS

A8.3.a
Second British edition, first printing [1955]

THE | SOJOURNER | [star device] | MARJORIE KINNAN | RAWLINGS | THE COMPANION BOOK CLUB | LONDON

336 pp. 18.3 × 11.8 cm. *Binding:* Dark yellow calico-textured cloth. *Dust jacket:* Orange design on white background. *Publication:* 1955. Club price, 4s.6d. *Location:* RLT.

Note: Copyright page, p. 6: '*Made and printed in Great Britain | for The Companion Book Club (Odhams Press Ltd.) | by Morrison & Gibb Ltd. | London and Edinburgh | 955.VSB*'.

A8.3.b
Second British edition, second printing [1955]

London: The Companion Book Club, n.d. [1955].

On copyright page: '... *by Odhams (Watford) Limited | Watford, Herts | 955.ZT*'. *Location:* RLT.

A8.4
First Australian edition, only printing [1956]

Hawthorn, Victoria, Australia: Readers Book Club, n.d. [1956].

336 pp. On p. 1: 'This edition, issued in 1956, is for | members of The Readers Book | Club.' *Locations:* National Library of Australia, RLT.

A 8.5
Second British edition, only printing [1959]

London: Landsborough Publications, n.d. [1959].

287 pp. 'FOUR SQUARE BOOKS'. *Location*: BL.

A 8.6
Second American edition, only printing [1965]

[author and title in white on black sunburst] MARJORIE | KINNAN | RAWLINGS | THE | Sojourner | POPULAR LIBRARY · NEW YORK

383 pp. *Binding*: Multicolor wrappers, edges stained red. *Publication*: 1965. 95¢. 'POPULAR LIBRARY EDITION', E128. *Location*: RLT.

A9 THE SECRET RIVER

A9.1.a
First edition, first printing [1955]

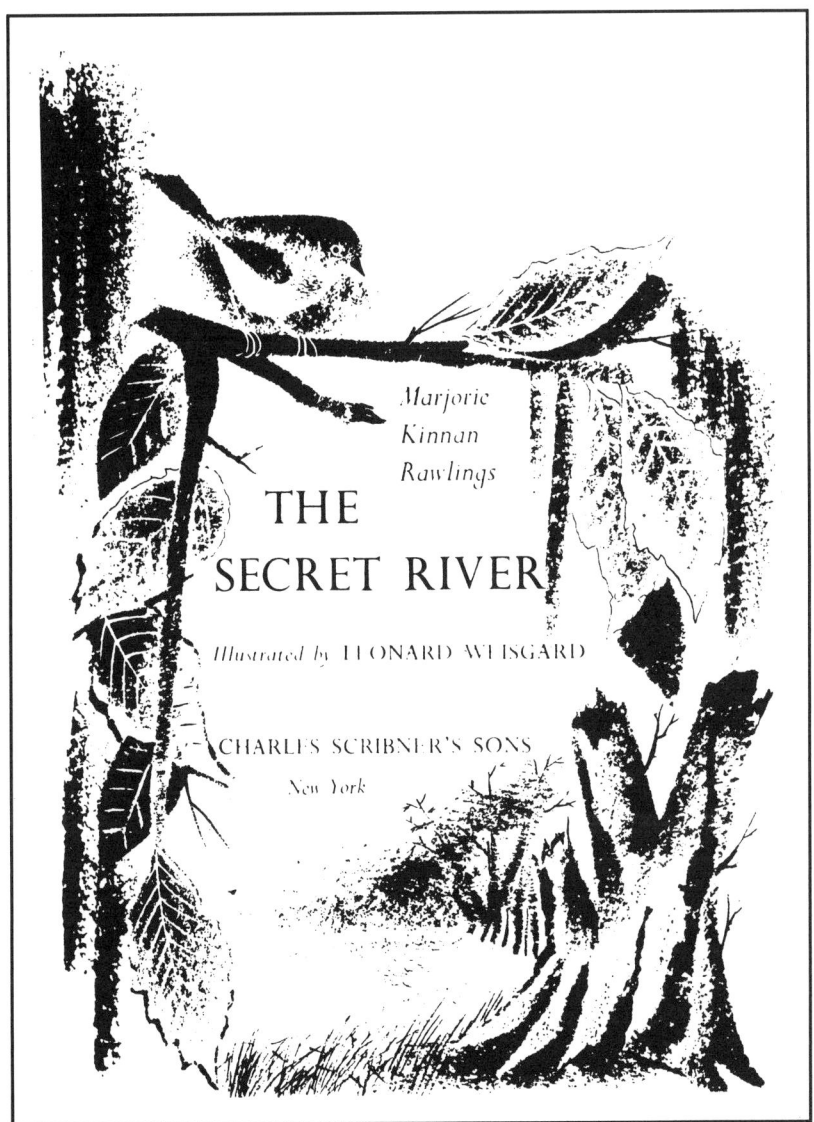

A 9.1.a: 20.4 × 15.0 cm. The border area is in light brown; the illustration and print are in black on a white background.

> Copyright 1955
> by Charles Scribner's Sons
> and Leonard Weisgard
>
> All rights reserved. No part of this book may be reproduced in any form without the permission of Charles Scribner's Sons
>
> Printed in the United States of America
> A
>
> Library of Congress Catalog Card
> No. 55-6916

[1–64]

[1–4]⁸; 32 leaves.

Contents: p. 1: blank; p. 2: 'BOOKS BY MARJORIE KINNAN RAWLINGS', followed by a list of eight; p. 3: half title: 'The | Secret River | [illustration of a frog]'; p. 4: blank; p. 5: title page; p. 6: copyright page; pp. 7–8: introduction by Julia Scribner Bigham; p. 9: section title: 'The | Secret River'; p. 10: illustration of a egret; pp. 11–63: text; p. 64: blank.

Typography and paper: (13.2) × 10.7 cm.; thick stock light brown wove paper; 16 lines per page. No running heads. Sheet bulk: title page: .165 mm; p. 1: .159 mm.

Binding: Light brown calico-textured cloth. Front cover: stamped in white at left, top to bottom: illustration of a girl sitting beneath a tree playing with a puppy: '[upper right] THE | SECRET RIVER'; spine (vertical top to bottom) stamped in white: '*Rawlings* The Secret River SCRIBNERS'; back cover: blank. Light brown endpapers. All edges trimmed.

Dust jacket: Multicolor (in black, brown, and light green) continuous cover: illustration of a girl fishing in a secluded scene. Front cover: '[upper center left in light green] The | Secret | River | [bottom center left in black] *by* | MARJORIE | KINNAN | RAWLINGS'; spine (vertical top to bottom): '[in white] RAWLINGS The Secret River SCRIBNERS'; back cover: scene continuous with front cover and spine; front flap: black on white background: '[upper right] '$2.50 | THE SECRET RIVER | *by* | MARJORIE KINNAN RAWLINGS |

A 9.1.d *The Secret River* 145

illustrated by LEONARD WEISGARD | [20-line blurb]'; rear flap: black on white background: 'MARJORIE KINNAN RAWLINGS | [14-line biography]'.

Publication: 18,000 copies published 23 May 1955. $2.50. Copyright A188535 on 26 April 1955. Listed in *Publishers' Weekly*, 167 (21 May 1955), 2284.

Printing: Printed by Affiliated. Bound by Bohn.

Locations: DLC (deposit-stamped 1 June 1955) FU (dj), InU (dj), PM (dj), RLT (2, dj), RM (dj).

Note one: 17,500 dust jackets printed by Affiliated on 31 April 1955.

Note two: The Secret River was named runner-up for the Newbery Medal, given to the most distinguished children's book of the year.

Note three: Printed in braille and recorded in Toronto: CNIB, n.d. [197–?]. Recording narrated by Janet Barkhouse.

A9.1.b
First edition, second printing [1955]

New York: Charles Scribner's Sons, 1955. *Copyright, binding, and dust jacket*: Same as A9.1.a. Sheet bulk: title page: .164 mm; p. 1: .165 mm.

Note: The difference in sheet bulk from the first printing indicates that this is a separate printing. The first and second printings exhibit the same batter on p. 1.

A9.1.c
First edition, third printing [1956]

New York: Charles Scribner's Sons, n.d. [1956]. *Binding*: Light orangish brown. *Location*: FU.

Note: Copyright page: 'B-10.56[AB]'. There is no mention in Scribners Records of this printing.

A9.1.d
First edition, fourth printing [1971]

New York: Charles Scribner's Sons, n.d. [1971].

19.7 × 13.3 cm. Copyright page: 'A-9.71[ML] | Library of Congress Catalog Card | No. 55-6916 | SBN684-12636-2'. *Binding*: Glossy printed wrappers, olive background. Front cover: same as A9.1.a, except at bottom left: '95¢'; spine, vertical top to bottom: 'SBF-8 RAWLINGS THE SECRET RIVER SCRIBNERS'; back cover: 'THE SECRET RIVER | By Marjorie Kinnan Rawlings | Illustrated by Leonard Weisgard | [16-line blurb] | [next four words inside an illustration of a pennant] '[lamp] SCRIBNER | BOOK FAIR | EDI-

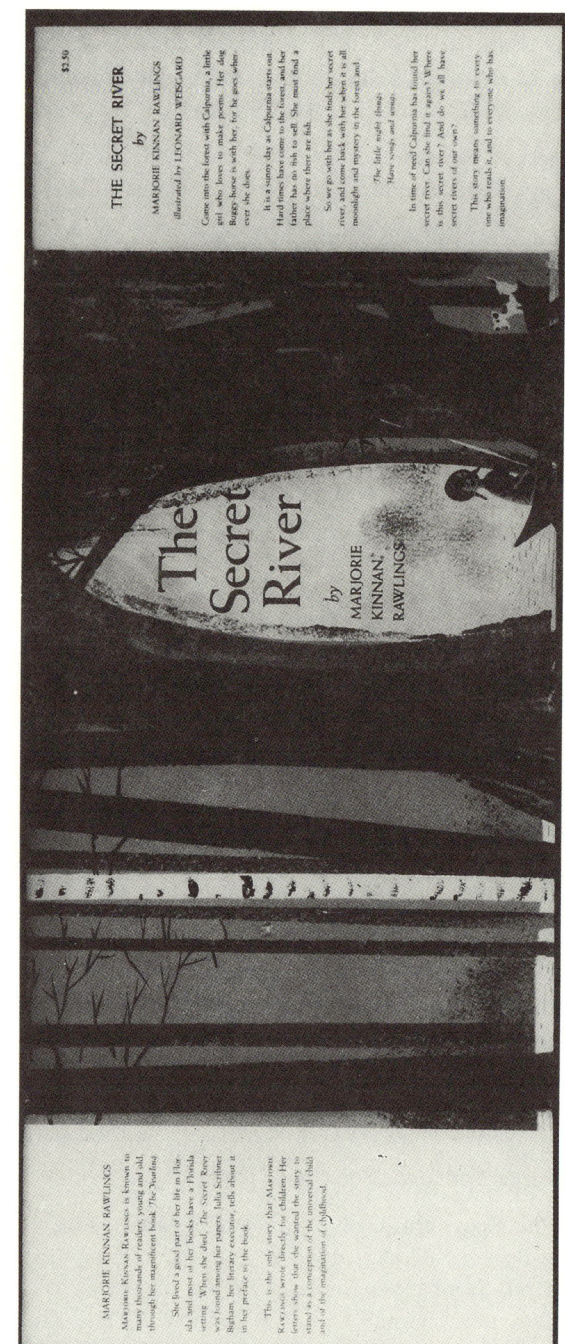

Dust jacket for a 9.1.a

Front cover for a 9.1.d

TIONS | Charles Scribner's Sons | SBN684-12636-2'. *Locations*: MKRH, PM, RLT.

Note: The batter and the sheet bulk (title page: .133 mm.; p. 1: .136 mm.) indicate that this is a separate printing. The sheets have been trimmed to fit the wrapper format. This printing is not listed in Scribners Records.

A 9.1.e
First edition, fifth printing [n.d.]

New York: Charles Scribner's Sons, n.d. *Binding*: Light olive calico-textured cloth. *Location*: Collection of Patricia, Lady Acton.

Note: Copyright page: '91 113151719 RD/C 201816141210 | SBN 684-13119-6 (R B, Cloth)'.

A9.1.f
First edition, sixth printing [1987]

Jacksonville, Florida: San Marco Book Store, n.d. [1987].

Facsimile reprint of A9.1.a, except for the title page alteration: 'San Marco Bookstore | P. O. Box 5842 | *Jacksonville, FL 32247-5842*'. *Binding*: Facsimile, except on spine: 'SAN MARCO | BOOKSTORE' replaces 'SCRIBNERS'. Front flap indicates 'REINFORCED BINDING'. White endpapers. *Dust jacket*: Facsimile. 2,176 copies. $9.95.

Note: 1983 appears on the copyright page, but the actual date of publication is 1987.

A9.1.g
First edition, seventh printing [1987]

Jacksonville, Florida: San Marco Book Store, n.d. [1987].

Note: A second facsimile reprint of 2,160 copies, ordered after the stock of the first facsimile was sold.

A 10 SELECTED LETTERS

A 10.1.a
First edition, first printing [1983]

```
selected
* letters
* * of * * * *
marjorie
kinnan * *
rawlings

edited by
Gordon E. Bigelow
and Laura V. Monti


A University of Florida Book
University Presses of Florida/Gainesville
```

A 10.1.a: 23.5 × 15.5 cm.

Frontispiece, Marjorie Kinnan Rawlings at her orange grove in Cross Creek, Florida, ca. 1933-34.

Most of the photographs in this book belong to the Rawlings Collection at the University of Florida Library, Gainesville, and are published through the courtesy of the library's Department of Rare Books and Manuscripts.

Library of Congress Cataloging in Publication Data
Rawlings, Marjorie Kinnan, 1896–1953.
  Selected letters of Marjorie Kinnan Rawlings.

"A University of Florida book."
  1. Rawlings, Marjorie Kinnan, 1896–1953—Correspondence. 2. Authors, American—20th century—Correspondence. I. Bigelow, Gordon E. II. Monti, Laura Virginia. III. Title.
PS3535.A845Z48   1982   813'.52 [b]   82-2674
ISBN 0-8130-0728-3   AACR2

University Presses of Florida, the agency of the State of Florida's university system for the publication of scholarly and creative works, operates under the policies adopted by the Board of Regents. Its offices are located at 15 Northwest 15th Street, Gainesville, Florida 32603.

Copyright © 1983 by the Board of Regents of the State of Florida
Printed in U.S.A. on acid-free paper

[i–vi] [1] 2 [3] 4–8 [9] 10–11 [12–14] 15–90 [91] 92–404 [405] 406–414 [415–418]

$[1-12]^{16}$ $[13]^4$ $[14]^{16}$; 212 leaves.

Contents: p. i: blank; p. ii: photograph of Rawlings; p. iii: title page; p. iv: copyright page; p. v: 'contents'; p. vi: blank; pp. 1–2: 'preface'; pp. 3–8: 'introduction'; pp. 9–11: 'chronology'; p. 12: photograph of Rawlings; p. 13: section title: 'the letters'; p. 14: blank; pp. 15–90: text; p. 91: photograph of Rawlings; pp. 92–404: text; pp. 405–414: 'index'; pp. 415–418: blank.

Typography and paper: 18.5 (17.7) × 10.5 cm.; acid free wove paper; 39 lines per page. Running heads: rectos: pp. 5–7: '*Introduction*'; p. 11: '*Chronology*'; pp. 407–413: '*Index*'; versos: p. 2: '*Preface*'; pp. 4–8: '*Introduction*'; p. 10: '*Chronology*'; pp. 406–414: '*Index*'.

A 10.1.c *Selected Letters*   151

Binding: Dark brownish orange calico-textured cloth, not embossed. Front cover: goldstamped lower center: '[rule] | m [in script, follwed by an asterisklike device] k [in script, followed by an asterisklike device] r | [rule]'; goldstamped spine: '[names, diagonal, in script] Bigelow | & | Monti | [title vertical in two lines, top to bottom] [top line] selected letters of [four asterisklike devices] [bottom line] marjorie kinnan rawlings | [horizontal] [press logo] | florida'; back cover: blank. Endpapers laid paper (2.0 cm. vertical chainlines). All edges trimmed.

Dust jacket: Emerald lines running horizontal, across the whole of the cover, on off-white background: front cover: in red two vertical rules at left edge running top to bottom: '[title and author in black script] selected | [single asterisklike device in red] letters | [two asterisklike devices in light red] of [four asterisklike devices in light red] | marjorie | kinnan [two asterisklike devices in red] rawlings | [in dark brownish orange] edited by | [in emerald in script, diagonal] Gordon E. Bigelow | & Laura V. Monti'; spine: the same as the spine of the binding, except the editors names are in emerald, the title and author in black, the asterisklike devices in light red, the press logo in dark brownish orange, and the press name in emerald]; back cover: in red two vertical rules at left edge running top to bottom: '[in black five separate blurbs comprising 40 lines] | [in emerald at lower left] A University of Florida Book | University Presses of Florida | ISBN 0-8130-0728-3'; front flap: '[title dark brownish orange] *Selected Letters of* | *Marjorie Kinnan Rawlings* | [next two lines in emerald] Edited by Gordon E. Bigelow and | Laura V. Monti | [39-line blurb in black] | [in black] continued on back flap | [in black] ISBN 0-8130-0728-3'; rear flap: '[in black] continued from front flap | [in black] 21-line blurb | [in emerald] *About the Editors* | [in black, 9-line biography] | [in dark brownish orange] University Presses of Florida | 15 NW 15 St. | Gainesville, FL 32603'.

Publication: 1,050 copies published May 1983. $30.00.

Locations: ISNU, PM (dj), RLT (dj).

A 10.1.b
First edition, second printing [1984]

Gainesville, Florida: University Presses of Florida, n.d. [1984]. *Binding and dust jacket*: Same as A10.1.a. $30.00. *Location:* RLT (dj).

Note: 984 copies.

A 10.1.c
First edition, third printing [1988]

Gainesville, Florida: University Presses of Florida, n.d. [1988]. *Binding:* Wrappers. $15.00. *Location:* PC.

Note: 1,435 copies.

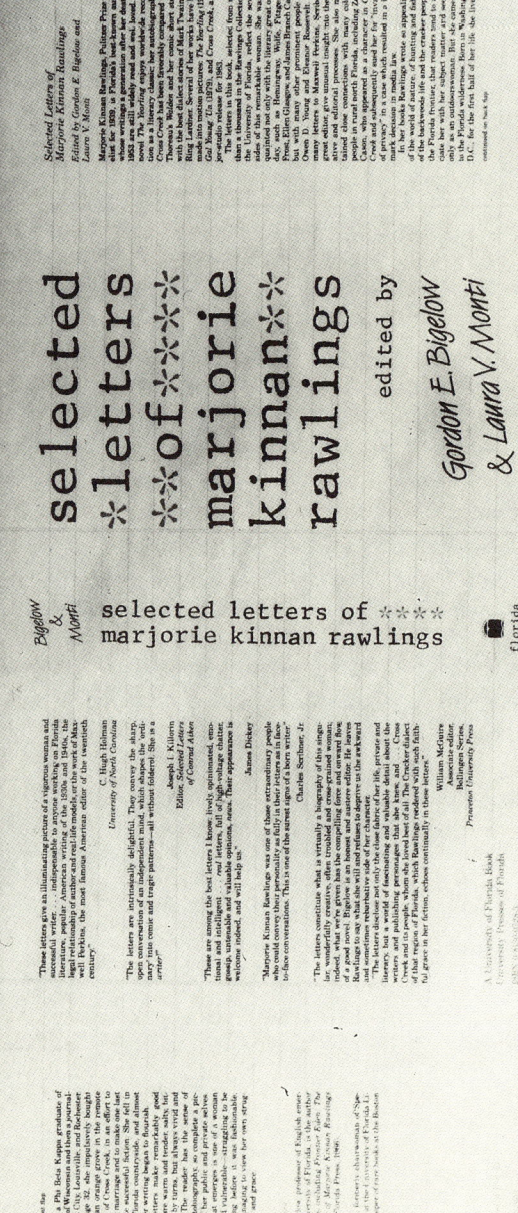

Dust jacket for A 10

A 11 UNIVERSITY OF FLORIDA ADDRESS

A 11
First edition, only printing (1991)

> AN ADDRESS DELIVERED BY
> # MARJORIE KINNAN RAWLINGS
> AT THE DEDICATION OF
> A NEW ADDITION TO THE
> UNIVERSITY OF FLORIDA LIBRARY
> MARCH 30, 1950
>
>
>
> PUBLISHED IN HONOR OF
> ## SENATOR GEORGE A. SMATHERS
>
> UNIVERSITY OF FLORIDA LIBRARIES
> GAINESVILLE · FLORIDA
> MAY 10, 1991

A 11: 22.9 × 15.0 cm.

> ONE THOUSAND COPIES OF THIS KEEPSAKE
> HAVE BEEN PRINTED AND BOUND BY THE STINEHOUR PRESS
> FOR DISTRIBUTION TO ATTENDEES AT THE CELEBRATORY DINNER
> HONORING THE ENDOWMENT OF THE UNIVERSITY OF FLORIDA LIBRARIES
> BY SENATOR GEORGE A. SMATHERS,
> MAY 10, 1991.
>
> THE TYPE IS LINOTRONIC-300 JANSON AND
> THE PAPER MOHAWK SUPERFINE.
> THE DESIGN IS BY PAUL G. HOFFMANN WITH
> PRODUCTION COORDINATION BY CARMEN RUSSELL HURFF.
>
> ~~~~~~~~~~~~~~~~~~~~~~~~~~~~~
>
> THE TEXT OF THE MARJORIE KINNAN RAWLINGS SPEECH,
> HERE PRINTED FOR THE FIRST TIME, IS PUBLISHED
> WITH THE PERMISSION OF NORTON BASKIN.
>
> © 1991, NORTON BASKIN

[1–8]

Stapled; [A]⁴; 4 leaves.

Contents: p. 1: title page; p. 2: copyright page; p. 3: 'INTRODUCTION' by Dale B. Canelas; p. 4: photo of Rawlings; pp. 5–7: address by Rawlings; p. 8: 'THE MARJORIE KINNAN RAWLINGS | LITERARY ARCHIVE' at the University of Florida, described by Carmen Russell Hurff.

Typography and paper: (17.1) × 11.0; wove paper; 35 lines per page. No running heads.

Binding: Dark blue imitation thick calico-weave wrappers; goldstamped front cover, upper center, in script: 'M·K·R'.

Cover for A 11

A11 *University of Florida Address* 155

Publication: 1,000 copies published on 10 May 1991.

Printing: Stinehour Press.

Locations: FU, PM, RLT.

Note: The address was delivered by Rawlings on 30 March 1950 on the occasion of the gift of her books and papers to the University of Florida.

AA. Collections

None of these volumes includes first publication of material by Rawlings.

AA 1 GAL YOUNG UN AND OTHER FAMOUS STORIES
1954

[on the verso] Gal Young Un | [decorated rule] | [publisher's device: rooster in a black box] | BANTAM BOOKS | NEW YORK | [on the recto] *by* | *MARJORIE KINNAN RAWLINGS* | *and Other Famous Stories of* | *the Cross Creek Country* | [decorated rule]

17.8 × 10.5 cm.

[i–viii] 1–182 [183–184]

On copyright page: 'A Bantam Book Published March, 1954 | FIRST EDITION'.

Contents: p. i: blurb; pp. ii–iii: title page; p. iv: copyright page; p. v: contents; p. vi: blank; p. vii: section title; p. viii: blank; pp. 1–4: "Antses in Tim's Breakfast"; pp. 5–75: "Jacob's Ladder"; pp. 76–85: "The Pardon"; pp. 86–103: "A Crop of Beans"; pp. 104–121: "The Enemy"; pp. 123–159: "Gal Young Un"; pp. 160–182: "Cocks Must Crow"; p. 183: advertisement; p. 184: blank.

Typography and paper: 16.2 (15.6) × 10.7 cm.; 39 lines per page; wove paper. Running heads: rectos: pp. 3: *'ANTSES IN TIM'S BREAKFAST'*; pp. 7–75: *'JACOB'S LADDER'*; pp. 77–85: *'THE PARDON'*; pp. 87–103: *'A CROP OF BEANS'*; pp. 105–119: *'THE ENEMY'*; pp. 123–159: *'GAL YOUNG UN'*; pp. 161–181: *'COCKS MUST CROW'*; versos: pp. 2–74, 78–84, 88–102, 106–120, 124–158, 162–182: *'GAL YOUNG UN'*.

Binding: Multicolor coated wrappers. Front cover on cream background: '[in black at upper right corner] A1209 | [in black] MARJORIE KINNAN RAW- LINGS | [inside a red box in black below A1209] A BANTAM | GIANT | [a rooster in white in a black box inside the red box] | [in ornamental white over an illustration of a woman soaking her foot in a tub] Gal Young Un | *and Other Famous Stories of* | *the Cross Creek Country* | [below illustration in black] A BANTAM GIANT | COMPLETE AND UNABRIDGED'; spine (top to bottom): '[horizontal in black] A1209 | [vertical on light blue background, black over red] GAL YOUNG UN [top] AND OTHER [bottom] STORIES [in black] Marjorie Kinnan Rawlings | [horizontal in black, illustration of a rooster] | [horizontal on cream background, black over red] 35¢'; back cover: '[in black, illustration of a rooster] 35¢ [dot in black over red] A BANTAM GIANT | [all in a light blue box] MARJORIE KINNAN RAWLINGS [in red] | [in black] 20-line blurb] | [device in red] | [in black] Mrs. Rawlings' publisher in the United States is Charles Scribner's Sons. | [bottom right in black on cream background] PRINTED IN U.S.A. | BANTAM BOOKS'. All edges trimmed. Perfect binding.

Publication: Number of copies printed unknown. 35¢. 'A BANTAM GIANT'. Listed in *Publishers' Weekly*, 165 (6 March 1954), 1310.

Printing: 'PRINTED IN THE UNITED STATES OF AMERICA'.

Location: RLT (4).

Cover for AA 1

AA 2 RAWLINGS READER
1956

MARJORIE KINNAN RAWLINGS | THE | *Marjorie Rawlings* | READER | *Selected and Edited* | *with* | *an Introduction* | *by* | JULIA SCRIBNER BIGHAM | CHARLES SCRIBNER'S SONS | NEW YORK

20.9 × 14.0 cm.

[i–viii] ix–xix [xx] [1–2] 3–270 [271–272] 273–313 [314–316] 317–351 [352–354] 355–374 [375–376] 377–504 [505–508]

[1–15]¹⁶ [16]⁸ [17]¹⁶; 264 leaves.

Contents: p. i: half title: '*The* | *Marjorie Rawlings* | *Reader*'; p. ii: '*Books by Marjorie Kinnan Rawlings* | [nine titles listed]'; p. iii: title page; p. iv: copyright page: ' © *Copyright 1956 by Charles Scribner's Sons* | [8 lines of copyright information] | [3-line rights statement | A-9.56 [H] | PRINTED IN THE UNITED STATES OF AMERICA | *Library of Congress Catalog Card Number 56-10198* | [2 lines of copyright information]'; p. v: '*Contents*'; p. vi: blank; p. vii: section title: '*INTRODUCTION*'; p. viii: blank; pp. ix–xix: '*Introduction*'; p. xx: blank; p. 1: section title: '*SOUTH MOON UNDER*'; p. 2: blank; pp. 3–270: '*SOUTH MOON UNDER*'; p. 271: 'from *CROSS CREEK*'; p. 272: blank; pp. 273–287: '*Hyacinth Drift*'; pp. 288–291: '*Antses in Tim's Breakfast*'; pp. 292–304: ' '*Geechee*'; pp. 305–313: '*Taking Up the Slack*'; p. 314: blank; p. 315: 'from *THE YEARLING*'; p. 316: blank; pp. 317–334: '*Penny Is Bitten by a Rattlesnake*'; pp. 335–351: '*Jody Finds the Fawn*'; p. 352: blank; p. 353: 'Hitherto Uncollected: | JESSAMINE SPRINGS | THE PELICAN'S SHADOW | THE SHELL'; p. 354: blank; pp. 355–360: '*Jessamine Springs*'; pp. 361–368: '*The Pelican's Shadow*'; pp. 369–374: '*The Shell*'; p. 375: 'from *When the Whippoorwill*'; p. 376: blank; pp. 377–413: '*Gal Young Un*'; pp. 414–435: '*Cocks Must Crow*'; pp. 436–504: '*Jacob's Ladder*'; pp. 505–508: blank.

Typography and paper: 17.6 (17.2) × 9.7 cm.; wove paper; 37 lines per page. Running heads: rectos: xi–xix: '*INTRODUCTION*'; pp. 5–269: '*SOUTH MOON UNDER*'; pp. 275–287: '*HYACINTH DRIFT*'; pp. 289–291: '*ANTSES IN TIM'S BREAKFAST*'; pp. 293–303: ' "*GEECHEE*'; pp. 307–313: '*TAKING UP THE SLACK*'; pp. 319–333: '*PENNY IS BITTEN BY A RATTLESNAKE*'; pp. 337–351: '*JODY FINDS THE FAWN*'; pp. 357–359: '*JESSAMINE SPRINGS*'; pp. 363–367: '*THE PELICAN'S SHADOW*'; pp. 371–373: '*THE SHELL*'; pp. 379–413: '*GAL YOUNG UN*'; pp. 415–435: '*COCKS MUST CROW*'; pp. 437–503: '*JACOB'S LADDER*'; versos: pp. x–xviii: '*INTRODUCTION*'; pp. 4–270, 274–286, 290, 294–312, 318–350, 356–374, 378–412, 416–434, 438–504: '*THE RAWLINGS READER*'.

Binding: Light olive and olive imitation marble paper (right half front cover, left half back cover) over bluish green calico-textured cloth. Front cover: '[goldstamped , upper left center] THE | MARJORIE | RAWLINGS | READER'; spine: '[title bluish green in goldstamped box] THE | MARJORIE | RAWLINGS | READER | [goldstamped] EDITED BY | [name bluish green in goldstamped box] JULIA | SCRIBNER | BIGHAM | [goldstamped] SCRIBNERS'; back cover: blindstamped: Scribner logo. Top and bottom edges trimmed. Fore-edge rough trimmed.

Dust jacket: Front cover and spine: white on bluish green background: continuous swamp scene depicting cranes and a fawn; in gold box continuous on front cover and spine: '[title in black lettering] THE | MARJORIE | RAWLINGS | READER'; [all in black in a gold box at bottom right] SELECTED AND EDITED, | WITH AN INTRODUCTION, BY | JULIA SCRIBNER BIGHAM'; spine: in continuous gold box: '[all in black lettering] THE | MARJORIE | RAWLINGS | READER | EDITED BY | JULIA | SCRIBNER | BIGHAM | SCRIBNERS'; back cover: on white background: '[bluish green] What THE MARJORIE RAWLINGS READER contains | [2-line blurb in black, preceded by a bluish green dot] | [2-line blurb in black, preceded by a bluish green dot] | [6-line blurb in black, preceded by a bluish green dot] | [4-line blurb in black, preceded by a bluish green dot] | [5-line blurb in black, preceded by a bluish green dot] | [5-line blurb in black, preceded by a bluish green dot] | [in bluish green] PUBLISHED BY CHARLES SCRIBNER'S SONS NEW YORK'; front flap: on white background: '[upper right corner, in black] $5.00 | [title in bluish green] THE | MARJORIE RAWLINGS | READER | [next two lines in black] SELECTED AND EDITED, | WITH AN INTRODUCTION, BY | [in bluish green] Julia Scribner Bigham | [26-line blurb in black] | [in bluish green] *(continued on back flap)*'; rear flap: '[in bluish green] *(continued from front flap)* | [29-line blurb in black] | [in bluish green] About the Editor | [9-line biography in black] | [in bluish green] *Jacket by Greta and Reynard Biemiller*'.

Publication: Unknown number of copies printed. Published 24 September 1956. $5. Copyright page: 'A-9.56[H]'. Copyright A255346. Listed in *Publishers' Weekly*, 170 (29 October 1956), 2084.

Locations: PM (dj), RLT (2, dj), RM (2, dj).

SECOND PRINTING:

New York: Charles Scribner's Sons, 1967. $4.50. *Binding*: Black calico-textured cloth, not embossed, with pink spirals on gray paper overlaid on right

Dust jacket for AA 2

front half and left back half of the cover. Dust jacket: 'MODERN STANDARD AUTHORS'. *Locations*: RLT(2), RM.

Note: Copyright: 'B-3.67[H]'.

THIRD PRINTING:

New York: Charles Scribner's, 1968. $2.95. *Binding*: Dark and light blue coated wrappers. '*The Scribner Library*' Omnibus Volume SL 159. Copyright page: 'A-6.68[COL]'. *Location*: RLT.

FOURTH PRINTING:

Jacksonville, Florida: San Marco Bookstore, 1988. $19.95. Facsimile of the first printing, except the Scribner's imprint on the title page is removed and replaced with 'SAN MARCO BOOKSTORE | P. O. BOX 5842 | JACKSONVILLE, FLORIDA 32247-5842'. *Binding*: Facsimile, but without the paper overlay. *Dust jacket*: Facsimile.

AA3 FLORIDA ENDOWMENT FOR THE HUMANITIES READER
1988

A Marjorie Kinnan Rawlings Reader | [rule] | [lower left] F · E · H · [below initials an illustration of an arch] | [to the right of the arch] Florida Endowment for the Humanities | 3102 N. Habana Avenue · Suite 300 | Tampa, Florida 33607

27.8 × 21.3 cm.

On copyright page: '© 1989 Florida Endowment for the Humanities'.

viii + 143 pp.

Contents: Both primary and secondary material. The primary material includes: pp. e–f: "A Word about my Life and Work as a Novelist"; pp. 3–11: "Jody Finds the Fawn" from *The Yearling*; pp. 13–29: "Gal Young Un"; pp. 31–39: "Benny and the Bird Dogs"; pp. 41–56: "Our Daily Bread" from *Cross Creek*; pp. 59–62: "Florida: A Land of Contrasts"; pp. 65–66: "About Fabulous Florida"; pp. 69–70: "Portrait of a Magnificent Editor as Seen in His Letters"; pp. 73–82: "Autobiographical Sketches" from the *Los Angeles Times*. See A3, C594, C597, A4, C628, C637, C641, C645.

Collections 165

Binding: Light brown wrappers, spiral-bound.

Publication: Unknown number of copies printed. No price.

Locations: PM, RLT.

Note: Prepared by Dorothy Abbott.

AA 4 SHORT STORIES
1994

[title page continuous from p. ii to p. iii, with a sketch of a house and surrounding rural scene extending from p. ii to p. iii] '[on p. ii, below sketch] University Press of Florida | *Gainesville / Tallahassee / Tampa / Boca Raton / Pensacola / Orlando / Miami / Jacksonville*'; [on p. iii, above and to right of the sketch] *Short Stories by* Marjorie ['M' in large font] | Kinnan ['K' in large font] | Rawlings ['R' in large font] | *Edited by Rodger L. Tarr*

22.2 × 14.5 cm.

On copyright page: 'Copyright 1994 by the Board of Regents of the State of Florida'. ISBN 0-8130-1252-X (cloth); ISBN 0-8130-1253-8 (paper).

[i–viii] ix–x [1–2] 3–373 [374] 375–376 [377–382]

[1–9]^{16} [10]^{4} [11–13]^{16}; 196 leaves.

Contents: p. i: half title: '*Short Stories by* | MARJORIE KINNAN RAWLINGS'; pp. ii–iii: title page; p. iv: copyright page; p. v: dedication page; p. vi: blank; p. vii: 'CONTENTS'; p. viii: blank; pp. ix–x: 'PREFACE'; p. 1: section title: same as half title; p. 2: blank; pp. 3–27: 'INTRODUCTION'; pp. 28–40: 'CRACKER CHIDLINGS'; pp. 41–107: 'JACOB'S LADDER'; pp. 108–123: 'LORD BILL OF THE SUWANNEE RIVER'; pp. 124–130: 'A PLUMB CLARE CONSCIENCE'; pp. 131–147: 'A CROP OF BEANS'; pp. 148–183: 'GAL YOUNG UN'; pp. 184–197: 'ALLIGATORS'; pp. 198–215: 'BENNY AND THE BIRD DOGS'; pp. 216–225: 'THE PARDON'; pp. 226–242: 'VARMINTS'; pp. 243–251: 'A MOTHER IN MANNVILLE'; pp. 252–272: 'COCKS MUST CROW'; pp. 273–289: 'FISH FRY AND FIREWORKS'; pp. 290–297: 'THE PELICAN'S SHADOW'; pp. 298–314: 'THE ENEMY'; pp. 315–319: 'IN THE HEART'; pp. 320–325: 'JESSAMINE SPRINGS'; pp. 326–337: 'THE PROVIDER'; pp. 338–343: 'THE SHELL'; pp. 344–351: 'BLACK SECRET'; pp. 352–358: 'MIRIAM'S HOUSES'; pp. 359–367: 'MISS MOFFATT STEPS OUT'; pp. 368–373: 'THE FRIENDSHIP'; p. 374: blank; pp. 375–376: 'PUBLICATION NOTES'; pp. 377–382: blank.

Typography and paper: Running heads at the bottom: 18.6 (17.6) × 10.2 cm.;

wove paper; 36 lines per page. Running heads: rectos: pp. 5–25: 'Introduction'; p. 26: 'Works Cited'; pp. 29–39: 'Cracker Chidlings'; pp. 43–107: 'Jacob's Ladder'; pp. 109–123: 'Lord Bill of the Suwannee River'; pp. 125–129: 'A Plumb Clare Conscience'; pp. 133–147: 'A Crop of Beans'; pp. 149–183: 'Gal Young Un'; pp. 185–197: 'Alligators'; pp. 199–215: 'Benny and the Bird Dogs'; pp. 217–225: 'The Pardon'; pp. 227–241: 'Varmints'; pp. 245–251: 'A Mother in Mannville'; pp. 253–271: 'Cocks Must Crow'; pp. 275–289: 'Fish Fry and Fireworks'; pp. 291–297: 'The Pelican's Shadow'; pp. 299–313: 'The Enemy'; pp. 317–319: 'In the Heart'; pp. 321–325: 'Jessamine Springs'; pp. 327–337: 'The Provider'; pp. 339–343: 'The Shell'; pp. 345–351: 'Black Secret'; pp. 353–357: 'Miriam's Houses'; pp. 361–367: 'Miss Moffatt Steps Out'; pp. 369–373: 'The Friendship'; versos: p. x: 'Preface'; pp. 4–24: 'Introduction'; p. 26: 'Works Cited'; pp. 30–106, 110–122, 126–146, 150–182, 186–196, 200–214, 218–224, 228–250, 254–288, 292–296, 300–318, 322–324, 328–336, 340–342, 346–350, 354–366, 370–372: 'Marjorie Kinnan Rawlings'; p. 376: 'Publication Notes'.

Binding: Two styles have been noted:

Binding A (hardcover): Brownish mustard calico-textured cloth; gold-stamped spine: '[horizontal] TARR | [vertical] Short Stories by [underneath] Marjorie Kinnan Rawlings | [horizontal] UPF'. All edges trimmed. Light brown uncoated endpapers.

Binding B (coated wrappers): The front cover and spine of the paperback are the same as the dust jacket of the hardback. The back cover is rearranged and includes the blurbs, photo, abbreviated description of the contents, biography, and description of the illustrations. At bottom left: '[in purple] University Press of Florida | [in light olive] ISBN 0-8130-1253-8'; at the bottom right: bar code in purple. All edges are trimmed.

Dust jacket: All on light cream background, sketch in light olive of a house in a rural setting begins on the back cover and continues on front flap; front cover: '[all printing in purple] Short Stories by | Marjorie ['M' in large font] | Kinnan ['K' in large font] | Rawlings ['R' in large font] | [five sketches, boxed in purple on dark cream background, extend from top right to bottom middle to left middle] | [bottom right] Edited by | Rodger L. Tarr'; spine: '[vertical top to bottom in purple] Short Stories by [underneath] Marjorie Kinnan Rawlings | [horizontal in purple] TARR | [horizontal in light olive] UPF'; back cover: [all in purple, except IBSN number, which is in light olive: 10-line blurb by James Dickey; 4-line blurb by Margaret Mitchell; 2-line blurb from the *New Republic*; 2-line blurb from the *Boston Transcript*; 1-line blurb from the *Atlantic Monthly*; photo of Rawlings is to the right of the first two blurbs] University Press of Florida | ISBN 0-8130-1252-X | [bar code in the lower right corner]'; front flap: '[47-line description in purple] | [in light olive] *continued on back flap*'; rear flap: '[all in purple, except in light olive] *continued from front flap* | [17-line description] | *About the editor* | [8-line biography] | [14-line description of the illustrations] | *Order books from* | University Press of Florida | 15 Northwest 15th Street | Gainesville, FL 32611'.

Publication: 1,233 copies in hardback and 4,681 copies in paperback published February 1994. $44.95 (hardback); $24.95 (paperback).

Printing: 'Printed in the United States of America on acid-free paper'.

Location: Bindings A–B: RLT.

Note: The hardback and the paperback were published simultaneously. There is no difference in the pagination and contents.

B. First-Appearance Contributions to Books and Pamphlets

Titles in which material by Rawlings appears for the first time in a book or pamphlet, arranged chronologically. Previously published items are so identified. The first printings only of these titles are noted, but the English editions are also noted.

B 1 O. HENRY PRIZE STORIES OF 1933
1933

O. HENRY | MEMORIAL AWARD | [in script] Prize Stories of 1933 | SELECTED AND EDITED BY | HARRY HANSEN | *Literary Editor of the* | NEW YORK WORLD-TELEGRAM | [publisher's device] | DOUBLEDAY, DORAN & COMPANY, INC. | GARDEN CITY, NEW YORK | 1933

On copyright page: 'COPYRIGHT, 1933'.

"Gal Young Un," pp. 1–44. See AA1–4, C594. Statement by Rawlings, p. 2—previously unpublished.

Location: IMacoW.

B 2 EDITOR'S CHOICE
1934

[enclosed in a double rule frame] EDITOR'S | CHOICE | [illustration] | ALFRED DASHIELL | [publisher's device] | G · P · PUTNAM'S SONS | NEW YORK

On copyright page: 'Copyright, 1934 . . . FIRST EDITION'.

"Benny and the Bird Dogs," pp. 292–311. See AA3–4, C597.

Location: RLT.

Note: A brief commentary on the story by Dashiell appears on p. 311.

B 3 THE BEST POEMS OF 1936
1937

The | [bold] BEST POEMS | *of* 1936 | *Selected by* | THOMAS MOULT | & *decorated by* | ELIZABETH MONTGOMERY | AND | AGNES MILLER

PARKER | [publisher's device] | NEW YORK | HARCOURT BRACE AND COMPANY

Published in 1937.

"Having Left Cities Behind Me" (poem), p. 40. See C600.

Location: RLT (2).

B 4 POST STORIES OF 1939
1939

[enclosed in triple rule frame] *POST STORIES | OF 1939* | [publisher's device] | BOSTON | LITTLE, BROWN AND COMPANY | 1940

On copyright page: 'COPYRIGHT, 1939'.

"Cocks Must Crow," pp. 198–200. See AA1–2, AA4, C610.

Location: RLT.

B 5 SHORT STORIES FROM THE NEW YORKER
1940

[title bold] SHORT STORIES | FROM | THE | NEW YORKER | 19 [publisher's device] 40 | SIMON AND SCHUSTER · NEW YORK

On copyright page: 'COPYRIGHT, 1940'.

"The Pelican's Shadow," pp. 291–297. See AA2, AA4, C611.

British edition: London: Victor Gollancz, 1951.

Location: RLT.

B 6 THIS IS MY BEST
1942

America's 93 Greatest Living Authors Present | [in script] This Is My Best | [leaf device] OVER 150 SELF-CHOSEN AND | COMPLETE MASTER-PIECES, TOGETHER WITH | THEIR REASONS FOR THEIR SELECTIONS | [cupid riding a lion inside an ornate oval frame] | *Edited by Whit Burnett* | Burton C. Hoffman THE DIAL PRESS New York, 1942

On copyright page: 'Copyright, 1942'.

"Hyacinth Drift" from *Cross Creek*, pp. 393–406. See A5, AA2, C595. Note by Rawlings on the reason for her selection. Previously unpublished.

Location: RLT.

B7 VOGUE'S FIRST READER
1942

[title bold in script] Vogue's | First | Reader | [bold rule] | [bold] INTRODUCTION BY FRANK CROWNINSHIELD | [in script] Julian Messner, Incorporated [star device] 1942 [star device] New York

On copyright page: 'COPYRIGHT 1942'.

" 'Fanny—You Fool!,' " pp. 319–321; "I Sing While I Cook," pp. 457–461. See C622; C609.

British edition: Vogue's Fireside Book. London: Hammond, Hammond & Co., 1944.

Location: RLT.

B8 LETTERS FROM CALEB MILNE
1944

[hollow font] *"I Dream of the Day . . ."* | LETTERS FROM | CALEB MILNE | AFRICA, 1942–1943 | WOODSTOCK, NEW YORK | 1944

On the copyright page: 'Copyright, 1944'.

Untitled introduction on p. v. Previously unpublished.

Locations: IU, RLT.

B9 KATHERINE MANSFIELD STORIES
1946

KATHERINE MANSFIELD | STORIES | [Illustration of a woman playing a guitar] | A SELECTION MADE BY *J. Middleton Murry* | WITH ILLUSTRATIONS BY *Leon Jacobson* | INTRODUCTION BY *Marjorie Kinnan Rawlings* | CLEVELAND AND NEW YORK | THE WORLD PUBLISHING COMPANY

On copyright page: 'First Printing October 1946'.

Introduction, "The Living Mansfield," pp. 9–12. Previously unpublished.

Locations: PM, RLT (2), RM.

B 10 GREAT FARM STORIES
1946

[enclosed in a double frame interlaced with leaves, letters in ornate font] *FURROW'S END* | *An anthology of* | *Great Farm Stories* | *edited by DAVID B. GREENBERG* | *introduction by LOUIS BROMFIELD* | *new york* | GREENBERG: PUBLISHER

On copyright page: 'Copyright 1946'.

"A Crop of Beans," pp. 131–150. See AA1, AA4, C593.

Location: RLT.

B 11 O. HENRY PRIZE STORIES OF 1946
1946

O. HENRY MEMORIAL AWARD | *PRIZE STORIES* | OF | *1946* | [rule with a decorated loop in the center] | SELECTED AND EDITED BY | HERSCHEL BRICKELL | ASSISTED BY | MURIEL FULLER | [rule with a decorated loop in the center] | [publisher's device] | DOUBLEDAY & COMPANY, INC. | GARDEN CITY 1946 NEW YORK

On copyright page: 'COPYRIGHT, 1946 . . . FIRST EDITION'.

"Black Secret," pp. 226–232. See AA4, C631.

Locations: FU, RLT.

B 12 HERE WE ARE
1947

HERE WE ARE | STORIES FROM | *Scholastic Magazine* | EDITED BY | *Ernestine Taggard* | WITH AN INTRODUCTION BY | *Dorothy Canfield Fisher* | [publisher's device] | ROBERT M. McBRIDE & COMPANY | *New York*

On copyright page: 'FIRST EDITION'.

"A Mother in Mannville," pp. 205–218. See AA4, C602.

Locations: ISNU, IU, RLT.

First-Appearance Contributions to Books and Pamphlets 175

B 13 AMERICAN AUTHORS TODAY
1947

[bold] *American Authors Today* | *By* WHIT BURNETT | *Editor of* Story | *and* CHARLES E. SLATKIN | *Formerly Instructor of English,* | *Julia Richman High School, New York City* | *Co-ordinator of the School Museum Program* | *in New York City* | [publisher's device] | [bold] GINN AND COMPANY | BOSTON · NEW YORK · CHICAGO · ATLANTA · DALLAS | COLUMBUS · SAN FRANCISCO · TORONTO · LONDON

On copyright page: 'COPYRIGHT, 1947'.

"A Mother in Mannville," pp. 179–188. See AA4, C602. There is a 17-line comment by Rawlings on the story, p. 179. Previously unpublished.

Location: RLT.

B 14 WORDS TO LIVE BY
1948

[enclosed in a frame decorated at the top and the bottom] | Words | to Live By | *A Little Treasury of Inspiration* | *and Wisdom* | *Selected and Interpreted by* | *Eighty-four Eminent Men and Women* | *Edited by* | William Nichols | SIMON AND SCHUSTER · 1948

From copyright page: 'COPYRIGHT . . . 1948'.

"The Key," p. 129. A 10-line comment on *1 Corinthians 13:1–2*. Previously unpublished.

Location: NdFA

B 15 BOOK OF KNOWLEDGE
1948

[thick-thin frame broken at upper right by title and at lower left by information on the publisher] THE BOOK | OF | KNOWLEDGE | ANNUAL | 1948 | *editor: e. v. mcloughlin* | THE GROLIER SOCIETY | *new york* | *toronto*

On copyright page: 'Copyright 1948'.

"If You Want to Be a Writer," pp. 247–249. Previously unpublished.

Location: DLC.

B 16 HISTORY OF GILCHRIST COUNTY
1986

The History of Gilchrist County | by | Kevin M. McCarthy | 1986 | The Historical Committee of the Trenton Women's Club

On copyright page: 'Copyright 1986 Kevin M. McCarthy'.

"Lord Bill of the Suwannee River," pp. 218–232. See AA4, C648.

Location: PC.

Note: In typescript. This is the first complete text of the story, the text of C648 being incomplete.

B 17 FLORIDA STORIES
1989

Florida Stories | edited by | Kevin McCarthy | University of Florida Press | Gainesville

On copyright page: 'Copyright 1989'.

"A Plumb Clare Conscience," pp. 248–254. See AA4, C591.

Location: RLT.

C. First Appearances in Journals, Magazines, and Newspapers

C1
"The Best Spell." *Washington Post*, Sunday Magazine Section, 2 January 1910, p. 5.

Signed: 'FIDELITY'.

Note: See Rodger L. Tarr, "Marjorie Kinnan Rawlings and the *Washington Post*," *Analytical & Enumerative Bibliography*, n.s. 4, no. 4 (1990), 163–168.

C2
"[Letter to Aunt Anna]." *Washington Post*, Sunday Magazine Section, 30 January 1910, p. 5.

Signed: 'FIDELITY.'.

C3
"[Letter to Aunt Anna]." *Washington Post*, Sunday Magazine Section, 22 May 1910, p. 5.

Signed: 'FIDELITY.'.

C4
"[Letter to Aunt Anna]." *Washington Post*, Sunday Magazine Section.

Signed: 'FIDELITY. | (Marjorie Kinnan, age 14)'.

C5
"[Letter to Aunt Anna]." *Washington Post*, Sunday Magazine Section, 4 September 1910, p. 5.

Signed: 'FIDELITY (Marjorie Kinnan)'.

C6
"The Traveler." *Washington Post*, Sunday Magazine Section, 11 September 1910, p. 5. Poem.

Signed: 'FIDELITY | (Marjorie Kinnan, age 14)'.

C 7
"[Letter to Aunt Anna]." *Washington Post*, Sunday Magazine Section, 25 September 1910, p. 5.

Signed: 'FIDELITY.'.

C 8
"[Letter to 'Everybody (Granny included)']." *Washington Post*, Sunday Magazine Section, 9 October 1910, p. 6.

Signed: 'FIDELITY.'.

C 9
"[Letter to 'Everybody']." *Washington Post*, Sunday Magazine Section, 30 October 1910, p. 6.

Signed: 'MARJORIE KINNAN (age 14)'.

C 10
"The Reincarnation of Miss Hetty." *Washington Post*, Miscellany Section, 12 February 1911, p. 5.

Signed: 'FIDELITY (age 14 years) | (Marjorie Kinsman [sic])'.

C 11
"Carmenite." *Washington Post*, Sunday Magazine Section, 19 March 1911, p. 7.

Signed: 'FIDELITY. | Marjorie Kinnan (age 14).'.

C 12
"Our Cloak-room Looking-glass." *Western*, 16, no. 1 (November 1911), 22. Poem.

Signed: 'Marjorie Kinnan, '14'.

Note: The Western is the literary publication of Western High School, *Washington*, D.C., from which Rawlings, née Kinnan, was graduated in 1914. Rawlings is listed as an associate editor in 1911–1912, and as a literary editor in 1913–1914.

C 13
"A Battle for Life." *Washington Post*, Sunday Magazine Section, 25 February 1912, p. 5.

Signed: 'FIDELITY. | (Marjorie Kinnan, age 15)'.

First Appearances in Journals, Magazines, and Newspapers 181

C 14
"The Reforming of a Mala Puella: Being the Confessions of the Reformer." *Western*, 16, no. 5 (March 1912), 17–20. Poem.

Signed: 'M. K., '14'.

C 15
"Old Friends Are Best." *Washington Post*, Sunday Magazine Section, 3 March 1912, p. 6.

Signed: 'FIDELITY. | (Marjorie Kinnan, age 15)'.

C 16
"[Letter to Aunt Anna]." *Washington Post*, Sunday Magazine Section, 10 March 1912, p. 6.

Signed: 'FIDELITY. | (Marjorie Kinnan)'.

C 17
"[Letter to 'Aunt Anna and Everybody']." *Washington Post*, Sunday Magazine Section, 2 June 1912, p. 6.

Signed: 'FIDELITY. | (Marjorie Kinnan, age 15)'.

C 18
"Sad Story of Little Pip." *Washington Post*, Sunday Magazine Section, 16 June 1912, p. 6.

Signed: 'FIDELITY. Marjorie Kinnan (age 15)'.

C 19
"The Last Day of School." *Washington Post*, Sunday Magazine Section, 14 July 1912, p. 4. Poem.

Signed: 'FIDELITY (age 15) | Marjorie Kinnan'.

C 20
"The Love of Adventure." *Washington Post*, Sunday Magazine Section, 28 July 1912, p. 4.

Signed: 'FIDELITY. | (Marjorie Kinnan, age 15)'.

C 21
"The Reincarnation of Miss Hetty." *McCall's Magazine*, 39, no. 2 (August 1912), 27, 72.

Signed: 'Marjorie Kinnan'.

Note: This is an expanded version of C10.

C22
"[Letter to 'Aunt Anna and Cousins']." *Washington Post*, Sunday Magazine Section, 11 August 1912, p. 4.

Signed: 'FIDELITY. | (Marjorie Kinnan.)'.

C23
"The Freshman's Side of It." *Western*, 17, no. 1 (October 1912), 24–26. Poem.

Signed: 'M. K., '14'.

C24
"To James Whitcomb Riley." *Washington Post*, Sunday Magazine Section, 27 October 1912, p. 6. Poem.

Signed: 'FIDELITY. | (MARJORIE KINNAN)'.

C25
"Company, Halt!" *Western*, 17, no. 2 (November 1912), 18–19. Poem.

Signed: 'M. K. '14'.

C26
"Our Triumph." *Washington Post*, Sunday Magazine Section, 17 November 1912, p. 6.

Signed: 'FIDELITY. | MARJORIE KINNAN (age 16)'.

C27
"H'it's a Bear, H'it's a Bear, H'it's a Bear, There!" *Western*, 17, no. 3 (December 1912), 10–11. Poem.

Signed: 'M. K., '14'.

C28
"Once Upon a Time a Black Demon Invented Powder, and ———" *Western*, 17, no. 4 (January 1913), 27. Poem.

Signed: 'M. K., '14'.

First Appearances in Journals, Magazines, and Newspapers   183

C 29
"Perse and the Baseball Game." *Western*, 17, no. 5 (February 1913), 25–28. Poem.

Signed: 'M. K., '14'.

C 30
"A Romance." *Western*, 17, no. 5 (May 1913), 21–24.

Signed: 'M. K., '14'.

C 31
"A Surprise." *Washington Post*, Sunday Magazine Section, 8 June 1913, p. 4.

Signed: 'Marjorie Kinnan, age 16'.

C 32
"Class Song: To the Tune of 'Believe Me, if all those enduring young charms.'" *Western*, 18, no. 8 (June 1914), 19.

Signed: 'MARJORIE KINNAN.'

Note: In the previous issue, May 1914, there is a dedicatory poem by 'Zeke' entitled "Little Marjorie" (14). In the June 1914 issue, Rawlings is mentioned in the "Class Poem" by K. E. Beach: "How Marjorie Kinnan is quite / The genius of us all, / The wondrous tales which she can write, / Do all the class enthrall" (18). Rawlings was the class vice-president in 1914.

C 33
"Alonzo Perceval Van Clyne." *Washington Post*, Sunday Magazine Section, 10 May 1914, p. 7.

Signed: 'Marjorie Kinnan, age 17'.

C 34
"Who Will Take This Money." *Wisconsin Magazine*, 1 (October 1915), 24.

Signed: 'M. K. and D. B.'.

C 35
"Curls and the Curlers." *Wisconsin Magazine*, 13 (March 1916), 3–5, 31–33.

Signed: 'Marjorie Kinnan, '18'.

C 36
"The Captivating Odors of the Kitchen." *Wisconsin Literary Magazine*, 16, no. 2 (November 1916), 41–42, 56, 58, 60, 87–88, 100, 102.

Signed: 'MARJORIE KINNAN.'.

C 37
"The Real Thing." *Wisconsin Literary Magazine*, 16, no. 5 (February 1917), 149.

Signed: 'MARJORIE KINNAN.'.

C 38
"When the Muse Knocks." *Wisconsin Literary Magazine*, 17, no. 1 (October 1917), 6.

Signed: 'MARJORIE KINNAN.'.

C 39
"The Miracle." *Wisconsin Literary Magazine*, 17, no. 1 (October 1917), 7. Poem.

Signed: 'MARJORIE KINNAN.'.

C 40
"The Singer." *Wisconsin Literary Magazine*, 17, no. 1 (October 1917), 7. Poem.

Signed: 'MARJORIE KINNAN.'.

C 41
"Little Grey Town of Tumbledown." *Wisconsin Literary Magazine*, 17, no. 2 (November 1917), 39. Poem.

Signed: 'MARJORIE KINNAN.'.

C 42
"Ephemera." *Wisconsin Literary Magazine*, 17, no. 2 (November 1917), 42.

Signed: 'MARJORIE KINNAN.'.

C 43
"Plays of Gods and Men." *Wisconsin Literary Magazine*, 17, no. 2 (November 1917), 48, 50.

Signed: 'M. K.'.

First Appearances in Journals, Magazines, and Newspapers 185

Note: Review of Edward J. Dunsany, *Plays of God and Men.* James W. Luce Company, 1917.

C 44
"[On American Drama]." *Wisconsin Literary Magazine*, 17, no. 3 (December 1917), 58.

Signed: 'M. K.'.

C 45
"Korlah." *Wisconsin Literary Magazine*, 17, no. 3 (December 1917), 66. Poem.

Signed: 'MARJORIE KINNAN.'.

C 46
"The Lullaby." *Wisconsin Literary Magazine*, 17, no. 3 (December 1917), 66. Poem.

Signed: 'MARJORIE KINNAN.'.

C 47
"Born to Blush Unseen." *Wisconsin Literary Magazine*, 17, no. 3 (December 1917), 69–70.

Signed: 'MARJORIE KINNAN.'.

C 48
"Nance of the Slums and the Smile." *Wisconsin Literary Magazine*, 17, no. 3 (December 1917), 78, 80.

Signed: 'M. K.'.

Note: Review of Alice H. Rice, *Calvary Alley.* New York: Century, 1918.

C 49
"[On Women's Suffrage]." *Wisconsin Literary Magazine*, 17, no. 4 (January 1918), 86.

Signed: 'M. K.'.

C 50
"The Gypsy." *Wisconsin Literary Magazine*, 17, no. 4 (January 1918), 91. Poem.

Signed: 'MARJORIE KINNAN.'.

C 51

"Fizz." *Wisconsin Literary Magazine*, 17, no. 5 (February 1918), 129. Poem.

Signed: 'MARJORIE KINNAN.'.

C 52

"Effectiveness." *Wisconsin Literary Magazine*, 17, no. 5 (February 1918), 132–33.

Signed: 'MARJORIE KINNAN.'.

C 53

"[Letter to Theodore M. Hammond]." *Wisconsin Literary Magazine*, 17, no. 5 (February 1918), 136.

Signed: 'M. KINNAN' and Board of Editors, *Wisconsin Literary Magazine*.

C 54

"Laughter." *Wisconsin Literary Magazine*, 17, no. 6 (March 1918), 154. Poem.

Signed: 'MARJORIE KINNAN.'.

C 55

"[On Poetry and Vachel Lindsay]." *Wisconsin Literary Magazine*, 17, no. 7 (April 1918), 169–170.

Signed: 'M. K.'.

C 56

"Witter Binner and Vachel Lindsay." *Wisconsin Literary Magazine*, 17, no. 7 (April 1918), 174.

Signed: 'M. K.'.

C 57

"Babylon Undying." *Wisconsin Literary Magazine*, 17, no. 7 (April 1918), 183. Poem.

Signed: 'MARJORIE KINNAN.'.

C 58

"The Monastery." *Wisconsin Literary Magazine*, 17, no. 8 (May 1918), 205–06. Poem.

Signed: 'MARJORIE KINNAN.'.

C 59
"Mother's Misplaced Confidence." *Wisconsin Literary Magazine*, 18, no. 1 (October 1918), 11. Poem.

Signed: 'MARJORIE KINNAN.'.

C 60
"Beginning Early." *Wisconsin Literary Magazine*, 18, no. 1 (October 1918), 11. Poem.

Signed: 'MARJORIE KINNAN.'.

C 61
"The Blue Triangle Follows the Switchboard." *Telephone Topics* (28 March 1919), 312–313.

Signed: 'MARJORIE KINNAN'.

Note: Reprinted in the *Pacific Telephone Magazine, not seen.*

C 62
"Found: A Practical Artist." *Everybody's Magazine*, 41 (October 1919), 124.

Signed: '*Marjorie Kinnan*'.

C 63
"Good Things for Church Suppers." *Woman's Magazine*, (June 1919), 24, 54.

Signed: 'MARJORIE KINNAN'.

C 64
"Women as Constructionists." *New France*, (1919), 434–36.

Signed: 'Marjorie Kinnan'.

C 65
"Eight-Week Clubs; Community Service." *St. Nicholas Magazine*, 46, no. 7 (May 1919), 619–21.

C 66
"Through Three Revolutions: A Woman's Experiences in Modern Russia." *Designer*, 50, no. 3 (July 1919), 1, 26, 29.

C 67
Getting in Touch With the Boys: The Confessions of a Welfare Worker—Part

One [—Part Two]." *Home Sector*, 1, no. 6 (20 December 1919), 7–9, 46–47; 1, no. 7 (27 December 1919), 9–11, 34–35.

Signed: 'A WELFARE WORKER.'

C 68
"A Sanatorium Without Mud Baths or Mineral Water." *Louisville Courier-Journal*, 24 October 1920, p. 5.

C 69
"Live Women in Live Louisville: The Only Woman State Bacteriologist in the United States." *Louisville Courier-Journal*, 6 February 1921, p. 6.

C 70
"Live Women in Live Louisville: A Roentgenological Technician." *Louisville Courier-Journal*, 13 February 1921, p. 4.

C 71
"Live Women in Live Louisville: The Chief Probation Officer for Jefferson County." *Louisville Courier-Journal*, 6 March 1921, p. 6.

C 72
"Live Women in Live Louisville: The Cashier for One of the South's Largest Manufacturing Concerns." *Louisville Courier-Journal*, 13 March 1921, p. 4.

C 73
"Live Women in Live Louisville: A Member of the Louisville Board of Fire Underwriters." *Louisville Courier-Journal*, 27 March 1921, p. 4.

C 74
"Live Women in Live Louisville: A Pioneer Booster of Women in Business." *Louisville Courier-Journal*, Sunday Magazine, 10 April 1921, p. 13.

C 75
" 'Flapping Is Merely Joy of Living.' " [Newspaper not located].

Note: Only a clipping has been seen. From the content, almost certainly published in a Rochester, N.Y., newspaper.

C 76
" 'Women Are Spoiled' Protests the Romantic Lou Tellegren." [Newspaper not located.]

First Appearances in Journals, Magazines, and Newspapers   189

Note: Only a clipping has been seen. From the content, almost certainly published in a Rochester, N.Y., newspaper.

C 77
"The Vagrant of Romance Finds Large City Harsh." [Newspaper not located.]

Note: Only a clipping has been seen. From the content, definitely a Rochester, N.Y., newspaper.

C 78
"Do American Women Appreciate Good Points of Their Men?" *Rochester* (N.Y.) *Evening Journal*, 19 September 1922.

Note: Only a clipping has been seen.

C 79
"Wives' School First Aid for Peeved Hubbies." *Rochester Sunday American*, 1 October 1922.

Note: Only a clipping has been seen.

C 80
"The Rev. Clinton Wunder Is Pioneer Efficiency Pastor." *Rochester Sunday American*, 8 October 1922, p. C-3.

C 81
"Romance of Fifty Years Ago Key to Lonely Life of Spinster Slain in Bethany." *Rochester Evening Journal*, 20 October 1922.

Note: Only a clipping has been seen.

C 82
"Lonely Spinster Had Premonition of Death." *Rochester Sunday American*, 22 October 1922, pp. 1, 3.

C 83
"No Place on Campus for Knickers or Cigarettes, Say Graduates." *Rochester Evening Journal*, 2 November 1922.

Note: Only a clipping has been seen.

C 84
"Tragic Drama at the Corinthian Stirs Rochester's Elite." *Five O'Clock*, 1 (22 April 1924), 9, 15.

Signed: 'LADY ALICIA THWAITE'.

Note: See Rodger L. Tarr, "Marjorie Kinnan Rawlings and the Rochester (NY) Magazine *Five O'Clock*," *American Periodicals*, 1, no. 1 (Fall 1991), 83–85.

C 85
"Our Center of Culture and Mike Dempsey." *Five O'Clock*, 1 (6 May 1924), 12.

Signed: 'LADY ALICIA THWAITE'.

C 86
"Society Divides Between Opera and Wrestling." *Five O'Clock*, 1 (13 May 1924), 7.

Signed: 'LADY ALICIA THWAITE'.

C 87
"Paint Jobs That Bloom in the Spring." *Five O'Clock*, 1 (20 May 1924), 9.

Signed: 'LADY ALICIA THWAITE'.

C 88
"The Smell of Country Sausage." *Rochester Times-Union*, 24 May 1926, p. 26. Poem.

C 89
"Other Women's Babies." *Rochester Times-Union*, 25 May 1926, p. 26. Poem.

'Reprinted by Request' in *Rochester Times-Union*, 9 September 1927, p. 34.

C 90
"Ancestral Pies." *Rochester Times-Union*, 26 May 1926, p. 36. Poem.

C 91
"The Kitchen Rocking Chair." *Rochester Times-Union*, 27 May 1926, p. 38. Poem.

'Reprinted by Request' in *Rochester Times-Union*, 6 September 1927, p. 31.

C 92
"Apples in the Cellar." *Rochester Times-Union*, 28 May 1926, p. 37. Poem.

C 93
"All Boy." *Rochester Times-Union*, 29 May 1926, p. 19. Poem.

First Appearances in Journals, Magazines, and Newspapers   191

C 94
"After Breakfast." *Rochester Times-Union*, 1 June 1926, p. 28. Poem.

'Reprinted by Request' in *Rochester Times-Union*, 20 September 1927, p. 31.

C 95
"Prize Jelly." *Rochester Times-Union*, 2 June 1926, p. 29. Poem.

C 96
"The Stove." *Rochester Times-Union*, 3 June 1926, p. 28. Poem.

C 97
"The Maple Tree." *Rochester Times-Union*, 4 June 1926, p. 33. Poem.

C 98
"Sunday Night Tea." *Rochester Times-Union*, 5 June 1926, p. 19. Poem.

C 99
"The Family's Return." *Rochester Times-Union*, 7 June 1926, p. 23. Poem.

C 100
"Envy." *Rochester Times-Union*, 8 June 1926, p. 29. Poem.

C 101
"Making the Beds." *Rochester Times-Union*, 9 June 1926, p. 31. Poem.

C 102
"Loving." *Rochester Times-Union*, 10 June 1926, p. 34. Poem.

C 103
"The Menagerie." *Rochester Times-Union*, 11 June 1926, p. 33. Poem.

C 104
"Houses." *Rochester Times-Union*, 12 June 1926, p. 20. Poem.

C 105
"Neighbor's Dogs." *Rochester Times-Union*, 14 June 1926, p. 25. Poem.

C 106
"Smell of Old Houses." *Rochester Times-Union*, 15 June 1926, p. 23. Poem.

C 107
"Twins." *Rochester Times-Union*, 16 June 1926, p. 32. Poem.

C 108
"Neighbors." *Rochester Times-Union*, 17 June 1926, p. 36. Poem.

C 109
"Baby Sue's Bath." *Rochester Times-Union*, 18 June 1926, p. 33. Poem.

C 110
"Picnics." *Rochester Times-Union*, 19 June 1926, p. 19. Poem.

C 111
"June Strawberries." *Rochester Times-Union*, 21 June 1926, p. 26. Poem.

C 112
"The Passer-By." *Rochester Times-Union*, 22 June 1926, p. 28. Poem.

C 113
"If I Were Queen." *Rochester Times-Union*, 23 June 1926, p. 36. Poem.

C 114
"Footprints." *Rochester Times-Union*, 24 June 1926, p. 36. Poem.

C 115
"Official Opening." *Rochester Times-Union*, 25 June 1926, p. 32. Poem.

C 116
"The Back Door." *Rochester Times-Union*, 26 June 1926, p. 25. Poem.

C 117
"Signs of Company." *Rochester Times-Union*, 28 June 1926, p. 28. Poem.

C 118
"No School!" *Rochester Times-Union*, 29 June 1926, p. 26. Poem.

C 119
"A Cup of Tea." *Rochester Times-Union*, 30 June 1926, p. 31. Poem.

C 120
"A Private Corner." *Rochester Times-Union*, 1 July 1926, p. 38. Poem.

C 121
"For Rent." *Rochester Times-Union*, 2 July 1926, p. 23. Poem.

First Appearances in Journals, Magazines, and Newspapers   193

C 122
"Independence Day." *Rochester Times-Union*, 3 July 1926, p. 25. Poem.

C 123
"Out of Things." *Rochester Times-Union*, 6 July 1926, p. 30. Poem.

C 124
"Understanding." *Rochester Times-Union*, 7 July 1926, p. 26. Poem.

C 125
"Unseen Visitors." *Rochester Times-Union*, 8 July 1926, p. 34. Poem.

C 126
"The Kids Across the Track." *Rochester Times-Union*, 9 July 1926, p. 20. Poem.

C 127
"Candle-Light." *Rochester Times-Union*, 10 July 1926, p. 21. Poem.

C 128
"Cherry Pie." *Rochester Times-Union*, 12 July 1926, p. 27. Poem.

C 129
"Going Barefoot." *Rochester Times-Union*, 13 July 1926, p. 23. Poem.

C 130
"Lickin' Good." *Rochester Times-Union*, 14 July 1926, p. 31. Poem.

C 131
"Waking Up." *Rochester Times-Union*, 15 July 1926, p. 31. Poem.

C 132
"Cooking Confession." *Rochester Times-Union*, 16 July 1926, p. 19. Poem.

C 133
"Coxey's Army." *Rochester Times-Union*, 17 July 1926, p. 20. Poem.

C 134
"The Kitchen Window." *Rochester Times-Union*, 19 July 1926, p. 18. Poem.

C 135
"The Order Man." *Rochester Times-Union*, 20 July 1926, p. 23. Poem.

C 136
"Home-Made Ice Cream." *Rochester Times-Union*, 21 July 1926, p. 24. Poem.

C 137
"Cleaning the Attic." *Rochester Times-Union*, 22 July 1926, p. 26. Poem.

C 138
"Lemon Pie." *Rochester Times-Union*, 23 July 1926, p. 14. Poem.

C 139
"Wasting Time." *Rochester Times-Union*, 24 July 1926, p. 18. Poem.

C 140
"When Mary Makes Molasses Cake." *Rochester Times-Union*, 26 July 1926, p. 40. Poem.

C 141
"Darning the Socks." *Rochester Times-Union*, 27 July 1926, p. 18. Poem.

C 142
"The Surprise Garden." *Rochester Times-Union*, 28 July 1926, p. 23. Poem.

C 143
"Dewberries." *Rochester Times-Union*, 29 July 1926, p. 27. Poem.

C 144
"Perch Fishing." *Rochester Times-Union*, 30 July 1926, p. 14. Poem.

C 145
"The Rose Jar." *Rochester Times-Union*, 31 July 1926, p. 18. Poem.

C 146
"Shelling Peas." *Rochester Times-Union*, 2 August 1926, p. 34. Poem.

C 147
"For Exchange: Rubbish." *Rochester Times-Union*, 3 August 1926, p. 18. Poem.

C 148
"The Mint Bed." *Rochester Times-Union*, 4 August 1926, p. 26. Poem.

C 150
"Always Hungry." *Rochester Times-Union*, 5 August 1926, p. 26. Poem.

First Appearances in Journals, Magazines, and Newspapers   195

C 150
"Perennials." *Rochester Times-Union*, 6 August 1926, p. 15. Poem.

C 151
"Bread and 'Lasses." *Rochester Times-Union*, 7 August 1926, p. 18. Poem.

C 152
"Mending." *Rochester Times-Union*, 9 August 1926, p. 22. Poem.

C 153
"Trees." *Rochester Times-Union*, 10 August 1926, p. 23. Poem.

C 154
"Hide and Seek." *Rochester Times-Union*, 11 August 1926, p. 30. Poem.

C 155
"Witchcraft." *Rochester Times-Union*, 12 August 1926, p. 31. Poem.

C 156
"A Rainy Day." *Rochester Times-Union*, 13 August 1926, p. 14. Poem.

C 157
"Washings on the Line." *Rochester Times-Union*, 14 August 1926, p. 18. Poem.

C 158
"Jealousy." *Rochester Times-Union*, 16 August 1926, p. 21. Poem.

C 159
"Canning." *Rochester Times-Union*, 17 August 1926, p. 18. Poem.

C 160
"The Point of View." *Rochester Times-Union*, 18 August 1926, p. 31. Poem.

C 161
"A Knack." *Rochester Times-Union*, 19 August 1926, p. 26. Poem.

C 162
"Grandma's Chair." *Rochester Times-Union*, 20 August 1926, p. 18. Poem.

C 163
"Neighbors' Cats." *Rochester Times-Union*, 21 August 1926, p. 18. Poem.

C 164
"Six Daisies." *Rochester Times-Union*, 23 August 1926, p. 23. Poem.

C 165
"Dusting." *Rochester Times-Union*, 24 August 1926, p. 22. Poem.

C 166
"Tomorrow, Rain." *Rochester Times-Union*, 25 August 1926, p. 26. Poem.

C 167
"A Busy Day." *Rochester Times-Union*, 26 August 1926, p. 27. Poem.

C 168
"Buckwheat Honey." *Rochester Times-Union*, 27 August 1926, p. 19. Poem.

C 169
"The Humming Bird." *Rochester Times-Union*, 28 August 1926, p. 18. Poem.

C 170
"Flowers on the Table." *Rochester Times-Union*, 30 August 1926, p. 23. Poem.

C 171
"A Prayer for Housewives." *Rochester Times-Union*, 31 August 1926, p. 18. Poem.

'Reprinted by Request' in *Rochester Times-Union*, 8 September 1927, p. 31.

C 172
"Postponed by Rain." *Rochester Times-Union*, 1 September 1926, p. 23. Poem.

C 173
"Wheat Fields." *Rochester Times-Union*, 2 September 1926, p. 31. Poem.

C 174
"Window Shades." *Rochester Times-Union*, 3 September 1926, p. 26. Poem.

C 175
"Petunia-Vain." *Rochester Times-Union*, 4 September 1926, p. 18. Poem.

C 176
"The Price of Marguerite." *World Magazine* (5 September 1926), pp. 12ff.

Note: Only a clipping has been seen.

First Appearances in Journals, Magazines, and Newspapers   197

C 177
"Corn Roasts." *Rochester Times-Union*, 7 September 1926, p. 24. Poem.

C 178
"When I Grow Old." *Rochester Times-Union*, 8 September 1926, p. 31. Poem.

C 179
"The Pioneer Picnic." *Rochester Times-Union*, 9 September 1926, p. 29. Poem.

C 180
"A Neighbor's Duties." *Rochester Times-Union*, 10 September 1926, p. 33. Poem.

C 181
"Keeping Hold." *Rochester Times-Union*, 11 September 1926, p. 21. Poem.

C 182
"Relatives." *Rochester Times-Union*, 13 September 1926, p. 25. Poem.

C 183
"My Dog." *Rochester Times-Union*, 14 September 1926, p. 26. Poem.

C 184
"A Cricket in the House." *Rochester Times-Union*, 15 September 1926, p. 33. Poem.

C 185
"Old Clothes." *Rochester Times-Union*, 16 September 1926, p. 31. Poem.

C 186
"The Touch." *Rochester Times-Union*, 17 September 1926, p. 35. Poem.

C 187
"Taking Down the Clothes." *Rochester Times-Union*, 18 September 1926, p. 20. Poem.

C 188
"Morning Friends." *Rochester Times-Union*, 20 September 1926, p. 23. Poem.

C 189
"Pots and Pans." *Rochester Times-Union*, 21 September 1926, p. 27. Poem.

C 190
"Color-Mad." *Rochester Times-Union*, 22 September 1926, p. 35. Poem.

C 191
"The Old Red Tablecloth." *Rochester Times-Union*, 23 September 1926, p. 34. Poem.

C 192
"Apples." *Rochester Times-Union*, 24 September 1926, p. 33. Poem.

'Reprinted by Request' in *Rochester Times-Union*, 17 September 1927, p. 12.

C 193
"Burning the Grass." *Rochester Times-Union*, 25 September 1926, p. 20. Poem.

C 194
"Rain on the Roof." *Rochester Times-Union*, 27 September 1926, p. 23. Poem.

C 195
"Household Arithmetic." *Rochester Times-Union*, 28 September 1926, p. 27. Poem.

C 196
"Blue Pitchers." *Rochester Times-Union*, 29 September 1926, p. 31. Poem.

C 197
"Starting School." *Rochester Times-Union*, 30 September 1926, p. 30. Poem.

C 198
"October, Friend of Housewives." *Rochester Times-Union*, 1 October 1926, p. 37. Poem.

C 199
"Gold and Blue." *Rochester Times-Union*, 2 October 1926, p. 21. Poem.

C 200
"When Housewives Work Together." *Rochester Times-Union*, 4 October 1926, p. 25. Poem.

C 201
"The Old Home." *Rochester Times-Union*, 5 October 1926, p. 26. Poem.

First Appearances in Journals, Magazines, and Newspapers 199

C 202
"The Willing Escort." *Rochester Times-Union*, 6 October 1926, p. 31. Poem.

C 203
"My Postman." *Rochester Times-Union*, 7 October 1926, p. 35. Poem.

C 204
"Gray Skies." *Rochester Times-Union*, 8 October 1926, p. 37. Poem.

C 205
"Hooked Rugs." *Rochester Times-Union*, 9 October 1926, p. 17. Poem.
'Reprinted by Request' in *Rochester Times-Union*, 7 September 1927, p. 37.

C 206
"A Rendezvous." *Rochester Times-Union*, 11 October 1926, p. 26. Poem.

C 207
"Upstairs and Down." *Rochester Times-Union*, 12 October 1926, p. 26. Poem.

C 208
"Time." *Rochester Times-Union*, 13 October 1926, p. 29. Poem.

C 209
"A Field of Stubble." *Rochester Times-Union*, 14 October 1926, p. 29. Poem.

C 210
"Down the Pike." *Rochester Times-Union*, 15 October 1926, p. 53. Poem.

C 211
"Pockets." *Rochester Times-Union*, 16 October 1926, p. 21. Poem.

C 212
"The Festal Board." *Rochester Times-Union*, 18 October 1926, p. 27. Poem.

C 213
"Waffle Hunger." *Rochester Times-Union*, 19 October 1926, p. 26. Poem.

C 214
"Apples Dropping." *Rochester Times-Union*, 20 October 1926, p. 30. Poem.

C 215
"The Early Christmas Shopper." *Rochester Times-Union*, 21 October 1926, p. 34. Poem.

C 216
"One Sunny Window." *Rochester Times-Union*, 22 October 1926, p. 53. Poem.

C 217
"No Cats Today." *Rochester Times-Union*, 23 October 1926, p. 22. Poem.

C 218
"Cheating Summer." *Rochester Times-Union*, 25 October 1926, p. 31. Poem.

C 219
"Out-Grown." *Rochester Times-Union*, 26 October 1926, p. 31. Poem.

C 220
"A Sandwich Soul." *Rochester Times-Union*, 27 October 1926, p. 30. Poem.

C 221
"Bells." *Rochester Times-Union*, 28 October 1926, p. 39. Poem.

C 222
"Plant Orphans." *Rochester Times-Union*, 29 October 1926, p. 52. Poem.

C 223
"Swapping Recipes." *Rochester Times-Union*, 30 October 1926, p. 21. Poem.

C 224
"The Queen's Breakfast." *Rochester Times-Union*, 1 November 1926, p. 26. Poem.

C 225
"Mother's Kiss." *Rochester Times-Union*, 2 November 1926, p. 22. Poem.

C 226
"The Measuring Spoon." *Rochester Times-Union*, 3 November 1926, p. 33. Poem.

C 227
"Treasure." *Rochester Times-Union*, 4 November 1926, p. 35. Poem.

First Appearances in Journals, Magazines, and Newspapers 201

C 228
"Worrying." *Rochester Times-Union*, 5 November 1926, p. 57. Poem.

C 229
"It Takes a Thief." *Rochester Times-Union*, 6 November 1926, p. 20. Poem.

C 230
"Four Walls." *Rochester Times-Union*, 8 November 1926, p. 22. Poem.

C 231
"Tucked-In Letters." *Rochester Times-Union*, 9 November 1926, p. 27. Poem.

C 232
"A Dress-Shop Angel." *Rochester Times-Union*, 10 November 1926, p. 30. Poem.

C 233
"Night-Times." *Rochester Times-Union*, 11 November 1926, p. 35. Poem.

C 234
"Child Wisdom." *Rochester Times-Union*, 12 November 1926, p. 57. Poem.

C 235
"The What-Not." *Rochester Times-Union*, 13 November 1926, p. 22. Poem.

C 236
"Friends by Sight." *Rochester Times-Union*, 15 November 1926, p. 27. Poem.

C 237
"Pleasant Street." *Rochester Times-Union*, 16 November 1926, p. 27. Poem.

C 238
"There Are No Lonely Hours." *Rochester Times-Union*, 17 November 1926, p. 30. Poem.

'Reprinted by Request' in *Rochester Times-Union*, 10 September 1927, p. 22.

C 239
"Secrets." *Rochester Times-Union*, 18 November 1926, p. 34. Poem.

C 240
"White Houses." *Rochester Times-Union*, 19 November 1926, p. 51. Poem.

C 241
"The Symphony of Suppertime." *Rochester Times-Union*, 20 November 1926, p. 11. Poem.

C 242
"Only Mother." *Rochester Times-Union*, 22 November 1926, p. 30. Poem.

C 243
"Good Company." *Rochester Times-Union*, 23 November 1926, p. 22. Poem.

C 244
"A Housewife's Thanksgiving." *Rochester Times-Union*, 24 November 1926, p. 22. Poem.

C 245
"No System!" *Rochester Times-Union*, 26 November 1926, p. 37. Poem.

C 246
"Demand and Supply." *Rochester Times-Union*, 27 November 1926, p. 20. Poem.

C 247
"Family Quarrels." *Rochester Times-Union*, 29 November 1926, p. 25. Poem.

C 248
"The Hound." *Rochester Times-Union*, 30 November 1926, p. 22. Poem.

C 249
"Pillow Fights." *Rochester Times-Union*, 1 December 1926, p. 27. Poem.

C 250
"Window Sewing." *Rochester Times-Union*, 2 December 1926, p. 30. Poem.

C 251
"Clothes and the Work." *Rochester Times-Union*, 3 December 1926, p. 54. Poem.

C 252
"Aunt Ida's Letters." *Rochester Times-Union*, 4 December 1926, p. 21. Poem.

C 253
"A Common Language." *Rochester Times-Union*, 6 December 1926, p. 20. Poem.

First Appearances in Journals, Magazines, and Newspapers   203

C 254
"Cold Turkey." *Rochester Times-Union*, 7 December 1926, p. 22. Poem.

C 255
"Little Barbee." *Rochester Times-Union*, 8 December 1926, p. 30. Poem.

C 256
"Pumpkin Pie and Cider." *Rochester Times-Union*, 9 December 1926, p. 38. Poem.

C 257
"Sewing Carpet Rags." *Rochester Times-Union*, 10 December 1926, p. 59. Poem.

C 258
"Old Magazines." *Rochester Times-Union*, 11 December 1926, p. 20. Poem.

C 259
"Getting Meals." *Rochester Times-Union*, 13 December 1926, p. 26. Poem.

C 260
"Sunset and Friends." *Rochester Times-Union*, 14 December 1926, p. 31. Poem.

C 261
"A Geranium on the Shelf." *Rochester Times-Union*, 15 December 1926, p. 34. Poem.

C 262
"The Old Mirror." *Rochester Times-Union*, 16 December 1926, p. 34. Poem.

C 263
"Fruit Cake." *Rochester Times-Union*, 17 December 1926, p. 61. Poem.

C 264
"The Gift Chest." *Rochester Times-Union*, 18 December 1926, p. 21. Poem.

C 265
"Gifts for Children." *Rochester Times-Union*, 20 December 1926, p. 31. Poem.

C 266
"Santa's Last Call." *Rochester Times-Union*, 21 December 1926, p. 29. Poem.

C 267
"Christmas Plum Pudding." *Rochester Times Union*, 22 December 1926, p. 26. Poem.

C 268
"Trimming the Tree." *Rochester Times-Union*, 23 December 1926, p. 22. Poem.

C 269
"Christmas Carols." *Rochester Times-Union*, 24 December 1926, p. 20. Poem.

C 270
"The Week after Christmas (With Apologies to the Old Classic)." *Rochester Times-Union*, 27 December 1926, p. 22. Poem.

C 271
"Winter Visits." *Rochester Times-Union*, 28 December 1926, p. 20. Poem.

C 272
"The Spice Box." *Rochester Times-Union*, 29 December 1926, p. 27. Poem.

C 273
"Burning the Greens." *Rochester Times-Union*, 30 December 1926, p. 19. Poem.

C 274
"New Year's Resolve." *Rochester Times-Union*, 31 December 1926, p. 21. Poem.

C 275
"The Weak Spot." *Rochester Times-Union*, 3 January 1927, p. 26. Poem.

C 276
"My Neighbor's Voice." *Rochester Times-Union*, 4 January 1927, p. 22. Poem.

C 277
"Winter Sun." *Rochester Times-Union*, 5 January 1927, p. 26. Poem.

C 278
"Deviltries." *Rochester Times-Union*, 6 January 1927, p. 26. Poem.

C 279
"Cold Mornings." *Rochester Times-Union*, 7 January 1927, p. 26. Poem.

First Appearances in Journals, Magazines, and Newspapers   205

C 280
"At Night." *Rochester Times-Union*, 8 January 1927, p. 20. Poem.

C 281
"Wondering." *Rochester Times-Union*, 10 January 1927, p. 22. Poem.

C 282
"Trees in Winter." *Rochester Times-Union*, 11 January 1927, p. 22. Poem.

C 283
"Lazy Bones." *Rochester Times-Union*, 12 January 1927, p. 26. Poem.

C 284
"Greetings." *Rochester Times-Union*, 13 January 1927, p. 26. Poem.

C 285
"South for the Winter." *Rochester Times-Union*, 14 January 1927, p. 31. Poem.

C 286
"Your Way and Mine." *Rochester Times-Union*, 15 January 1927, p. 21. Poem.

C 287
"Old Doctor Parker." *Rochester Times-Union*, 17 January 1927, p. 22. Poem.

C 288
"Grace before Meals." *Rochester Times-Union*, 18 January 1927, p. 22. Poem.

C 289
"Wind Tantrums." *Rochester Times-Union*, 19 January 1927, p. 26. Poem.

C 290
"Recipe for Home-Making." *Rochester Times-Union*, 20 January 1927, p. 30. Poem.

C 291
"Next Door." *Rochester Times-Union*, 21 January 1927, p. 30. Poem.

C 292
"Mother's Helper." *Rochester Times-Union*, 24 January 1927, p. 20. Poem.

C 293
"Old Brooms." *Rochester Times-Union*, 25 January 1927, p. 22. Poem.

C 294
"Bread and Jam." *Rochester Times-Union*, 26 January 1927, p. 28. Poem.

C 295
"My Day." *Rochester Times-Union*, 27 January 1927, p. 30. Poem.

C 296
"Dressing for School." *Rochester Times-Union*, 28 January 1927, p. 30. Poem.

C 297
"Sounds in Silence." *Rochester Times-Union*, 29 January 1927, p. 20. Poem.

C 298
"The Busiest Woman." *Rochester Times-Union*, 31 January 1927, p. 22. Poem.

C 299
"Strangers." *Rochester Times-Union*, 1 February 1927, p. 26. Poem.

C 300
"Winter Vegetables." *Rochester Times-Union*, 2 February 1927, p. 30. Poem.

C 301
"Green Things Growing." *Rochester Times-Union*, 3 February 1927, p. 30. Poem.

C 302
"Licking the Pans." *Rochester Times-Union*, 4 February 1927, p. 32. Poem.

C 303
"Firelight." *Rochester Times-Union*, 5 February 1927, p. 21. Poem.

C 304
"A Hectic Day." *Rochester Times-Union*, 7 February 1927, p. 22. Poem.

C 305
"Love's Needs." *Rochester Times-Union*, 8 February 1927, p. 22. Poem.

C 306
"The Family Album." *Rochester Times-Union*, 9 February 1927, p. 30. Poem.

C 307
"A Man Goes Singing." *Rochester Times-Union*, 10 February 1927, p. 34. Poem.

First Appearances in Journals, Magazines, and Newspapers 207

C 308
"Pot Luck." *Rochester Times-Union*, 11 February 1927, p. 32. Poem.

C 309
"Mis' Meekin's Dumplings." *Rochester Times-Union*, 12 February 1927, p. 20. Poem.

C 310
"To My Valentine." *Rochester Times-Union*, 14 February 1927, p. 22. Poem.

C 311
"Nose News." *Rochester Times-Union*, 15 February 1927, p. 20. Poem.

C 312
"Love Insurance." *Rochester Times-Union*, 16 February 1927, p. 28. Poem.

C 313
"Happiness." *Rochester Times-Union*, 18 February 1927, p. 31. Poem.

C 314
"Me in the Kitchen." *Rochester Times-Union*, 19 February 1927, p. 20.

C 315
"Friends Who Drop In." *Rochester Times-Union*, 21 February 1927, p. 38. Poem.

C 316
"The Need of Change." *Rochester Times-Union*, 22 February 1927, p. 18. Poem.

C 317
"Excuses." *Rochester Times-Union*, 23 February 1927. p. 30. Poem.

C 318
"The Look of Spring." *Rochester Times-Union*, 24 February 1927, p. 26. Poem.

C 319
"Good Pie." *Rochester Times-Union*, 25 February 1927, p. 30. Poem.

C 320
"Just Kids." *Rochester Times-Union*, 26 February 1927, p. 21. Poem.

C 321
"Some Days." *Rochester Times-Union*, 28 February 1927, p. 18. Poem.

C 322
"Can-Fed Husbands." *Rochester Times-Union*, 1 March 1927, p. 19. Poem.

C 323
"Samaritans Needed." *Rochester Times-Union*, 2 March 1927, p. 30. Poem.

C 324
"Pride Makes a Wall." *Rochester Times-Union*, 3 March 1927, p. 30. Poem.

C 325
"Last Night's Dishes." *Rochester Times-Union*, 4 March 1927, p. 30. Poem.

C 326
"Memory's Attic." *Rochester Times-Union*, 5 March 1927, p. 21. Poem.

C 327
"Dear Friend." *Rochester Times-Union*, 7 March 1927, p. 22. Poem.

C 328
"A Flying Start." *Rochester Times-Union*, 8 March 1927, p. 22. Poem.

C 329
"At the Door." *Rochester Times-Union*, 9 March 1927, p. 30. Poem.

C 330
"A Hankering to Know." *Rochester Times-Union*, 10 March 1927, p. 30. Poem.

C 331
"Economy." *Rochester Times-Union*, 11 March 1927, p. 34. Poem.

C 332
"The Noisy Kitchen." *Rochester Times-Union*, 12 March 1927, p. 20. Poem.

C 333
"Unanswerable." *Rochester Times-Union*, 14 March 1927, p. 22. Poem.

C 334
"Fashions in Food." *Rochester Times-Union*, 15 March 1927, p. 26. Poem.

First Appearances in Journals, Magazines, and Newspapers 209

C 335
"Temptation." *Rochester Times-Union*, 16 March 1927, p. 30. Poem.

C 336
"Sal Jenks' Window." *Rochester Times-Union*, 17 March 1927, p. 31. Poem.

C 337
"A Rainy Evening." *Rochester Times-Union*, 18 March 1927, p. 32. Poem.

C 338
"Spring in the Larder." *Rochester Times-Union*, 19 March 1927, p. 21. Poem.

C 339
"The First Tooth (For Evelyn)." *Rochester Times-Union*, 21 March 1927, p. 22. Poem.

C 340
"Me and Mine." *Rochester Times-Union*, 22 March 1927, p. 22. Poem.

C 341
"The Garden." *Rochester Times-Union*, 23 March 1927, p. 30. Poem.

C 342
"Spring Cleaning." *Rochester Times-Union*, 24 March 1927, p. 30. Poem.

C 343
"Fat Folks." *Rochester Times-Union*, 25 March 1927, p. 36. Poem.

C 344
"Spring Tonics." *Rochester Times-Union*, 26 March 1927, p. 21. Poem.

C 345
"The Fault." *Rochester Times-Union*, 28 March 1927, p. 23. Poem.

C 346
"Pleasing Everybody." *Rochester Times-Union*, 29 March 1927, p. 22. Poem.

C 347
"Shining the Silver." *Rochester Times-Union*, 30 March 1927, p. 5. Poem.

C 348
"Reminders." *Rochester Times-Union*, 31 March 1927, p. 29. Poem.

C 349
"Sitting in the Sun." *Rochester Times-Union*, 1 April 1927, p. 55. Poem.

C 350
"A Boy, a Dog, an April Day." *Rochester Times-Union*, 2 April 1927, p. 20. Poem.

C 351
"Bargaining." *Rochester Times-Union*, 4 April 1927, p. 23. Poem.

C 352
"Sweet in the Evening." *Rochester Times-Union*, 5 April 1927, p. 26. Poem.

C 353
"The Bottomless Pit." *Rochester Times-Union*, 6 April 1927, p. 34. Poem.

C 354
"Half-Way Through." *Rochester Times-Union*, 7 April 1927, p. 31. Poem.

C 355
"Queen of the Kitchen." *Rochester Times-Union*, 9 April 1927, p. 20. Poem.

C 356
"Busy Households." *Rochester Times-Union*, 11 April 1927, p. 22. Poem.

C 357
"A Busy Old Lady." *Rochester Times-Union*, 12 April 1927, p. 22. Poem.

C 358
"Shabby Streets." *Rochester Times-Union*, 13 April 1927, p. 34. Poem.

C 359
"A Kitchen Artist." *Rochester Times-Union*, 14 April 1927, p. 32. Poem.

C 360
"Easter Clothes." *Rochester Times-Union*, 15 April 1927, p. 32. Poem.

C 361
"Easter Lilies." *Rochester Times-Union*, 16 April 1927, p. 21. Poem.

C 362
"No Adults, Unaccompanied." *Rochester Times-Union*, 18 April 1927, p. 22. Poem.

First Appearances in Journals, Magazines, and Newspapers   211

C 363
"Ballade of Accomplished Work." *Rochester Times-Union*, 19 April 1927, p. 23. Poem.

C 364
"The Hypocrite." *Rochester Times-Union*, 20 April 1927, p. 31. Poem.

C 365
"Interruptions." *Rochester Times-Union*, 21 April 1927, p. 34. Poem.

C 366
"The Hurdy-Gurdy." *Rochester Times-Union*, 22 April 1927, p. 30. Poem.

C 367
"A House High-Up." *Rochester Times-Union*, 23 April 1927, p. 21. Poem.

C 368
"My Cook Stove." *Rochester Times-Union*, 25 April 1927, p. 22. Poem.

C 369
"Bugbears." *Rochester Times-Union*, 26 April 1927, p. 27. Poem.

C 370
"New Neighbors." *Rochester Times-Union*, 27 April 1927, p. 31. Poem.

C 371
"Please!" *Rochester Times-Union*, 28 April 1927, p. 31. Poem.

C 372
"Closed Doors." *Rochester Times-Union*, 29 April 1927, p. 32. Poem.

C 373
"Clocks." *Rochester Times-Union*, 30 April 1927, p. 21. Poem.

C 374
"Rag Rugs." *Rochester Times-Union*, 5 May 1927, p. 33. Poem.

C 375
"The Lazy Garden." *Rochester Times-Union*, 6 May 1927, p. 32. Poem.

C 376
"To Mother." *Rochester Times-Union*, 7 May 1927, p. 21. Poem

C 377
"Spring Is a Housewife." *Rochester Times-Union*, 9 May 1927, p. 22. Poem.

C 378
"My Cat." *Rochester Times-Union*, 10 May 1927, p. 23. Poem.

C 379
"Voices I Love." *Rochester Times-Union*, 11 May 1927, p. 39. Poem.

C 380
"Laughter in the Cupboard." *Rochester Times-Union*, 12 May 1927, p. 28. Poem.

C 381
"The Children's Washing." *Rochester Times-Union*, 13 May 1927, p. 37. Poem.

C 382
"The Beauty Parlor." *Rochester Times-Union*, 14 May 1927, p. 21. Poem.

C 383
"The Jolly Tramp." *Rochester Times-Union*, 16 May 1927, p. 26. Poem.

C 384
"A Kitchen Facing West." *Rochester Times-Union*, 17 May 1927, p. 26. Poem.

C 385
"Hyacinths for the Soul." *Rochester Times-Union*, 18 May 1927, p. 35. Poem.

C 386
"Travel." *Rochester Times-Union*, 19 May 1927, p. 28. Poem.

C 387
"When Company Helps." *Rochester Times-Union*, 20 May 1927, p. 35. Poem.

C 388
"Every Wanderer." *Rochester Times-Union*, 21 May 1927, p. 21. Poem.

C 389
"Perverse Appetites." *Rochester Times-Union*, 23 May 1927, p. 23. Poem.

C 390
"Small Hands." *Rochester Times-Union*, 24 May 1927, p. 23. Poem.

First Appearances in Journals, Magazines, and Newspapers   213

C 391
"Work and the Weather." *Rochester Times-Union*, 25 May 1927, p. 37. Poem.

C 392
"The Home Town." *Rochester Times-Union*, 26 May 1927, p. 35. Poem.

C 393
"Grandma in the Doorway." *Rochester Times-Union*, 28 May 1927, p. 20. Poem.

C 394
"This Morning's Pancakes." *Rochester Times-Union*, 31 May 1927, p. 27. Poem.

C 395
"Because It's Home." *Rochester Times-Union*, 1 June 1927, p. 25. Poem.

C 396
"Fooling Around." *Rochester Times-Union*, 2 June 1927, p. 31. Poem.

C 397
"Handsome Is as Handsome Does." *Rochester Times-Union*, 3 June 1927, p. 30. Poem.

C 398
"Lilac Time." *Rochester Times-Union*, 4 June 1927, p. 20. Poem.

C 399
"The Unfortunate Liar." *Rochester Times-Union*, 6 June 1927, p. 23. Poem.

C 400
"The Face on the Pansy." *Rochester Times-Union*, 7 June 1927, p. 23. Poem.

C 401
"Not for Long Years." *Rochester Times-Union*, 8 June 1927, p. 34. Poem.

C 402
"Bedlam." *Rochester Times-Union*, 9 June 1927, p. 34. Poem.

C 403
"A Sixth Sense." *Rochester Times-Union*, 10 June 1927, p. 32. Poem.

C 404
"Sportsmen's Wives." *Rochester Times-Union*, 11 June 1927, p. 21. Poem.

C 405
"June Is So Sweet." *Rochester Times-Union*, 13 June 1927, p. 25. Poem.

C 406
"Browsing in the Attic." *Rochester Times-Union*, 14 June 1927, p. 29. Poem.

C 407
"For Days Like This." *Rochester Times-Union*, 15 June 1927, p. 31. Poem.

C 408
"Spilt Milk." *Rochester Times-Union*, 16 June 1927, p. 29. Poem.

C 409
"The Old Huckster." *Rochester Times-Union*, 17 June 1927, p. 29. Poem.

C 410
"The Perversity of Objects." *Rochester Times-Union*, 18 June 1927, p. 20. Poem.

C 411
"The Horrors." *Rochester Times-Union*, 20 June 1927, p. 23. Poem.

C 412
"A Guilty Conscience." *Rochester Times-Union*, 21 June 1927, p. 27. Poem.

C 413
"One Step More." *Rochester Times-Union*, 22 June 1927, p. 30. Poem.

C 414
"Some Day." *Rochester Times-Union*, 23 June 1927, p. 33. Poem.

C 415
"A Pitcher Full of Cream." *Rochester Times-Union*, 24 June 1927, p. 32. Poem.

C 416
"The Twelve O'Clock Whistle." *Rochester Times-Union*, 25 June 1927, p. 21. Poem.

C 417
"Two Pictures." *Rochester Times-Union*, 27 June 1927, p. 22. Poem.

First Appearances in Journals, Magazines, and Newspapers 215

C 418
"Walled Gardens." *Rochester Times-Union*, 28 June 1927, p. 22. Poem.

C 419
"The Breath of Summer." *Rochester Times-Union*, 29 June 1927, p. 29. Poem.

C 420
"Just Strawberries!" *Rochester Times-Union*, 30 June 1927, p. 37. Poem.

C 421
"Earth Lovers." *Rochester Times-Union*, 1 July 1927, p. 27. Poem.

C 422
"Safe and Sane." *Rochester Times-Union*, 2 July 1927, p. 21. Poem.

C 423
"Hoodlums." *Rochester Times-Union*, 5 July 1927, p. 25. Poem.

C 424
"Mutual Affection Needed." *Rochester Times-Union*, 6 July 1927, p. 23. Poem.

C 425
"A Mute Housewife." *Rochester Times-Union*, 7 July 1927, p. 27. Poem.

C 426
"Sweet William." *Rochester Times-Union*, 8 July 1927, p. 19. Poem.

C 427
"Good Flowers and Bad." *Rochester Times-Union*, 9 July 1927, p. 21. Poem.

C 428
"A Next-Door Optimist." *Rochester Times-Union*, 11 July 1927, p. 20. Poem.

C 429
"To Each His Gift." *Rochester Times-Union*, 12 July 1927, p. 23. Poem.

C 430
"Luck." *Rochester Times-Union*, 13 July 1927, p. 27. Poem.

C 431
"Sounds on Our Street." *Rochester Times-Union*, 14 July 1927, p. 30. Poem.

C 432
"Bread on the Waters." *Rochester Times-Union*, 15 July 1927, p. 18. Poem.

C 433
"Fat Tea-Pots." *Rochester Times-Union*, 16 July 1927, p. 21. Poem.

C 434
"The Improvident Housewife." *Rochester Times-Union*, 18 July 1927, p. 39. Poem.

C 435
"Riches." *Rochester Times-Union*, 19 July 1927, p. 18. Poem.

C 436
"Help Yourself!" *Rochester Times-Union*, 20 July 1927, p. 25. Poem.

C 437
"Vegetables and Sunshine." *Rochester Times-Union*, 21 July 1927, p. 27. Poem.

C 438
"Appreciative Guests." *Rochester Times-Union*, 22 July 1927, p. 18. Poem.

C 439
"Strangers." *Rochester Times-Union*, 26 July 1927, p. 22. Poem.

C 440
"Neighborhood Noise." *Rochester Times-Union*, 27 July 1927, p. 23. Poem.

C 441
"Hospitality." *Rochester Times-Union*, 28 July 1927, p. 31. Poem.

C 442
"White Bedspreads." *Rochester Times-Union*, 29 July 1927, p. 22. Poem.

C 443
"Shopping Blinders." *Rochester Times-Union*, 30 July 1927, p. 10. Poem.

C 444
"The Heart on the Sleeve." *Rochester Times-Union*, 1 August 1927, p. 29. Poem.

First Appearances in Journals, Magazines, and Newspapers 217

C 445
"The Sin of Neatness." *Rochester Times-Union*, 2 August 1927, p. 22. Poem.

C 446
"The Mocking Cat-Bird." *Rochester Times-Union*, 3 August 1927, p. 27. Poem.

C 447
"The Pup." *Rochester Times-Union*, 4 August 1927, p. 33. Poem.

C 448
"A Bit of Blue." *Rochester Times-Union*, 5 August 1927, p. 18. Poem.

C 449
"Blissful Ignorance." *Rochester Times-Union*, 6 August 1927, p. 10. Poem.

C 450
"The Wastebasket." *Rochester Times-Union*, 8 August 1927, p. 22. Poem.

C 451
"Old Lace." *Rochester Times-Union*, 9 August 1927, p. 21. Poem.

C 452
"Almost." *Rochester Times-Union*, 10 August 1927, p. 29. Poem.

C 453
"A Very Useful Pie." *Rochester Times-Union*, 11 August 1927, p. 33. Poem.

C 454
"House Fronts." *Rochester Times-Union*, 12 August 1927, p. 19. Poem.

C 455
"After Dinner." *Rochester Times-Union*, 13 August 1927, p. 7. Poem.

C 456
"A Problem." *Rochester Times-Union*, 15 August 1927, p. 25. Poem.

C 457
"After the Rain." *Rochester Times-Union*, 16 August 1927, p. 21. Poem.

C 458
"A Peaceful House." *Rochester Times-Union*, 17 August 1927, p. 23. Poem.

C 459
"The Gadabout." *Rochester Times-Union*, 18 August 1927, p. 25. Poem.

C 460
"Company's Coming!" *Rochester Times-Union*, 19 August 1927, p. 19. Poem.

C 461
"A Housewife's Luxuries." *Rochester Times-Union*, 20 August 1927, p. 7. Poem.

C 462
"The Day's Work." *Rochester Times-Union*, 22 August 1927, p. 21. Poem.

C 463
"The Railroad Station." *Rochester Times-Union*, 23 August 1927, p. 22. Poem.

C 464
"Em Seaton's Cake Tree." *Rochester Times-Union*, 24 August 1927, p. 25. Poem.

C 465
"Death Has No Power." *Rochester Times-Union*, 25 August 1927, p. 29. Poem.

C 466
"The Two Tongues." *Rochester Times-Union*, 26 August 1927, p. 19. Poem.

C 467
"Belief." *Rochester Times-Union*, 27 August 1927, p. 7. Poem.

C 468
"The Secret Gardeners." *Rochester Times-Union*, 30 August 1927, p. 23. Poem.

C 469
"One Song." *Rochester Times-Union*, 31 August 1927, p. 29. Poem.

C 470
"Crazy Nell." *Rochester Times-Union*, 1 September 1927, p. 27. Poem.

C 471
"Bouquets." *Rochester Times-Union*, 2 September 1927, p. 30. Poem.

C 472
"The Jesters." *Rochester Times-Union*, 3 September 1927, p. 21. Poem.

First Appearances in Journals, Magazines, and Newspapers 219

C 473
"Mother's Linens." *Rochester Times-Union*, 12 September 1927, p. 18. Poem.

C 474
"Handsome Madam Earth." *Rochester Times-Union*, 14 September 1927, p. 27. Poem.

C 475
"The Nurse." *Rochester Times-Union*, 15 September 1927, p. 31. Poem.

C 476
"A Snippy Neighbor." *Rochester Times-Union*, 16 September 1927, p. 39. Poem.

C 477
"Apples in the Cellar." *Rochester Times-Union*, 17 September 1927, p. 12. Poem.

C 478
"Too Much Energy." *Rochester Times-Union*, 19 September 1927, p. 25. Poem.

C 479
"After Breakfast." *Rochester Times-Union*, 20 September 1927, p. 31. Poem.

C 480
"A Cure for Work." *Rochester Times-Union*, 21 September 1927, p. 37. Poem.

C 481
"The New Roof." *Rochester Times-Union*, 22 September 1927, p. 33. Poem.

C 482
"Too Much Energy." *Rochester Times-Union*, 23 September 1927, p. 37. Poem.

C 483
"The Queen of Hearts." *Rochester Times-Union*, 24 September 1927, p. 18. Poem.

C 484
"Thinking Times." *Rochester Times-Union*, 26 September 1927, p. 23. Poem.

C 485
"Fooling Myself." *Rochester Times-Union*, 27 September 1927, p. 25. Poem.

C 486
"Killed with Kindness." *Rochester Times-Union*, 30 September 1927, p. 37. Poem.

C 487
"The Day's Work." *Rochester Times-Union*, 1 October 1927, p. 18. Poem.

C 488
"My Friend." *Rochester Times-Union*, 3 October 1927, p. 23. Poem.

C 489
"The Chatelaine." *Rochester Times-Union*, 4 October 1927. Poem.

C 490
"Important! Rush!" *Rochester Times-Union*, 5 October 1927, p. 28. Poem.

C 491
"An Old-Fashioned Bouquet." *Rochester Times-Union*, 6 October 1927, p. 30. Poem.

C 492
"The Last Vegetable." *Rochester Times-Union*, 7 October 1927, p. 35. Poem.

C 493
"The Folks Who'll Feed a Fellow." *Rochester Times-Union*, 8 October 1927, p. 18. Poem.

C 494
"The Deserted House." *Rochester Times-Union*, 10 October 1927, p. 21. Poem.

C 495
"Stolen Fruit." *Rochester Times-Union*, 11 October 1927, p. 26. Poem.

C 496
"But Not Forgotten." *Rochester Times-Union*, 12 October 1927, p. 28. Poem.

C 497
"Autumn's Carpet." *Rochester Times-Union*, 14 October 1927, p. 35. Poem.

C 498
"Company's Coming." *Rochester Times Union*, 1 November 1927, p. 23. Poem.

First Appearances in Journals, Magazines, and Newspapers   221

C 499
"One Way to Reduce." *Rochester Times-Union*, 2 November 1927, p. 25. Poem.

C 500
"Another Woman's House." *Rochester Times-Union*, 3 November 1927, p. 30. Poem.

C 501
"My Conscience." *Rochester Times-Union*, 4 November 1927, p. 37. Poem.

C 502
"Wisdom." *Rochester Times-Union*, 5 November 1927, p. 14. Poem.

C 503
"Too Many Cooks." *Rochester Times-Union*, 7 November 1927, p. 22. Poem.

C 504
"Candlelight." *Rochester Times-Union*, 8 November 1927, p. 25. Poem.

C 505
"Unaccustomed Splendor." *Rochester Times-Union*, 9 November 1927, p. 33. Poem.

C 506
"The Failure." *Rochester Times-Union*, 10 November 1927, p. 31. Poem.

C 507
"Breakfast in Bed." *Rochester Times-Union*, 11 November 1927, p. 33. Poem.

C 508
"It Isn't Work." *Rochester Times-Union*, 12 November 1927, p. 21. Poem.

C 509
"The Kitchen at Morning." *Rochester Times-Union*, 14 November 1927, p. 22. Poem.

C 510
"A Change of Diet." *Rochester Times-Union*, 15 November 1927, p. 29. Poem.

C 511
"The Master Artist." *Rochester Times-Union*, 16 November 1927, p. 33. Poem.

C 512
"Strayed: A Pup." *Rochester Times-Union*, 17 November 1927, p. 37. Poem.

C 513
"The Perpetual Hat-Lining." *Rochester Times-Union*, 18 November 1927, section 2, p. 4. Poem.

C 514
"The Bend of the Road." *Rochester Times-Union*, 19 November 1927, p. 19. Poem.

C 515
"A Thoughtless Hostess." *Rochester Times-Union*, 21 November 1927, p. 22. Poem.

C 516
"Past Our Place." *Rochester Times-Union*, 22 November 1927, p. 26. Poem.

C 517
"The Family Look." *Rochester Times-Union*, 23 November 1927, p. 12. Poem.

C 518
"Caught." *Rochester Times-Union*, 26 November 1927, p. 19. Poem.

C 519
"Earth's Children." *Rochester Times-Union*, 29 November 1927, p. 23. Poem.

C 520
"Waiting Dinner." *Rochester Times-Union*, 30 November 1927, p. 29. Poem.

C 521
"The Gift." *Rochester Times-Union*, 1 December 1927, p. 37. Poem.

C 522
"Diplomacy." *Rochester Times-Union*, 2 December 1927, sec. 2, p. 7. Poem.

C 523
"The Easiest Way." *Rochester Times-Union*, 3 December 1927, p. 21. Poem.

C 524
"At Breakfast." *Rochester Times-Union*, 5 December 1927, p. 22. Poem.

First Appearances in Journals, Magazines, and Newspapers   223

C 525
"Every-Day Babies." *Rochester Times-Union*, 6 December 1927, p. 27. Poem.

C 526
"Cold Turkey." *Rochester Times-Union*, 7 December 1927, p. 29. Poem.

C 527
"Aunt Em's Antiques." *Rochester Times-Union*, 9 December 1927, p. 8. Poem.

C 528
"Picture-Kitchens." *Rochester Times-Union*, 10 December 1927, p. 18. Poem.

C 529
"New Curtains." *Rochester Times-Union*, 12 December 1927, p. 22. Poem.

C 530
"Useful Gifts." *Rochester Times-Union*, 13 December 1927, p. 29. Poem.

C 531
"A Glimpse of Santa." *Rochester Times-Union*, 14 December 1927, p. 29. Poem.

C 532
"Come in, Friend." *Rochester Times-Union*, 15 December 1927, p. 35. Poem.

C 533
"Scent-Memories." *Rochester Times-Union*, 16 December 1927, sec. 2, p. 8. Poem.

C 534
"The Sorry House." *Rochester Times-Union*, 17 December 1927, p. 18. Poem.

C 535
"Duty Books." *Rochester Times-Union*, 19 December 1927, p. 22. Poem.

C 536
"Uncle Abner." *Rochester Times-Union*, 20 December 1927, p. 29. Poem.

C 537
"The Perfect Guest." *Rochester Times-Union*, 21 December 1927, p. 27. Poem.

C 538
"Three Bowls of Milk." *Rochester Times-Union*, 22 December 1927, p. 35. Poem.

C 539
"The Old Dog." *Rochester Times-Union*, 23 December 1927, p. 18. Poem.

C 540
"Fire on the Hearth." *Rochester Times-Union*, 24 December 1927, p. 14. Poem.

C 541
"Holiday Left-Overs." *Rochester Times-Union*, 27 December 1927, p. 22. Poem.

C 542
"Close Margins." *Rochester Times-Union*, 28 December 1927, p. 20. Poem.

C 543
"Solid Comfort." *Rochester Times-Union*, 29 December 1927, p. 20. Poem.

C 544
"The Crucial Moment." *Rochester Times-Union*, 30 December 1927, p. 21. Poem.

C 545
"The Reason." *Rochester Times-Union*, 3 January 1928, p. 31. Poem.

C 546
"Old Folks." *Rochester Times-Union*, 4 January 1928, p. 26. Poem.

C 547
"Waffles on the Air." *Rochester Times-Union*, 5 January 1928, p. 22. Poem.

C 548
"Swearing Off." *Rochester Times-Union*, 6 January 1928, p. 29. Poem.

C 549
"The Lucky Housewife." *Rochester Times-Union*, 7 January 1928, p. 19. Poem.

C 550
"The Struggle." *Rochester Times-Union*, 9 January 1928, p. 22. Poem.

First Appearances in Journals, Magazines, and Newspapers   225

C 551
"Friends for Tea." *Rochester Times-Union*, 10 January 1928, p. 21. Poem.

C 552
"Warming Up the Engine." *Rochester Times-Union*, 11 January 1928, p. 26. Poem.

C 553
"Mistress and House." *Rochester Times-Union*, 12 January 1928, p. 26. Poem.

C 554
"Winter Twilight." *Rochester Times-Union*, 13 January 1928, p. 27. Poem.

C 555
"Some Other Time." *Rochester Times-Union*, 14 January 1928, p. 19. Poem.

C 556
"A Clean House." *Rochester Times-Union*, 16 January 1928, p. 22. Poem.

C 557
"The Miser." *Rochester Times-Union*, 17 January 1928, p. 18. Poem.

C 558
"Shut in." *Rochester Times-Union*, 18 January 1928, p. 17. Poem.

C 559
"Born Cooks." *Rochester Times-Union*, 19 January 1928, p. 26. Poem.

C 560
"My Friend's Relations." *Rochester Times-Union*, 20 January 1928, p. 24. Poem.

C 561
"Mother's Cooking." *Rochester Times-Union*, 21 January 1928, p. 19. Poem.

C 562
"Every-Day Melodies." *Rochester Times-Union*, 23 January 1928, p. 19. Poem.

C 563
"A Rattling Good Hint." *Rochester Times-Union*, 25 January 1928, p. 16. Poem.

C 564
"Itching for a Spanking." *Rochester Times-Union*, 26 January 1928, p. 26. Poem.

C 565
"The Little Girl I Used to Be." *Rochester Times-Union*, 27 January 1928, p. 26. Poem.

C 566
"Up Against It." *Rochester Times-Union*, 30 January 1928, p. 22. Poem.

C 567
"Poor Proportions." *Rochester Times-Union*, 31 January 1928, p. 19. Poem.

C 568
"Old-Fashioned Neighbors." *Rochester Times-Union*, 1 February 1928, p. 25. Poem.

C 569
"The Scientific Lecturer." *Rochester Times-Union*, 2 February 1928, p. 31. Poem.

C 570
"My Children." *Rochester Times-Union*, 3 February 1928, p. 24. Poem.

C 571
"A Full House." *Rochester Times-Union*, 4 February 1928, p. 19. Poem.

C 572
"A Housewife's Hands." *Rochester Times-Union*, 7 February 1928, p. 20. Poem.

C 573
"A Meal of Almost Nothing." *Rochester Times-Union*, 8 February 1928, p. 27. Poem.

C 574
"The Girls." *Rochester Times-Union*, 9 February 1928, p. 29. Poem.

C 575
"Spoiled Pets." *Rochester Times-Union*, 10 February 1928, p. 31. Poem.

First Appearances in Journals, Magazines, and Newspapers   227

C 576
"On the Job." *Rochester Times-Union*, 13 February 1928, p. 21. Poem.

C 577
"A Small Boy's Valentine." *Rochester Times-Union*, 14 February 1928, p. 10. Poem.

C 578
"Too Chatty." *Rochester Times-Union*, 17 February 1928, p. 29. Poem.

C 579
"Nasty-Nice." *Rochester Times-Union*, 18 February 1928, p. 18. Poem.

C 580
"Invited Out." *Rochester Times-Union*, 21 February 1928, p. 21. Poem.

C 581
"The Fallen Idol." *Rochester Times-Union*, 22 February 1928, p. 17. Poem.

C 582
"The Unrouted Enemy." *Rochester Times-Union*, 23 February 1928, p. 23. Poem.

C 583
"Aunt Em on Patchwork Quilts." *Rochester Times-Union*, 24 February 1928, p. 27. Poem.

C 584
"The Perfect Housekeeper." *Rochester Times-Union*, 25 February 1928, p. 19. Poem.

C 585
"The Housewife's Heaven." *Rochester Times-Union*, 27 February 1928, p. 20. Poem.

C 586
"Turn About." *Rochester Times-Union*, 28 February 1928, p. 23. Poem.

C 587
"The First Spring Sunshine." *Rochester Times-Union*, 29 February 1928, p. 13. Poem.

C 588
"Cracker Chidlings." *Scribner's Magazine*, 89, no. 2 (February 1931), 127–34.

Note: See AA4.

C 589
"[Letter to 'Editor Star']." *Ocala* (Florida) *Evening Star*, 2 February 1931, p. 2.

Note: The letter, 'Jan. 30, 1931', was written in response to an editorial criticizing the portrayal of the Cracker in "Cracker Chidlings."

C 590
"Jacob's Ladder." *Scribner's Magazine*, 89, no. 4 (April 1931), 351–66, 446–64.

Note: See A4, AA1–AA2, AA4.

C 591
"A Plumb Clare Conscience." *Scribner's Magazine*, 90, no. 6 (December 1931), 622–626.

Reprinted in *Golden Book Magazine*, 18, no. 104 (August 1933), 97–101.

Note: See A4, AA4.

C 592
"Dutch Oven Cookery." *Sunrise: The Florida Magazine*, 1, no. 4 (February 1932), 20, 46.

C 593
"A Crop of Beans." *Scribner's Magazine*, 91, no. 5 (May 1932), 283–90.

Note: See A4, AA1, AA4.

C 594
"Gal Young Un." *Harper's Monthly Magazine*, 165 (June 1932), 21–33, 225–34.

Note one: "Gal Young Un" was rejected by *Scribner's Magazine* before it was submitted to *Harper's*. It was subsequently awarded the O. Henry Memorial Prize for the best short story of 1932.

Note two: See A4, AA1–4.

C 595
"Hyacinth Drift." *Scribner's Magazine*, 94, no. 3 (September 1933), 169–173. Nonfiction.

Note: See A5, AA2.

C 596
"Alligators." *Saturday Evening Post*, 23 (September 1933), 16–17, 36, 38.

Signed: 'Marjorie Kinnan Rawlings and Fred Tompkins'.

Note: See A4, AA4.

C 597
"Benny and the Bird Dogs." *Scribner's Magazine*, 94, no. 4 (October 1933), 193–200.

Reprinted in *Scholastic*, 2 (March 1935), 4–6, 10.

Note: See A4, AA3–4.

C 598
"The Pardon." *Scribner's Magazine*, 96, no. 2 (August 1934), 95–98.

Note: See A4, AA1, AA4.

C 599
"Golden Apples." *Cosmopolitan*, 98 (April 1935), 18–22, 144–162; 98 (May 1935), 46–49, 130–134, 137–142; 98 (June 1935), 62–65, 122–132; 99 (July 1935), 82–84, 87–88, 90, 92, 94; 99 (August 1935), 82–84, 87–88, 90, 92, 94.

Note one: 'Illustrations by Harold von Schmidt'.

Note two: See A2.

C 600
"Having Left Cities Behind Me." *Scribner's Magazine*, 98, no. 4 (October 1935), 246. Poem.

C 601
"Varmints." *Scribner's Magazine*, 100, no. 6 (December 1936), 26–32, 84–85.

Reprinted in *Scholastic*, 31 (4 December 1937), 3–5, 34–37.

Note: See A4, AA4.

C 602
"A Mother in Mannville." *Saturday Evening Post*, 209 (12 December 1936), 7, 33.

Reprinted in *Scholastic*, 37 (16 September 1940), 29–30, 36–37; *Today's Woman*, 13 (January 1946), 27–28, 105–108; *Parent's Magazine*, 40 (April 1965), 59–63; *Reader's Digest*, 92 (February 1968), 124–128.

Note one: A dramatic reading of the story was given by Rawlings at Rollins College in 1937. See the *Rollins Animated Magazine*, 10, no. 1 (21 February 1937), [1–4]. The *Animated Magazine* did not print stories, it only announced them: '*In place of going to the expense of printing the Magazine the writers | have been invited to appear in person and read their contributions*'.

Note two: See A4, AA4.

C 603
"You Reckon This Mought Be the Same Man, Elmer?" *Tampa Morning Tribune*, 18 March 1937, p. 8.

Signed: 'The Widow Rawlings'.

C 604
"Bear Hunt." *Saturday Review of Literature*, 17, no. 20 (12 March 1938), 10–12.

Note: Excerpt from *The Yearling*, A3.

C 605
"Abe Traphagen's Farm." *Holly* (Michigan) *Herald*, Centennial Anniversary Edition, 30 June 1938, p. 35.

C 606
"Mountain Rain." *Scribner's Magazine*, 104, no. 1 (July 1938), 63. Poem.

C 607
"Old Slewfoot." *Scholastic*, 33, no. 6 (22 October 1938), 3–5, 32, 35, 37.

Note: Excerpt from *The Yearling*, A3.

C 608
"*The Yearling.*" New York *Post*, 5 June 1939, p. 16; 6 June, p. 9; 8 June, pp. 21, 25; 9 June, p. 8; 10 June, p. 21; 12 June, p. 19; 13 June, p. 17; 14 June, p. 22; 15 June, p. 26; 16 June, p. 20; 17 June, p. 4; 19 June, p. 11; 20 June, p. 19; 21 June, p. 19; 22 June, p. 17; 23 June, p. 15; 24 June, p. 11; 26 June, p. 16; 27 June, p. 8; 28 June, p. 18; 29 June, p. 13; 30 June, p. 14; 1 July, p. 17; 3 July, p. 6; 5 July, p. 23; 6 July, p. 23; 7 July, p. 16; 8 July, p. 19; 10 July, p. 6; 11 July, p. 18; 12 July, p. 20; 13 July, p. 23; 14 July, p. 16; 15 July, p. 17; 17 July, p. 7; 18 July, p. 8; 19 July, p. 10; 20 July, p. 8; 21 July, p. 11; 22 July, p. 22; 24 July, p. 10; 25 July, p. 12.

Note one: Serialization of A3, announced in the *New York Post*, 1 June 1939, p. 20.

First Appearances in Journals, Magazines, and Newspapers   231

Note two: Excerpts were read by Rawlings as part of a dramatic reading at Rollins College in 1938. See the *Rollins Animated Magazine*, 11, no. 1 (20 February 1938), [1–4].

C609
"I Sing While I Cook." *Vogue*, 93 (15 February 1939), 48–49. Nonfiction.

C610
"Cocks Must Crow." *Saturday Evening Post*, 212 (25 November 1939), 5–7, 58, 60, 62–64.

Note: See A4, AA1–2, AA4.

C611
"The Pelican's Shadow." *New Yorker*, 15 (6 January 1940), 17–19.

Note: See AA2, AA4.

C612
"The Enemy." *Saturday Evening Post*, 212 (20 January 1940), 12–13, 32, 36, 39.

Note: See AA1–4.

C613
"Regional Literature of the South." *English Journal*, 29, no. 2, pt. 1 (February 1940), 89–97.

Note: Also published in *College English*, 1, no. 5 (February 1940), 381–389.

C614
"In the Heart." *Collier's Magazine*, 105 (3 February 1940), 19, 39.

Note one: See AA4.

Note two: A dramatic reading of the story was given by Rawlings at Rollins College in 1941. See the *Rollins Animated Magazine*, 14, no. 1 (23 February 1941), [1–4].

C615
"Jessamine Springs." *New Yorker*, 17 (22 February 1941), 19–20.

Note: See AA2, AA4.

C616
"[Faherty's *Big Old Sun*]." *Saturday Review*, 23 (29 March 1941), 12.

Note: A review of Robert Faherty, *Big Old Sun.* New York: G. P. Putnam's Sons, 1941.

C 617
"The Provider." *Woman's Home Companion*, 68 (June 1941), 20–21, 44, 60–61.

Note: See AA4.

C 618
"Marjorie K. Rawlings, Author of 'The Yearling,' Places the Laurel on an Epic of Kentucky." *Chicago Daily News*, Christmas Book Section, 3 December 1941, p. 9B.

Note: A review of James Still, *On Troublesome Creek.* New York: Viking Press, 1941.

C 619
"My Friend Moe." *Scholastic*, 41, no. 1 (14 September 1942), 17–20.

Note: Excerpt from *Cross Creek*, A5.

C 620
"Here Is Home." *Atlantic Monthly*, 169 (March 1942), 277–285.

Note: Excerpt from *Cross Creek*, A5.

C 621
"Who Owns Cross Creek?" *Atlantic Monthly*, 169 (April 1942), 439–450.

Note: Excerpt from *Cross Creek*, A5.

C 622
"Fanny—You Fool!" *Vogue*, 100 (15 July 1942), 42. Nonfiction.

C 623
"Cross Creek Breakfasts." *Woman's Home Companion*, 69 (November 1942), 72–73.

Note: Excerpt from *Cross Creek Cookery*, A6.

C 624
"Sweet Talk, Honey." *Vogue*, 100 (1 December 1942), 77, 116–118.

Note: Excerpt from *Cross Creek Cookery*, A6.

First Appearances in Journals, Magazines, and Newspapers 233

C625
"Christmas at Cross Creek." *American Cookery*, 47 (December 1942), 168, 184.

C626
"Trees for Tomorrow." *Collier's Magazine*, 117 (8 May 1943), 14–15, 24, 25. Nonfiction.

C627
"A River That Flows Through Florida History." *New York Herald Tribune Book Review* (5 September 1943), sec. VIII, p. 3.

Note: A review of James Branch Cabell and A. J. Hanna, *The St. Johns*. New York: Farrar and Rinehart, 1943.

C628
"Florida: A Land of Contrast." *Transatlantic*, no. 14 (October 1944), 12–17.

Note: See AA2, AA4.

C629
"The Shell." *New Yorker*, 20 (9 December 1944), 29–31.

Note: See AA2, AA4.

C630
"Florida: An Affectionate Tribute." *Congressional Record* (U.S. House of Representatives), 2 March 1945, pp. 1692–93.

C631
"Black Secret." *New Yorker*, 21 (8 September 1945), 20–23.

Note: See AA4.

C632
"Miriam's Houses." *New Yorker*, 21 (24 November 1945), 29–31.

Note: See AA4.

C633
"Miss Moffatt Steps Out." *Liberty Magazine*, 23, no. 7 (February 1946), 31, 58–61.

Note: See AA4.

C634
"Parceling in Florida. How Napoleon's Nephew Ate Boiled Owl and Alligator and Served as a County Judge." *New York Herald Tribune Book Review*, 17 November 1946, sec. 4, p. 7.

Note: A review of A. J. Hanna, *A Prince in Their Midst: The Adventurous Life of Achille Murat on the American Frontier*. Norman: University of Oklahoma Press, 1946.

C635
"Mountain Prelude." *Saturday Evening Post*, 219 (26 April 1947), 15–17, 67–68, 70–72, 74; (3 May 1947), 36–37, 132, 134, 137, 139–40, 142; (10 May 1947), 38–39, 140, 142, 144–47; (17 May 1947), 40–41, 153, 155–56, 158–59, 161; (24 May 1947), 36–37, 83, 86, 90, 92, 95, 97; (31 May 1947), 40, 45–46, 48, 50.

Note: Scribners rejected "Mountain Prelude" after its serial publication. In an internal memo in the MGM archives, Culver City, California, 31 July 1947, Katherine Barnes writes that Scribners acknowledged their intention to publish under the new title *Mountain Home*, only to withdraw. In a letter, 14 July 1947, Samuel Tannenbaum writes to MGM informing them that "Family for Jock," the original title of "Mountain Prelude," was published by Doubleday, Doran. No such title has been located. See Appendix 1.

C636
"The Use of the Sitz-Bath: A Study Based on Experiments in the Brown's Hollow Laboratory." *Dumpling Magazine*, 11, no. 2 (6 July 1947), 3–7.

Signed: 'Dr. M. K. Rawlings Baskin'.

Note: The *Dumpling Magazine* was privately published by the family of Owen D. Young of Van Hornesville, N.Y. Only one copy of most issues was printed.

C637
"About Fabulous Florida: Study of One of the Strangest, Most Fascinating and Blood-Stained Regions of Our Continent." *New York Herald Tribune Book Review*, 30 November 1947, p. 4.

Note one: A review of Marjory Stoneman Douglas, *The Everglades: River of Grass*. New York: Rinehart and Company, 1947.

Note two: See AA3.

C638
"Apology to an Old House." *Dumpling Magazine*, 11, no. 4 (5 September 1948), 10. Poem.

First Appearances in Journals, Magazines, and Newspapers   235

C 639
"The Friendship." *Saturday Evening Post*, 221 (1 January 1949), 14–15, 44.

Note: See AA4.

C 640
"Lament of a Siamese Cat." *Dumpling Magazine*, 11, no. 5 (4 September 1949), 8. Poem.

C 641
"Portrait of a Magnificent Editor as Seen in His Letters." *Publisher's Weekly*, 157, no. 13 (1 April 1950), 1573–74.

Note one: See AA3.

Note two: A review of *Editor to Author: The Letters of Maxwell E. Perkins*. Edited by John Hall Wheelock. New York: Charles Scribner's Sons, 1950.

C 642
"Dubious Praise in Dubious Battle; or, 'Who Said That—and Why?'" *Dumpling Magazine*, 11, no. 8 (1 September 1950), 7. Poem.

Note: The running head gives the date as 'September 3, 1950'.

C 643
"I Remember Christmas." *Better Living*, 2, no. 12 (December 1952), 22–23.

C 644
"About *The Sojourner*." *Wings: The Literary Guild Review* (January 1953), 4–8.

Note: A promotional piece by John Beecroft about *The Sojourner* (pp. 1–3) precedes the above.

C 645
"[Autobiographical Sketches]." *Los Angeles Times*, 26 April 1953, p. 1; 3 May, p. 6; 10 May, p. 6; 17 May, p. 7; 24 May 1953, p. 6.

Note: See AA3.

C 646
"The Man and the Place." *Dumpling Magazine*, 12, no. 2 (5 July 1953), 10–11.

Signed: 'Notes from a brief talk | at Canton, June 7, 1953'.

Note: From a tribute to Owen D. Young, read at St. Lawrence University, Canton, New York, a ceremony at which Rawlings received an honorary Litt.D.

C647
"The Sojourner." *Omnibook Best-Seller Magazine*, 15, no. 8 (July 1953), 1–47.

Note: Excerpt from *The Sojourner*, A8.

C648
"Marjorie Kinnan Rawlings' 'Lord Bill of the Suwannee River.'" *Southern Folklore Quarterly*, 27, no. 2 (June 1963), 113–131.

Note one: See B16, AA4 for the complete text of the story.

Note two: Edited by Gordon E. Bigelow, the story appears on pp. 117–131. In a letter to Alfred Dashiell, 31 March 1931, Rawlings says that she is turning "incredible known facts into an impossible myth"; and on 15 June she writes to Dashiell that she has sent the manuscript to the *Scribner's Magazine* short story contest. On 12 August, Dashiell rejects the manuscript, finding it unconvincing (Scribners Archive).

C649
"Fish Fry and Fireworks." *Florida Quarterly*, 1 (Summer 1967), 1–18.

Note: Edited by Gordon E. Bigelow, the story appears on pp. 2–18. See AA4.

C650
"The Yearling." *Scholastic Scope*, 22, no. 12 (8 May 1975), 1–6.

Note: The cover of this magazine reproduces a studio still of film actor Claude Jarman, Jr., and Flag, the fawn. The story here, aimed at a juvenile audience, is described as a retelling by Ira Beck.

D. Blurbs

D1
Fitzgerald, F. Scott. *Tender is the Night*. New York: Charles Scribner's Sons, 1934.

Location: PM.

Note: The blurb is on the front flap of a later dust jacket. A copy of this jacket is reported in *J. Stephan Lawrence . . . Catalogue*, 38 (Winter, 1977–1978), item 510. See Matthew J. Bruccoli, *Supplement to F. Scott Fitzgerald: A Descriptive Bibliography*: (Pittsburgh, Pa.: University of Pittsburgh Press, 1980), p. 13, who reports the blurb. The blurb, a manuscript copy of which is in the Firestone Library, Princeton University, reads:

> 'Disturbing, bitter and beauti- | ful. I am totally unable to analyze | the almost over-powering effect | that some of his passages create. | There is something terrifying about it, | and the closest I can come | to understanding it is to think | that he visualizes people not in | their immediate setting, from the | human point of view—but in time | and space—almost, you might say, | with the divine detachment.'

D2
Sorensen, Virginia. *A Little Lower than the Angels*. New York: Grosset and Dunlap, 1942.

Location: FU.

Note: The blurb appears at the top of an advertisement in the *New York Herald Tribune Book Review*, 17 May 1942, sec. 9, p. 9, and reads: ' "I have read 'A Little Lower than the Angels' with pleasure. | It is completely mature, wise and vital." '

D3
Mansfield, Katherine. *Katherine Mansfield Stories*. Introduction by Rawlings. Cleveland and New York: World Publishing Company, 1946.

Locations: PM, RLT.

Note one: The blurb appears on the rear flap and reads: 'In her stimulating

Introduction, Marjorie | Kinnan Rawlings says, [20–line quotation from the Introduction].

Note two: Reprinted: '3 HC 953'.

D4

Moffett, Langston. *Devil by the Tale.* Philadelphia: J. B. Lippincott, 1947.

Location: Collection of David Nolan.

Note: The blurb on the back flap reads: 'I am most enthusiastic about Langston Mof- | fett's book and consider it utterly fascinating. | It packs a terrific wallop . . . instead of being | merely one psychological episode, it is the saga | of the wandering drunk.'

D5

Niggli, Josephina. *Step Down, Elder Brother.* New York and Toronto: Rinehart and Company, Inc., [1947].

Location: PM, RLT.

Note: The blurb on the back of the dust jacket reads: ' "I can only describe the book as enchanting, in the broadest sense . . . The | stories, in themselves, have the classic quality of Isak Dinesen's *Seven* | *Gothic Tales*, yet taken as a whole, they make a complete narrative." '

D6

Douglas, Marjory Stoneman. *Road to the Sun.* New York: Rinehart & Company, Inc., 1951.

Locations: PM, RLT.

Note: The blurb on the back of the dust jacket reads: Marjorie Kinnan Rawlings in the New York *Herald* | *Tribune* Book Section said, "This beautiful and bitter, | sweet and savage book may be recommended not only to | residents and tourists of Florida but to all readers con- | cerned with American life and general relation of man | to nature."

D7

Betts, Doris. *The Gentle Insurrection and Other Stories.* New York: G. P. Putnam's Sons, 1954.

Location: RLT.

Note: The blurb, Rawlings's response as judge to the Putnam–University of North Carolina Prize Contest, on the back of the dust jacket, reads: ' "The Doris Betts stories are completely mature and | effective. They are as fine as any stories

I have read in a | long time. I decidedly vote that the prize should go to | them. I feel these stories will receive a splendid critical | reception." '

Location: RLT.

E. Translations

Translations of a particular work by Rawlings are listed by language. Languages are alphabetical under Rawlings's titles, which are chronological.

SOUTH MOON UNDER

DANISH

E 1
Solens born. Trans. Soffy Topsoe. Copenhagen: Jespersen and Pios, 1941. 263 pp. *Location*: MnU.

FRENCH

E 2
Le whisky du clair de lune. Trans. Denise van Moppès. Paris: Albin Michel, 1950. 357 pp. *Location*: Bibliothèque Nationale, FU.

GERMAN

E 3
Spur unter Sternen. Trans. Jutta Kunst and Theodor Kunst. Hamburg: Marion von Schröder, 1965. 384 pp. *Location*: FU.

E 4
Spur unter Sternen. Translator undetermined. [Hamburg?]: Rowohlt, 1967. 179 pp. *Location*: World Catalogue, *not seen.*

ITALIAN

E 5
La Luna Nascosta. Trans. Beatrice Boffito Serra. Milan: Valentino Bompiani,

---

All foreign-language book titles are set in italics. Not all translations have been examined by the compiler, although locations are given for copies listed.

1948. 345 pp. *Location*: FU. *Note*: Brandt and Brandt records, 21 May 1940, indicate a Bompiani translation. No copy has been located. Reprint, 1955, as '6th ed.' *Location*: World Catalogue, *not seen*.

GOLDEN APPLES

DANISH

E 6
Gyldne frugter. Trans. Kirsten Restrup. Copenhagen: Jespersen and Pios, 1940. *Location*: MnU.

DUTCH

E 7
Gouden Oogst. Trans. Mien Labberton. The Hague: M. C. Stok, n.d. 435 pp. *Locations*: FU, RLT. *Note*: 'TWEEDE DRUNK', no other printings seen.

FINNISH

E 8
Kultaiset Hedelmät. Trans. Aune Brotherus. Helsinki and Porvoo: Werner Söderström, 1943. 373 pp. *Locations*: FU, GU. Reprint, 1956. *Locations*: FU, RLT.

FRENCH

E 9
Les pommes d'or. Trans. Madame Lebettre-Laporte. Paris: Albin Michel, 1948. 431 pp. *Location*: DLC.

E 10
Les pommes d'or. Trans. Madame Lebettre-Laporte. Verviers, Belgium: Gerard, n.d. 251 pp. *Locations*: FU, RLT.

Translations 247

GERMAN

E 11
Die Goldenen Äpfel. Trans. Wilhelm E. Süskind. Hamburg, Bielefeld, Stuttgart: Freunde der Weltliteratur, 1940. 322 pp. *Location*: RLT.

E 12
Neue Heimat-Florida. Trans. Wilhelm E. Süskind. Zurich: Scientia, 1940. 472 pp. *Location*: FU.

E 13
Im dunklen Laub die Goldorangen glühn. Translator undetermined. Munich: Wilhelm Goldmann, 1975. 284 pp. *Location*: FU.

HUNGARIAN

E 14
Uj Élet Floridában. Translator undetermined. N.p.: Horváth Zoltán, n.d. 334 pp. *Location*: FU.

ITALIAN

E 15
Le mele d'oro. Trans. Bruno Maffi and Edoardo Canali. Milan: Valentino Bompiani, 1945. 350 pp. *Location*: DLC. Reprints, 1975, 1983. *Locations*: Catalogue, FU.

E 16
Le mele d'oro. Trans. Bruno Maffi and Edoardo Canali. Verona: Arnoldo Mondadori, 1974. 288 pp. *Location*: FU. *Note*: Copyright page indicates earlier editions in 1942 and 1965, *not seen.*

SPANISH

E 17
Manzanas de Oro. Trans. Jorge Garzolini. Barcelona: Luis de Caralt, 1946. 335 pp. *Location*: FU.

THE YEARLING

ASSAMESE

E 18
[*The Yearling*]. Translator not given. Calcutta: Sribhumi, 1957. 214 pp. *Location*: FU. *Note*: Abridged.

BENGALI

E 19
[*The Yearling*]. Trans. Bimal Mitra. Calcutta: M. C. Sarkar, 1952. 163 pp. *Location*: RLT. *Note*: Abridged.

E 20
[*The Yearling*]. Trans. Shamsul Haque. Dacca: Diganta Publishing House, 1955. 121 pp. *Location*: FU.

E 21
[*The Yearling*]. Trans. Amir U. Ahmad. Dacca: Jinat Publishing House, 1965. 153 pp. *Location*: FU.

BURMESE

E 22
[*The Yearling*]. Translator unknown. Rangoon: Shumara Press, 1938. 280 pp. *Location*: World Catalogue, *not seen*.

CHINESE

E 23
Lu yuan chang chun. Trans. Eileen Chang. Hong Kong: Tienfeng Press, 1953. vi + 184 pp. *Locations*: FU, MKRH. *Note*: Second printing, Taipei: Taiwan Ying, 1988. *Location*: World Catalogue, *not seen*.

E 24
Lu yuan chang chun. Trans. Longming Li. Beijing: Foreign Literature Publisher, 1980. 508 pp. *Location*: RLT.

E 25
Lu yuan chang chun. Adaptation. [Taipei]: Hua i shu chu, [1980?]. 10 pp. *Location*: World Catalogue, *not seen*. Second printing, 1989. *Location*: World Catalogue, *not seen*.

E 26
Hsiao Lu Ti Ku Shih. Trans. Kuei-yun Huang. Kao-hsiung, [Taiwan]: Ta Chung Su Chu, 1983. 24 pp. *Note*: Adaptation.

E 27
Lu yuan chang chun. Adapted by Yi Jia Huang. Illustrated by Yi Yuan Xiao. Shanghai: People's Arts Publisher, 1984. 150 pp. *Location*: RLT. *Note*: Picture book (9.0 × 12.5 cm.) with commentary.

E 28
Lu yuan chang chun. Translator unknown. Taipei: Juan Jing, 1982. 490 pp. *Location*: World Catalogue, *not seen*. Second printing, Taipei: Shu hu chu pan, 1986. *Location*: World Catalogue, *not seen*.

CZECH

E 29
Dítě Divočiny. Trans. Jarmila Fastrová. Prague: Václav Petr, 1949. 376 pp. *Location*: FU. *Note*: Date on copyright page is 1949. Date on illustrations is 1969, indicating this copy is from oversheets or a later printing.

E 30
Dítě Divočiny. Trans. Jarmila Fastrová. Illus. Jan Krejci. Prague: Mladá Fronta, 1964. 303 pp. *Location*: MKRH.

E 31
Dítě Divočiny. Trans. Jamila Fastrová. Illus. Adolf Born. Prague: Mladá Fronta, 1967. 360 pp. *Location*: RLT.

E 32
Dieťa Divočiny. Trans. Draga Christovová. Illus. Lubomir Kellenberger. [Prague]: Mladé letá, 1964. 336 pp. *Location*: RLT. *Note*: A copy in wrappers has been seen. 308 pp. *Location*: RLT. Reprint, 1971. 351 pp. *Location*: MKRH.

DANISH

E 33
Livets Foraar. Trans. Aage Dons. Copenhagen: Jespersen and Pios, 1939. 342 pp. *Locations*: FU, GU, RLT. *Note*: Reprint, 1989. *Location*: FU.

DUTCH

E 34
Jody en het hertejong. Trans. Mein Labberton. The Hague: M. C. Stok: [1940?]. *Location*: On copyright page of the 1988 printing. *Note*: Second printing, Amsterdam: M. C. Stok, [1954?]. 450 pp. *Locations*: FU, RLT. Third printing, Elsevier Nederland, 1980. 352 pp. *Location*: MKRH. Fourth printing, 1981. 438 pp. *Location*: MKRH. Fifth printing, Amsterdam: Boekerij, 1988. 354 pp. *Location*: RLT.

FINNISH

E 35
Elämän Kevät. Trans. Aune Brotherus. Helsinki: Werner Söderström, 1939. 420 pp. *Location*: FU. Reprint, 1954. *Location*: RLT.

FRENCH

E 36
Jody et le faon. Trans. Denise van Moppès. Paris: Albin Michel, [1940?]. 365 pp. *Location*: MKRH. Reprint, 1946. 367 pp. *Locations*: Bibliothèque Nationale, FU, RLT. Reprints, 1955, 1964, and 1969. 431 pp. *Locations*: Bibliothèque Nationale, National Library of Canada.

E 37
Jody et la faon. Trans. Denise van Moppès. [Paris]: Club des libraires de France, [1950?]. 362 pp. *Locations*: Bibliothèque Nationale, RLT.

E 38
Jody et la faon. Paris: Club du livre du mois, 1956. 373 pp. *Location*: Bibliothèque Nationale.

E 39
Jody et la faon. Trans. Denise van Moppès. Illus. Paul Durand. [Paris]: Hachette, 1957. 278 pp. 'ÉDITION CONDENÉE'. *Location*: FU.

E 40
Jody et la faon. [Paris]: Club des jeunes amis du livre, 1959. 295 pp. *Location*: Bibliothèque Nationale, *not seen*.

E 41
Jody et la faon. Illus. Paul Durand. [Paris]: Hachette, 1961. 254 pp. *Location*: Bibliothèque Nationale, *not seen*.

E 42
Jody et la faon. Edition abrègèè. [Paris]: Mame, 1965. 211 pp. *Location*: Bibliothèque Nationale, *not seen*.

E 43
Jody et la faon. Illus. Yves Beaujard. [Paris]: Hachette, 1978. 154 pp. *Location*: Bibliothèque Nationale, *not seen*.

GERMAN

E 44
Frühling des Lebens. Trans. Maria Honeit. Hamburg: Marion von Schröder, 1939. 478 pp. *Location*: FU. Reprint, Berlin: C. A. Koch, n.d. 382 pp. *Location*: MKRH.

E 45
Jody und Flag. Trans. Maria Honeit. Illus. Alice Geist-Bechert. Braunschweig, Berlin, Hamburg, Kiel: Georg Westermann, 1951. 82 pp. *Location*: FU.

E 46
Frühling des Lebens. Translator undetermined. Hamburg: Rowohlt, 1955. 396 pp. *Location*: World Catalogue, *not seen*.

GREEK

E 47
[*The Yearling*]. Athens: Pechlivanides, 1963. 328 pp. *Location*: RLT.

E 48
Thryloitou dasous. Trans. G. Tsoukala. Illus. G. Giakoumatou. Athens: D. A. Papademetriou, 1969. 208 pp. *Location*: MB.

HUNGARIAN

E 49
Penny paradicsoma. Trans. Juhász Vilmos. Budapest: Pantheon Kiadás, [1940?]. 404 pp. *Location*: MB.

ITALIAN

E 50
Il Cucciolo. Trans. Carlo Coardi. [Milan]: Valentino Bompiani, 1939. 437 pp. *Location*: FU. Reprint, 1945. 319 pp. *Location*: DLC. Reprint, 1963. 232 pp. *Location*: RLT. Reprint, 1987. 311 pp. *Location*: MKRH. *Note*: This 1987 copy is called the 'LXXXXVII EDIZIONE'.

JAPANESE

E 51
The Yearling. Trans. Kaku Arai. Tokyo: Shigen-sha, 1939. 580 pp. *Locations*: Kinki University, RLT.

E 52
Iyaringu. Trans. Kenzo Kato. Tokyo: Seinen-shobo, 1939. 642 pp. *Location*: Kinki University, RLT. Reprint, Seinen-sha, 1940. pp. 642. *Location*: FU.

E 53
Iyaringu. Trans. Satoshi Ueda. Tokyo: Meisoh-sha, 1939. *Location*: From *Eibei Bungaku Honyaku Shomoku, not seen*.

E 54
The Yearling. Trans. Yasuo Ohkubo. Tokyo: Mikasa-shobo, 1939. 491 pp. *Locations*: Kinki University, RLT. *Note*: Abridged edition. Tokyo: Kokakan, 1970. 188 pp. *Location*: National Library of Canada.

E 55
Iyaringu. Trans. Saburo Yamaya. Tokyo: Shincho-sha, 1940. *Location*: From

Translations   253

Honyaku Amerika Bungaku Shomoku, not seen. Reprinted in 2 vols. in Tokyo: Shincho-sha, 1951. 297, 369 pp. *Locations*: FU, MKRH.

E 56
Iyaringu. Trans. Yasuo Ohkubo. Tokyo: Hibiyashuppan, 1949. 604 pp. *Location*: Kinki University. Reprint, in 2 vols., n.p.: Kadokawa Shoten, 1954, 1967; n.p: Heibonsha, 1960. *Location*: From a Japanese catalogue, *not seen.*

E 57
Kojikamonogatri. Trans. Kinetaro Yoshida. Illus. Koiso Ryōhei. Chugataban: Sekai no ehon, 1951. 80 pp. *Location*: DLC.

E 58
Kojikamonogatri. Trans. Yasuo Ohkubo. Tokyo: Mikasa-shobo, 1953. 351 pp. *Location*: Kinki University.

E 59
Kojikamonogatri. Trans. Saburo Yamaya. Tokyo: Arechishuppan-sha, 1958. 358 pp. *Location*: Kinki University.

E 60
Kojikamonogatri. Trans. Kinetaro Yoshida. Tokyo: Tokyosougen-sha, 1960. *Location*: From *Honyaku Amerika Bungaku Shomoku, not seen.*

E 61
Kojikamonogatri. Trans. Suzue Okaue. Tokyo: Iwasaki-shoten, 1964. *Location*: From *Honyaku Amerika Bangaku Shomoku, not seen.*

E 62
Kojikamonogatri. Trans. Tatsuzou Nasu. Tokyo: Koudan-sha, 1966. *Location*: From *Honyaku Amerika Bangaku Shomoku, not seen.*

E 63
Kojikamonogatri. Trans. Muraji Uchiki. Tokyo: Kaisei-sha, 1966. *Location*: From *Honyaku Amerika Bangaku Shomoku, not seen.* Reprint, 1983. *Location*: *Honyaku Tosho Mokuroku, not seen.*

E 64
Kojikamonogatri. Trans. Toshiko Yamanushi. Tokyo: Kaisei-sha, 1967. *Location*: From *Honyaku Amerika Bangaku Shomoku, not seen.*

E 65
Kojikamonogatri. Trans. Hisashi Shigeo. 2 vols. Tokyo: Obunsha, 1968, 1976.

320, 340 pp. Reprint, Tokyo: Kodansha, 1983. *Location*: From *National Diet Library*, *not seen*.

E 65a
Kojikamonogatri. Translator not determined. Tokyo: Shogaku-kan, 1970. 423 pp. *Location*: Canadian National Literary Catalogue, *not seen*.

E 66
Kojikamonogatri. Trans. Shunichi Yukimuro. Tokyo: Gakushu Kenkyusha, 1976. 134 pp. *Note*: A television script was made from this translation. 109 pp. Tokyo: Kodansha, 1984. *Location*: From *National Diet Library*, *not seen*.

E 67
Kojikamonogatri. Trans. Tsugiko Aizawa. Tokyo: Shunyodo Shoten, 1977. 278 pp. *Location*: From *Honyaku Tosho Mokuroku*, *not seen*.

E 68
Kojikamonogatri. Trans. Toshi Imada. Tokyo: Nihon Shobo, 1978. 212 pp. *Location*: From *National Diet Library*, *not seen*.

E 69
Kojikamonogatri. Trans. Hoji Nagai. Tokyo: Gyosei, 1983. 204 pp. *Location*: From *National Diet Library*, *not seen*.

E 70
Kojikamonogatri. Trans. Shinobu Segawa. Tokyo: Popurasha, 1983. 212 pp. *Location*: From *National Diet Library*, *not seen*.

E 71
Kojikamonogatri. Trans. Yasuo Ohkubo. Tokyo: Kaisei-sha, 1983. ix + 756 pp. *Location*: Kinki University. Reprint, 1990. 294 pp. *Location*: RLT.

E 72
Kojikamonogatri. Trans. Tomoji Abe. Tokyo: Kodansha, 1983. 280 pp. Reprint, 1984. *Location*: From *National Diet Library*, *not seen*.

E 73
Kojikamonogatri. Trans. Kotoko Yamada. Tokyo: Nihon Shobo, 1984. 176 pp. *Location*: From *National Diet Library*, *not seen*.

E 74
Kojikamonogatri. Trans. Yoshiko Hara. Tokyo: Orenji-Poko, 1984. 31 pp. *Location*: World Catalogue, *not seen*.

Translations   255

E 75
Kojikamonogatri. Trans. Setsuo Yazaki. Tokyo: Kinnohoshisha, 1985. 76 pp.
Location: From *National Diet Library, not seen.*

E 76
Kojikamonogatri. Trans. Shogo Hirata. N.p.: Nagaoka Shoten, 1988. 46 pp.
Reprint, n.p.: Butikkausha, 1990. 48 pp. *Location*: From *Nihon Shoseki Somokuroku, not seen.*

E 77
Kojikamonogatri. Trans. Miho Madarme. Tokyo: Popura-sha, 1989. 141 pp.
Location: RLT.

E 78
Kojikamonogatri. Trans. Takahisa Katsume. N.p.: Shogakukan, 1991. 176 pp.
Location: From *Honyaku Tosho Mokuroku, not seen.*

E 79
Kojikamonogatri. Trans. Yoshiko Ashizawa. Tokyo: Kodansha, 1992. 96 pp.
Location: From *Nihon Shoseki Somokuroku, not seen.*

KOREAN

E 80
Choon Ha Choo Dong. Trans. Seong Han Kim. Seoul: Sa Sang Ke Sa, n.d. 651 pp. *Location*: FU.

E 80a
Haroop sasum. Trans. Kim Tae Ju. Seoul: Yukyoungsa, 1974. 318 pp. *Location*: Canadian National Library Catalogue.

E 81
Agi Sasum Iyangi. Translator undetermined. Seoul: Kyerim Chulpansa, 1983. 250 pp. *Location*: World Catalogue, *not seen.*

E 82
Agi Sasum Iyangi. Translator undetermined. Seoul: Kumsong Chulpansa, 1984. 287 pp. *Location*: World Catalogue, *not seen.*

MALAYALAM

E 83
[*The Yearling*]. Trans. M. C. Nambudripad. Trichur: Mangalodayam, 1956. 284 pp. *Location*: FU.

MARATHI

E 84
[*The Yearling*]. Trans. Ram Patwardhan. Bombay: Mauj Prakashan Griha, [1949?]. iv + 398 pp. *Location*: MKRH.

NORWEGIAN

E 85
Gutten og Dakalven. Trans. Hans Krag. Oslo: H. Aschehoug, 1940. 428 pp. *Location*: MKRH.

E 86
[*The Yearling*]. Serialized in *Arbeidermagasinet*. *Note*: Referred to in Brandt and Brandt records, 28 February 1940, *not seen*.

POLISH

E 87
[*The Yearling*]. N.p., n.p. [1939?]. *Note*: Referred to in Brandt and Brandt records, 2 December 1938, *not seen*.

E 88
Roczniak. Trans. Adam Galis. Warsaw: Ksaiazka, 1947. 416 pp. *Location*: MB. *Reprint*, in 1949. *Location*: Copyright page of 1984 printing, *not seen*. Reprint, 1959. Illus. József Wilkon. Warsaw: Nasza Ksiegarnia, 1959. 439 pp. *Location*: FU. Reprint, 1984. Intro. by Izabella Korzak on pp. 5–7. 496 pp. *Location*: MKRH.

Translations   257

PORTUGUESE

E 89
Virtude Selvagem. Trans. Augusto Souza. São Paulo, Brazil: Instituto Progresso Editorial, 1947. 289 pp. *Locations*: FU, MKRH.

RUSSIAN

E 90
Sverstniki. Translator undetermined. Moscow: Detskaia litra, 1976. 381 pp. *Location*: World Catalogue, *not seen.* Reprint, 1970. *Location*: World Catalogue, *not seen.*

SERBIAN

E 91
[*The Yearling*]. Belgrade, Yugoslavia: USIS, 1953. 441 pp. *Locations*: MKRH, RLT.

SINHALESE

E 92
[*The Yearling*]. Colombo, Ceylon: Gunaratne and Company, 1954. 96 pp. *Location*: RLT. *Note*: Abridged.

SLOVENE

E 93
V pomladi Življenja. 2 vols. Trans. Fran Albreht. Ljubljana: Mladinska Knjiga, 1975. 207, 214 pp. *Location*: MKRH.

SPANISH

E 94
El Despertar. Trans. J. M. C. [Barcelona]: Luis de Caralt, 1953. 456 pp. *Location*: Libros Españoles en Venta, *not seen.*

E 95
[*The Yearling*]. Buenos Aires: Editorial Autorjus, 1938. *Note*: Referred to in Brandt and Brandt records, 30 November 1939, *not seen*.

E 96
Virtud Salvaje. Trans. Guillermo Maldonado. Buenos Aires: Editorial Claridad, 1945. 423 pp. *Location*: FU.

E 97
Cacharro. Trans. Guillermo Maldonado. [Barcelona]: Luis de Caralt, 1973. 290 pp. *Location*: Libros Españoles en Venta, *not seen*.

SWEDISH

E 98
[*The Yearling*]. N.p.: Albert Bonnier, 1938. *Note*: Referred to in Brandt and Brandt records, 6 June 1938, *not seen*.

E 99
Hjortkalven. Trans. Johannes Bäck. Hälsingborg: AB Lito-Reproduktion, 1967. *Location*: MKRH. *Note*: Text is from the 'Reader's Digest Aktiebolag | Stockholm', and appears on pp. 251–387.

E 100
Hjortkalven. Trans. Eva Larsson. Lindblands: De Klassiska Ungdomsbockerna, 1973. 160 pp. *Location*: MKRH.

TAMIL

E 101
[*The Yearling*]. Trans. Kalidasan. Madras: Jothi Nilayam, 1956. 155 pp. *Location*: FU. *Note*: Abridged.

E 102
[*The Yearling*]. Trans. Mayavi. Madras: Jothi Nilayam, 1967. 540 pp. *Location*: MKRH.

Translations

TELUGU

E 103
[*The Yearling*]. Trans. Kommuri S. Rao. Madras: Vidheshi S. Grandhamul, n.d. *Location*: FU.

VIETNAMESE

E 104
Con Nai To'. Trans. Tiêu Thuyēt. Ban Viet: Báo-Son, 1957. 278 pp. *Location*: FU. Reprint, [Saigon?]: Phuong-Giang, 1957. 276 pp. *Location*: MKRH.

WHEN THE WHIPPOORWILL—

FRENCH

E 105
Au premier cri de l'engoulevent. Trans. Madame Lebettre-Laporte. Paris: Albin Michel, 1954. 328 pp. *Locations*: Bibliothèque Nationale, RLT.

CROSS CREEK

DANISH

E 106
Det fortryllede Land. Trans. Poul P. M. Pedersen. Copenhagen: Jespersen and Pios, 1947. 300 pp. *Location*: FU.

FRENCH

E 107
Le pays enchanté. Trans. Jeanine Parot. Paris: Albin Michel, 1951. 408 pp. *Location*: Bibliothèque Nationale.

SECTION E

GERMAN

E 108
Cross Creek. Meine Pflanzererlebnisse in Florida. Trans. Anita Wiegand. Zurich: Rascher, 1944. 332 pp. *Location*: FU.

ITALIAN

E 109
Cross Creek. Trans. Orietta Guaita Alliata. Milan: Valentino Bompiani, 1965. 255 pp. *Location*: FU.

JAPANESE

E 110
Suigoumonogatri. Trans. Tetsuo Murakami. Tokyo: Hayakawashobou, 1951. 381 pp. *Location*: Kinki University. Reprint, Tokyo: Hayakawashobou, n.d. 388 pp. *Location*: FU.

THE SOJOURNER

ARABIC

111
[*The Sojourner*]. Translator undetermined. Damascus, Syria: USIS, 1955–1956. 318 pp. *Location*: FU.

DANISH

E 112
Gæst pa Jorden. Trans. Aage Dons. Copenhagen: Jespersen and Pios, 1954. 278 pp. *Location*: RLT.

Translations

DUTCH

E113
Als een vreemdeling op Aarde. Trans. Mien Labberton. The Hague: M. C. Stok, n.d. 384 pp. *Location*: FU.

FINNISH

E114
Matkamies. Trans. Aune Brotherus. Porvoo and Helsinki: Werner Söderström, 1954. 414 pp. *Location*: FU.

FRENCH

E115
Comme l'ombre sur la terre. Trans. Denise van Moppès. Paris: Albin Michel, 1956. 427 pp. *Locations*: Bibliothèque Nationale, FU.

GERMAN

E116
Der ewige Gast. Trans. Edmund T. Kauer. Vienna: Paul Zsolnay, 1953. 414 pp. *Locations*: FU, RLT. Second printing, Berlin and Darmstadt: Deutsche-Buch Gemeinschaft, 1953. 384 pp. *Locations*: FU, RLT. Reprint, 1955. *Location*: RLT. Reprint, [Hamburg]: Rowohlt, 1956. 267 pp. *Location*: FU.

ITALIAN

E117
L'Ospite Inatteso. Trans. Bruno Oddera. Milan: Valentino Bompiani, 1953. 537 pp. *Location*: MB. Reprints, 1959, 1974. *Locations*: World Catalogue, *not seen*; FU.

PORTUGUESE

E 118
O Peregrino. Trans. Virgínia Lefèvre. São Paulo and Rio de Janeiro: Editora Mérito, 1954. 356 pp. *Locations:* FU, RLT.

Note: Cover design is same as the Spanish edition.

SLAVIC

E 119
Neadani gost. Trans. Mirjana Cenov and Boris Ivankovic. Rijeka, Yugoslavia: Otokar Kersovani, 1957. 521 pp. *Location:* FU.

SPANISH

E 120
Pasajero a la Gloria. Trans. Vicente de Artadi. Mexico City: Editorial Cumbre, 1954. 368 pp. *Location:* FU.

THE SECRET RIVER

DANISH

E 121
Den Hemmelige Flod. Trans. Leonard Weisgard. Illus. Birte Svensson. Copenhagen: Glydendal, 1974. *Location:* FU.

GERMAN

E 122
Der verborgene Fluss. Trans. Christa Karasek-Schreiber. Illus. Erich Remmers Wuppertal. Konstanz: Friedrich Bahn, 1956. 51 pp. *Location:* FU.

E 123
Calpurnia lässt die Sonne wieder scheinen. Trans. and illus. Ruth von Hagen-Torn. Gütersloh: Sigbert Mohn, 1965. 63 pp. *Location:* FU.

Translations   263

ITALIC

E 124
Il Fiume Segreto. Trans. Nennele Piatti. Illus. L. Corbella. Milan: Fratelli Fabbri, 1959. 41 pp. *Location:* FU.

SHORT STORIES

BURMESE

E 125
[A Collection of Short Fiction]. Rangoon, Burma: Shumara Press, 1961. 124 pp. *Location:* RLT. *Note:* "A Mother in Mannville" appears on pp. 39–60.

DANISH

E 126
["Gal Young Un"]. Serialized in *Svenska Dagbladet. Note:* Referred to in Brandt and Brandt records, 4 April 1934, *not seen.*

DUTCH

E 127
Een handvol juwelen. Een bundel korte verhalen die lang in Uw herinnering zullen blijven. Translator undetermined. Amsterdam: Geïllustreerde Pers, n.d. 123 pp. *Location:* FU. *Note:* "A Mother in Mannville" appears on pp. 57–64.

FINNISH

E 128
Nuorten Novellisto. Cantervillen kummitus ja muita kuuluisia kertomuksia. Toimittanut Kerttu Manninen. Trans. A. Lindeberg. Porvoo and Helsinki: Werner Söderström, 1964. 286 pp. *Location:* FU. *Note:* "A Mother in Mannville" appears on pp. 83–93, under the title "Äitíni asuu Mannvillessa."

JAPANESE

E 129
"Furorida no Hitobito." Trans. Nobuko Kurihara. Tokyo: Shuppankyoudousha, 1958. *Location*: From *Honyaku Amerika Bungaku Shomoku*, *not seen*.

E 130
"Perikan no Kage [Pelican's Shadow]." Trans. Yasukuni Takakashi. N.p.: Hayakawa Shobo, 1969. *Location*: From *Honyaku Tosho Mokuroku*, *not seen*.

Appendixes / Index

Appendix 1
Movie Work

1.1
The Sun Comes Up. MGM. 1948.

Note: Rawlings was hired by MGM, contract dated 15 July 1946, to write a ' "Lassie" story'. She received $30,000 upon delivery of the manuscript. She was paid an additional $30,000 at the beginning of filming, with 'certain contingent additional compensation' not to exceed the sum of $150,000. The story was tentatively entitled "A Family for Jock," which was an expansion of her short story "A Mother in Mannville" (C602). The story was published under the title "Mountain Prelude" (C635). Although Rawlings was given screen credit, her script was altered significantly to suit the musical talents of the film's star Jeanette MacDonald.

1.2
A Bad Name Dog. MGM. Unproduced.

Note: The title is a working title. The script was rejected by MGM and the story by the *Saturday Evening Post.* See Elizabeth Silverthorne, *Marjorie Kinnan Rawlings: Sojourner at Cross Creek* (Woodstock, N.Y.: Overlook Press, 1988), p. 291, Appendix 4; and an unpublished letter from Rawlings to Clifford Lyons, 13 November 1948: "POST and M.G.M. have rejected the story, and it serves me right" (FU).

Appendix 2
Films Made from Rawlings's Work

2.1

The Yearling. MGM. 1946. Produced by Sidney Franklin. Directed by Clarence Brown. Screenplay by Paul Osborn. Music composed by Herbert Stothart and Frederick Delius.

Note: The Yearling was rereleased in 1956 as an 'M-G-M Masterpiece'; in 1975 by Films Inc. in an edited filmstrip format; in 1973 on the 'smf Holiday Network'; in 1985 by MGM on Beta and VHS formats; in 1988 by MGM on two videodiscs.

2.2

The Sun Comes Up. MGM. 1949. Produced by Robert Sisk. Directed by Richard Thorpe. Music composed by André Previn. Screenplay by William Ludwig and Margaret Fitts.

Note: The screen credits claim from the 'novel' by Rawlings. See 1.1.

2.3

Gal Young Un. A First-Run Features Release; Nuñez Films. 1979. Produced and directed by Victor Nuñez.

Note: In 1986 released by Academy Home Entertainment in VHS format.

2.4

Cross Creek. Thorn EMI Films. 1983. Produced by Robert B. Radnitz. Co-produced by Leonard Rosenman. Directed by Martin Ritt. Screenplay by Dalene Young.

Note: In 1983 released by Thorn EMI and HBO Video in Beta and VHS formats.

Films Made from Rawlings's Work

2.5
The Yearling. RHI Entertainment. 1994. Executive Producers: Robert Halmi, Sr.; Robert Halmi, Jr.; Sandra J. Birnhak; David R. Ames. Produced by Edwin Self. Directed by Ron Hardy. Teleplay by Joe Wiesenfeld. Music by Lee Holdridge.

Note: 'Presented as a Kraft General Foods Premier Movie on CBS-TV Sunday, April 24'.

Appendix 3
Radio Address

"In This I Believe." Overseas Voice of America.

Note: No recording of the broadcast has been located. The 4-page typed manuscript of the address, edited in Rawlings's hand, is at the University of Florida. Elizabeth Silverthorne claims the address was delivered in New York City in October 1951 (*Marjorie Kinnan Rawlings: Sojourner at Cross Creek* [Woodstock, N.Y.: Overlook Press, 1988], pp. 316–317).

Appendix 4
Unlocated Poem

"The Mouse Speaks."
Listed in *The Poets of the Future: A College Anthology for 1916–1917*. Edited by Henry T. Schnittkind. Boston: Stratford Co., 1917.

Note: The poem is cited on p. 319, under 'OTHER POEMS OF DISTINCTION'; composed by '*Marjorie Kinnan*'.

Appendix 5
Principal Books About Rawlings

Acton, Patricia Nassif, Lady. *Invasion of Privacy: The "Cross Creek" Trial of Marjorie Kinnan Rawlings*. Gainesville: University Presses of Florida, 1988.

Bellman, Samuel I. *Marjorie Kinnan Rawlings*. New York: Twayne Publishers, 1974.

Bigelow, Gordon E. *Frontier Eden: The Literary Career of Marjorie Kinnan Rawlings*. Gainesville: University Presses of Florida, 1966.

Parker, Idella, with Mary Keating. *Idella: Marjorie Rawlings' "Perfect Maid"*. Gainesville: University Press of Florida, 1992.

Silverthorne, Elizabeth. *Marjorie Kinnan Rawlings: Sojourner at Cross Creek*. Woodstock, N.Y.: Overlook Press, 1988.

Index

[AB], A 9.1.c
Abbott, Dorothy, AA 3
Abe, Tomoji, E 72
"Abe Traphagen's Farm," C 605
AB Lito-Reproduktion, E 99
"About Fabulous Florida," AA 3, C 637
"About *The Sojourner*," C 644
Academy Home Entertainment, Appendix 2.3
Æonian Press, A 4.1.i
Affiliated (printers), A 9.1.a
Agi Sasum Iyangi, E 81–82
Ahmad, Amir U., E 21
"Äitini asuu Mannvillessa," E 128
"Alanzo Perceval Van Clyne," C 33
Albert Bonnier, E 98
Albin Michel, E 2, E 9, E 36, E 105, E 107, E 115
Albreht, Fran, E 93
Alliata, Orietta G., E 109
"Alligators," A 4.1.a, A 4.2, AA 4, C 596
Als een vreemdeling op Aarde, E 113
Amereon Ltd., A 1.1.p, A 2.1.g, A 8.1.l
American Authors Today, B 12
American Cookery, C 625
American Foundation for the Blind, A 8.1.a$_2$
American Periodicals, C 84
American Printing House for the Blind, A 3.5.f
Ames, David R., Appendix 2.5
Analytical & Enumerative Bibliography, C 1
"The Ancient Enmity," A 5.1.a, A 5.2.a
"Antses in Tim's Breakfast," A 5.1.a, A 5.2.a, AA 1, AA 2
"Apology to an Old House," C 638
Arai, Kaku, E 51
Arbeidermagasinet, E 86
Arechishuppan-sha, E 59

"Armed Services Edition," A 1.3, A 3.1.a, A 3.6.a–b
Arnoldo Mondadori, E 16
Artadi, Vincent de, E 120
Arthur Baker Ltd., A 3.8.a, A 3.8.g
Aschehoug, H. E 85
Ashizawa, Yoshiko, E 79
Association for the Blind, A 2.2
Atlantic Monthly, AA 4, C 620–621
Au premier cri de l'engoulevent, E 105
"Autobiographical Sketches," AA 3, C 645
"Autumn," A 5.1.a, A 5.2.a
Ayers, Jessie, A 7

"Babylon Undying," C 57
Bäck, Johannes, E 99
A Bad Name Dog, Appendix 1.2
Ballantyne Books, A 4.3.a, A 5.6.a–j
"A Bantam Book," A 1.4, AA 1
Bantam Books, A 1.4, AA 1
"A Bantam Giant," AA 1
Báo-Son, E 104
Barkhouse, Janet, A 9.1.a
Barnes, Katherine, C 635
Baskin, Norton S., A 3.3.a, A 4.1.a, A 5.8.a$_1$–a$_3$
"A Battle for Life," C 13
Beach, K. E., C 32
"Bear Hunt," C 604
Beaujard, Yves, E 43
Beck, Ira, C 650
"Beginning Early," C 60
"Benny and the Bird Dogs," A 4.1.a, A 4.2, AA 3, AA 4, B 2, C 597
The Best Poems of 1936, B 3
"The Best Spell," C 1
Better Living, C 643
Betts, Doris, D 7
Biemiller, Greta and Reynard, AA 2
Bigelow, Gordon E., A 10.1.a, C 648–649
Bigham, Julia Scribner, A 9.1.a, AA 2

Big Old Sun, C 616
Binner, Witter, C 56
Birnhak, Sandra J., Appendix 2.5
"Black Secret," AA 4, B 11, C 631
"Black Shadows," A 5.1.a, A 5.2.a
"The Blue Triangle Follows the Switchboard," C 61
Boekerij (publishers), E 34
Bohn (binders), A 9.1.a
The Book Club, A 5.4
"Book Club Edition," A 8.1.e
"Book Fair Editions," A 9.1.d
Book of Knowledge Annual, B 15
Book-of-the-Month Club, A 1.1.a–d, A 2.1.a, A 3.1.a–b, A 3.1.d, A 5.1.a–b, A 5.1.h–i, A 8.1.a$_2$, A 8.1.e–g, A 8.1.l
Book of the Month Club Family Reading News, A 5.1.i, A 8.1.e
Born, Adolf, E 31
"Born to Blush Unseen," C 47
Boston Transcript, AA 4
Bowden, Ann, A 3.4
Braille Writing Association, A 3.2.a
Brandt and Brandt, A 1.2, E 5, E 86–87, E 95, E 98, E 126
"The Bread," A 5.1.a
Brickell, Herschel, B 11
Bromfield, Louis, B 10
Brotherus, Aune, E 8, E 35, E 114
Brown, Clarence, Appendix 2.1
Bruccoli, Matthew J., D 1
Bulmer and Baskerville, A 3.18
Burnett, Whit, B 6, B 12
Butikkausha, E 76
Butler and Tanner, A 1.2
The Butterfly Man, A 5.2.a

C., J. M., E 94
Cabell, James B., C 627
Cacharro, E 97
C. A. Koch, E 44
Caldwell, Taylor, A 3.1.a
Calpurnia lässt die Sonne wieder scheinen, E 123
Calvary Alley, C 48
Camp, Robert, Jr., A 5.1.a$_1$, A 6.1.a
Canali, Edoardo, E 15–16
Canby, Henry S., A 5.1.b
Canelas, Dale B., A 11
Canfield, Dorothy, B 12
"The Captivating Odors of the Kitchen," C 36

"Carmenite," C 11
"Catching One Young," A 5.1.a, A 5.2.a
CBS (Columbia Broadcasting System), Appendix 2.5
Cenov, Mirjana, E 119
"The Census," A 5.1.a, A 5.2.a
Chang, Eileen, E 23
Charles Scribner's Sons, A 1, A 2, A 3, A 4, A 5, A 6, A 8, A 9, AA 1, AA 2, C 641, D 1
Cherokee Publishing Co., A 8.1.m
Chicago Daily News, C 618
Chicago Daily Tribune, A 3.1.a
Choon Ha Choo Dong, E 80
"Christmas at Cross Creek," C 625
Christovová, Draga, E 32
Clark, Olin, A 3.1.a
"Class Song," C 32
Club des jeunes amis du livre, E 40
Club des libraires de France, E 37
Club du livre du mois, E 38
CNIB, A 9.1.a
Coardi, Carlo, E 50
"Cocks Must Crow," A 4.1.a, A 4.2, AA 1, AA 2, AA 4, B 4, C 610
College English, C 613
"Collier Books," A 5.1.q
Collier Macmillan, A 3.1.xx
Collier's Magazine, C 614, C 626
Colonial Printing Co., A 3.1.oo–uu, A 5.1.h, A 6.1.k, AA 2
Comme l'ombre sur la terre, E 115
Companion Book Club, A 8.3.a
"Company, Halt!", C 25
Congressional Record, C 630
Con Nai To', E 104
"Consul Book," A 2.3
Copyright Office, A 4.1.a
Cosmopolitan, A 2.1.b, C 599
The Council on Books in War Time, A 1.3, A 3.6.a, A 5.3
Cowles, Edith, A 3.10.a
Cox and Wyman (printers), A 6.2
"Cracker Chidlings," AA 4, C 588–589
"A Crop of Beans," A 4.1.a, A 4.2, AA 1, AA 4, B 10, C 593
Cross Creek, A 3.1.z, A 5, A 6.1.a, A 8.1.a$_1$, AA 2, AA 3, B 6, C 619–621, E 106–110
Cross Creek (film), Appendix 2.4
"Cross Creek" (chapter), A 5.1.a, A 5.2.a
"Cross Creek Breakfasts," C 623

Index

Cross Creek Cookery, A 3.1.z, A 6, C 623–624
Crothers, Joel, A 8.1.a₂
Crowninshield, Frank, B 7
Cumulative Book Index, A 1.1.h, A 2.1.c, A 5.1.q
"Curls and the Curlers," C 35

D. A. Papademetriou, E 4
Dashiell, Alfred, B 2, C 648
De Klassiska Ungdomsbockerna, E 100
Delius, Frederick, Appendix 2.1
Dell Publishing Co., A 3.1.yy
"Delux Edition" (*The Yearling*), A 3.3.o
Dempsey, Mike, C 85
Den Hemmelige Flod, E 121
DePietro, Thomas, A 3.20
Der ewige Gast, E 116
Der verborgene Fluss, E 122
Designer, C 66
Det fortryllede Land, E 106
Detskaia litra, E 90
Deutsche-Buch Gemeinschaft, E 116
Devil by the Tale, D 4
The Dial Press, B 6
Dickey, James, AA 4
Die Goldenen Äpfel, E 11
Dieta Divociny, E 32
Diganta Publishing House, E 20
Dinesen, Isak, D 5
Dite Divociny, E 29–31
"Do American Women Appreciate Good Points of Their Men," C 78
Dons, Aage, E 33, E 112
Doubleday & Co., B 11
Doubleday, Doran & Co., B 1, C 635
Douglas, Marjory Stoneman, C 637, D 6
"Dubious Praise in Dubious Battle," C 642
Dumpling Magazine, C 636, C 638, C 640, C 642, C 646
Dunsany, Edward J., C 43
Durand, Paul, E 39, E 41
"Dutch Oven Cookery," C 592
Dynasty of Death, A 3.1.a

Easton Press, A 3.19
Editora Mérito, E 118
Editorial Autorjus, E 95
Editorial Claridad, E 96
Editorial Cumbre, E 120
Editor's Choice, B 2

Editor to Author: The Letters of Maxwell E. Perkins, C 641
Een handvol juwelen, E 127
"Effectiveness," C 52
"Eight-Week Clubs," C 65
Elämän Kevät, E 35
El Despertar, E 94
Elsevier Nederland, E 34
"The Enemy," A 4.1.a, A 4.2, AA 1, AA 4, C 612
English Journal, C 613
"Ephemera," C 42
The Everglades: River of Grass, C 637
Everybody's Magazine, C 62
"The Evolution of Comfort," A 5.1.a, A 5.2.a

Faber and Faber, A 1.2
Faber and Faber Archives, A 1.2
Faber Library, A 1.2
Fadiman, W. S., A 3.1.a
Fagg, Mary L., A 3.10.a
Faherty, Robert, C 616
"[Faherty's *Big Old Sun*]," C 616
"Fall," A 5.1.a
"A Family for Jock," C 635, Appendix 1.1
"Fanny—You Fool," C 622
Farrar and Reinhart, C 627
Farrar, Straus, and Co., A 7
Fastrová, Jarmila, E 29–31
Fiddia, Leonard, A 1.1.a
Fidelity (pseudonym), C 1–8, C 10–11, C 13, C 16–20, C 22, C 24, C 26
Firestone Library (Princeton), D 1
1 Chronicles, A 8.1.f, A 8.2.a
1 Corinthians, B 14
"The First Edition Library," A 3.1.aaa
"Fish Fry and Fireworks," AA 4, C 649
Fitts, Margaret, Appendix 2.2
Fitzgerald, F. Scott, D 1
Five O'Clock, C 84–87
"Fizz," C 51
"Flapping is Merely Joy of Living," C 75
"Florida: A Land of Contrasts," AA 3, C 628
"Florida: An Affectionate Tribute," C 630
Florida Endowment for the Humanities, AA 3
Florida Quarterly, C 649
Florida Stories, B 16
Fontana (publishers), A 5.7
Foreign Literature Publisher, E 24

"For This Is An Enchanted Island,"
  A 5.1.a, A 5.2.a
For Whom the Bell Tolls, A 3.1.y$_2$
"Found: A Practical Artist," C 62
"A Four Square Book," A 3.8.f, A 8.5
Franklin, Sidney, Appendix 2.1
Franklin Library, A 3.16, A 3.17.a–b
"Franklin Library Limited Edition,"
  A 3.16
"Franklin Mint Pulitzer Prize Series,"
  A 3.17.a
Franklin Watts, A 3.12
Fratelli Fabbri, E 124
"The Freshman's Side of It," C 23
Freunde der Weltliteratur, E 11
Friedrich Bahn, E 122
"The Friendship," AA 4, C 639
Frühling des Lebens, E 44, E 46
Fuller, Muriel, B 11
"Furorida no Hitobito," E 129
Furrow's End: Great Farm Stories, B 10

Gæst pa Jorden, E 112
Gakushu Kenkyusha, E 66
Galis, Adam, E 88
"Gal Young Un," A 4.1.a, A 4.2, AA 1,
  AA 2, AA 3, AA 4, B 1, C 594, E 126, Appendix 2.3
Gal Young Un and Other Famous Stories of the Cross Creek Country, AA 1
Garzolini, Jorge, E 17
" 'Geeche," A 5.1.a, A 5.2.a, AA 2
Geïllustreerde Pers, E 127
Geist-Bechert, Alice, E 45
The Gentle Insurrection and Other Stories, D 7
Georg Westermann, E 45
Gerard (publishers), E 10
"Getting in Touch with the Boys: The
  Confessions of a Welfare Worker," C 67
Giakoumatou, G., E 48
Ginn and Co., B 13
Glisson, J. T., A 5.8.a$_1$–a$_3$
Glydendal (publisher), E 121
Golden Apples, A 2, A 3.1.a–b, A 4.2,
  C 599
Golden Book Magazine, C 591
"Good Things for Church Suppers," C 63
Gouden Oogst, E 7
G. P. Putnam's Sons, B 2, C 616
Graphic Offset Co., A 8.1.a$_1$, A 8.1.d

Grau, Shirley A., A 5.5
Greenberg, David B., B 10
Greenberg Publisher, B 10
Grolier Club Inc., A 3.12
The Grolier Society, B 15
Grosset and Dunlap, A 1.1.e–f, A 1.1.i–n,
  A 2.1.c, A 3.1.dd–ii, A 3.1.kk–ll,
  A 5.1.l–m, D 2
Gunaratne and Company, E 92
Gutten og Dakalven, E 85
Gyldne frugter, E 6
Gyosei (publishers), E 69
"The Gypsy," C 50

[H], A 5.1.n, AA 2
Hachette (publishers), E 39, E 41, E 43
Hagen-Torn, Ruth von, E 123
Halmi, Robert, Jr., Appendix 2.5
Halmi, Robert, Sr., Appendix 2.5
Hammond, Theodore, C 53
Hammond, Hammond, and Co., B 7
Hammond Publishing Co., A 6.2
Hanna, A. J., C 627, C 634
Hansen, Harry, B 1
Haque, Shamsul, E 20
Hara, Yoshiko, E 74
Harcourt, Brace and Co., B 3
Hardy, Ron, Appendix 2.5
Haroop sasum, E 80a
Harper's Monthly Magazine, C 594
Hartmann, Erich, A 8.1.a$_1$
"Having Left Cities Behind Me," B 3,
  C 600
Hayakawashobou, E 110
HBO Video, Apendix 2.4
Heinemann (publishers), A 2.2, A 3.2.a–
  h, A 3.1.j–n, A 3.8.a–e, A 3.9.a,
  A 3.14.a–c, A 4.2, A 5.2, A 8.2
Hemingway, Ernest, A 1.1.j, A 3.1.y$_2$
"Here Is Home," C 620
Here We Are, B 12
Hibiyashuppan, E 56
Hirata, Shogo, E 76
The Historical Committee of the Trenton's Women's Club, B 16
The History of Gilchrist County, B 16
"H'it's a Bear," C 27
Hjortkalven, E 99–100
Hoffman, Burton C., B 6
Holdridge, Lee, Appendix 2.5
Holly Herald, C 605

Index

Home Sector, C 67
Honeit, Maria, E 44–45
Hsiao Lu Ti Ku Shih, E 26
Hua i shu chu, E 25
Huang, Kuei-yun, E 26–27
Hurff, Carmen R., A 11
H. Wolff Manufacturing Co., A 7
"Hyacinth Drift," A 5.1.a, A 5.2.a, AA 2, B 6, C 595

"If You Want to Be a Writer," B 15
Il Cucciolo, E 50
Il Fiume Segreto, E 124
Imada, Toshi, E 68
Im dunklen Laub die Goldorangen glühn, E 13
Instituto Progresso Editorial, E 89
International Collectors Library, A 3.22
"In the Heart," AA 4, C 614
"In This I Believe," Appendix 3
Introduction (untitled) to "A Mother in Mannville," B 13
Introduction (untitled) to *Letters from Caleb Milne*, B 8
"I Remember Christmas," C 643
"I Sing While I Cook," B 7, C 609
Ivankovic, Boris, E 119
Iwasaki-shoten, E 61
Iyaringu, E 52–53, E 55–56

Jacksonville University Library, A 1.1.a
Jacob's Ladder, A 7, AA 1, C 590
"Jacob's Ladder," A 4.1.a, A 4.2, AA 2, AA 4
Jacobson, Leon, B 9
"[James Still's] Epic of Kentucky," C 618
James W. Luce Co., C 43
Jarman, Claude, Jr., A 3.1.hh, C 650
Jarman, Vera, A 3.9.a
J. B. Lippincott, D 4
Jespersen and Pios, E 1, E 6, E 33, E 106, E 112
"Jessamine Springs," AA 2, AA 4, C 615
Jinat Publishing House, E 21
Jody en het Hertejong, E 34
Jody et le faon, E 36–43
Jothi Nilayam, E 101–102
J. Stephan Lawrence Catalogue, D 1
Ju, Kim Tae, E 80a
Juan Jing, E 28
Julia Richmond High School, B 13

Kadokawa Shoten, E 56
Kaisei-sha, E 63–64, E 71
Kalidasan (translator), E 101
Karasek-Schreiber, Christa, E 122
Katherine Mansfield Stories, B 9, D 3
Kato, Kenzo, E 52
Katsume, Takahisa, E 78
Kauer, Edmund T., E 116
"A Keith Jennison Book," A 3.12
Kellenberger, Lubomir, E 32
"The Key," B 14
Kim, Seong Han, E 80
Kinnohoshisha, E 75
Kodansha, E 65–66, E 72. E 79
Kojikamonogatri, E 57–69
Kokakan (publisher), E 54
"Korlah," C 45
Korzak, Izabella, E 88
Koudan-sha, E 62
"Kraft General Foods Premier Movie on CBS," Appendix 2.5
Krag, Hans, E 85
Krejci, Jan, E 30
Ksaiazka (publisher), E 88
Kultaiset Hedelmät, E 8
Kumsong Chulpansa, E 82
Kunst, Jutta and Theodore, E 3
Kyerim Chulpansea, E 81

Labberton, Mien, E 7, E 34, E 113
Lady Alicia Thwaite (pseudonym), C 84–87
La Luna Nascosta, E 5
"Lament of Siamese Cat," C 640
Landsborough Publications Ltd., A 3.8.f, A 8.5
"Large Type Edition," A 3.12
Larsson, Eva, E 100
"Lassie," Appendix 1.1
"The Last Day of School," C 19
"Laughter," C 54
Lebettre-Laporte, Madame, E 9–10, E 105
Lefèvre, Virgínia, E 118
Le mele d'oro, E 15–16
Le pays enchanté, E 107
Les pommes d'or, E 9–10
Letters from Caleb Milne, B 8
"[Letter to Aunt Anna]," C 2–5, C 7, C 16–17, C 22
"[Letter to 'Editor Star']," C 589

"[Letter to 'Everybody']," C 8–9
"[Letter to Theodore M. Hammond]' " C 53
Le whiskey du clair de lune, E 2
Li, Longming, E 24
Liberty Magazine, C 633
Library of Congress, A 1.1.a, A 5.1.a, A 6.1.a, A 8.1.a$_2$, A 9.1.d, AA 2
Lindeberg, A., E 128
Lindsay, Vachel, C 55–56
Linotype Baskerville, A 3.3p, A 3.16
Little, Brown and Co., B 4
"Little Grey Town of Tumbledown," C 41
A Little Lower than the Angels, D 2
"Little Marjorie," C 32
Livets Foraar, E 33
"Live Women in Live Louisville," C 69–74
"The Living Mansfield," B 9
"Lonely Spinster Had Premonition of Death," C 82
"Lord Bill of the Suwannee River," AA 4, B 16, C 648
Los Angeles Times, AA 3, C 645
L'Ospite Inatteso, E 117
Louisville Courier-Journal, C 68–74
"The Love of Adventure," C 20
Low, William G., A 1.2
Ludwig, William, Appendix 2.2
Luis de Caralt, E 17, E 94, E 97
"The Lullaby," C 46
Lu yuan chang chun, E 23–25, E 27–28
Lyons, Clifford, Appendix 1.2

MacDonald, Jeanette, Appendix 1.1
Macmillan Publishing Co., A 5.1.r
Madarme, Miho, E 77
Maffi, Bruno, E 15–16
"The Magnolia Tree," A 5.1.a, A 5.2.a
Maldonado, Guillermo, E 96–97
Mame (publisher), E 42
Mammoth (publisher), A 3.9.b
"The Man and the Placem" C 646
Mangalodayam, E 83
Man's Courage, A 3.2.a
Mansfield, Katherine, B 9, D 3
Manzanas de Oro, E 17
Marion von Schröder, E 3, E 44
A Marjorie Kinnan Rawlings Reader, AA 3
Marjorie Rawlings Reader, AA 2

Marron, Joseph F., A 1.1.a
Matkamies, E 114
Mauj Prakashan Griha, E 84
May, Philip S., Jr., A 5.8.a$_1$
Mayavi (translator), E 102
McCall's Magazine, C 21
McCarthy, Kevin, B 17
McLoughlin, E. V., B 15
M. C. Sarkar, E 19
M. C. Stok, E 7, E 34, E 113
Meine Pflanzererlebnisse in Florida, E 108
Meisoh-sha, E 53
MGM (Metro-Goldwyn-Mayer), A 3.1.a, A 3.1.hh, C 635, Appendix 1.1–2
[MH], A 6.1.f–i
Mikasa-shobo, E 54, E 58
"The Miracle," C 39
"Miriam's Houses," AA 4, C 632
"Miss Moffatt Steps Out," AA 4, C 632
Mitchell, Margaret, AA 4
Mitra, Bimal, E 19
Mladá Fronta, E 30–31
Mladé letá, E 32
Mladinska Knjiga, E 93
"A Mockingbird Book," A 1.6.a, A 1.6.c, A 4.3.a, A 5.6.a–j
Mockingbird Books, A 1.6.a–c, A 4.3.c–d, A 5.6.a–j
Modern Book Co., A 3.21
Modern Library, A 3.7.a–b
"Modern Library Edition," A 3.7.b
"Modern Standard Authors," AA 2
Moffett, Langston, D 4
"The Monastery," C 58
Montgomery, Elizabeth, B 3
Monti, Laura, A 10.1.a
Moppès, Denise van, E 2, E 36–37, E 39, E 115
Morrison and Gibb Ltd., A 8.3.a
"A Mother in Mannville," A 4.1.a, A 4.2, AA 4, B 12–B13, C 602, E 125, E 127–128, Appendix 1.1
Moult, Thomas, B 3
Mountain Home, C 635
"Mountain Prelude," C 635, Appendix 1.1
"Mountain Rain," C 606
"The Mouse Speaks," Appendix 4
Murakami, Tetsuo, E 110
Murray, J. Middleton, B 9
"My Friend Moe," A 5.1.a, A 5.2.a, C 619

Index 279

Nagai, Hoji, E 69
Nagaoka Shoten, E 76
Nambudripad, M. C., E 83
"Nance of the Slums and the Smile," C 48
Nasu, Tatsuzou, E 62
Nasza Ksiegarnia, E 88
Native Son, A 1.1.l
Neadani gost, E 119
Neue Heimat-Florida, E 12
Newbery Medal, A 9.1.a
New France, C 64
New Republic, AA 4
"The New Windmill Series," A 3.9.a
New Yorker, C 611, C 615, C 629, C 631–632
New York Herald Tribune Books, A 1.1.a, A 3.1.a–b, A 4.1.a, A 5.1.a, D 6
New York Herald Tribune Book Review, C 627, C 634, C 637, D 2
New York Post, C 608
New York Times Book Review, A 2.1.a–b, A 3.1.a, A 5.1.a
New York World-Telegram, B 1
Nichols, William, B 14
Niggli, Josephine, D 5
Nihon Shobo, E 68, E 73
Noble, Mrs. Fred E., A 3.1.y_1
"No Place on Campus for Knickers or Cigarettes," C 83
Norman S. Berg (publisher), A 1.1.o, A 4.1.f, A 5.1.p, A 8.1.i, A 8.1.k
"Novels of Distinction," A 1.1.h
Nuñez, Victor, Appendix 2.3
Nuorten Novellisto, E 128

Obunsha, E 65
Ocala Evening Star, C 589
Ocala Morning Banner, A 1.1.b
Oddera, Bruno, E 117
Odhams Press Ltd., A 8.3.a–b
Oember, Marie C., A 5.2.a
O. Henry Memorial Award Prize Stories of 1933, B 1
O. Henry Memorial Award Prize Stories of 1946, B 11
O. Henry Memorial Prize, C 594
Ohkubo, Yasuo, E 54, E 56, E 58, E 71
Okaue, Suzue, E 61
"Old Slewfoot," C 607
Omnibook Best-Seller Magazine, C 647

"[On American Drama]," C 44
"Once Upon a Time a Black Demon Invented Powder," C 28
"[On Poetry and Vachel Lindsay]," C 55
On Troublesome Creek, C 618
"[On Women's Suffrage]," C 49
O Peregrino, E 118
Orenji-Poko, E 74
Osborn, Paul, Appendix 2.1
Otokar Kersovani, E 119
"Our Center of Culture and Mike Dempsey," C 85
"Our Cloak-room Looking-glass," C 12
"Our Daily Bread," A 5.1.a, A 5.2.a
"Our Friends Are Best," C 15
"Our Triumph," C 26
Overseas Voice of America, Appendix 3

"Paint Jobs That Bloom in the Spring," C 87
"Palmetto Edition," A 3.1.z–aa
Pan Books, A 3.15
Pantheon Kiadás, E 49
"Parceling in Florida," C 634
"The Pardon," A 4.1.a, A 4.2, AA 1, AA 4, C 598
Parent's Magazine, C 602
Parker, Agnes M., B 3
Parker, Idella, A 5.8.a_1–a_3, A 6.2
Parot, Jeanine, E 107
Pasajero a la Gloria, E 120
Patwardhan, Ram, E 84
"A Peacock Book," A 3.11
Pechlivanides (publisher), E 47
Peck, Gregory, A 3.1.hh
Pedersen, Poul P. M., E 106
"The Pelican's Shadow," AA 2, AA 4, B 5, C 611, E 130
Penguin Books, A 3.11
Penny paradicsoma, E 49
People's Arts Publisher, E 27
Peoples Book Club, A 8.1.h–i
"Perikan no Kage," E 130
Perkins, Maxwell E., C 641
"Perse and the Baseball Game," C 29
Phuong-Giang, E 104
Piatti, Nennele, E 124
"A Pig Is Paid For," A 5.1.a, A 5.2.a
"Plays of Gods and Men," C 43
"A Plumb Clare Conscience," A 4.1.a, A 4.2, AA 4, B 17, C 591

The Poets of the Future, Appendix 4
Popular Library, A 8.6
"Popular Library Edition," A 8.6
Popurasha, E 70, E 77
"Portrait of a Magnificent Editor as Seen in His Letters," AA 3, C 641
Post Stories of 1939, B 4
"The Pound Party," A 5.1.a, A 5.2.a
Powers, Harris, A 1.1.b
Prescott, Dessie Smith, A 5.8.a_1–a_3
Previn, André, Appendix 2.1
"The Price of Marguerite," C 176
A Prince in Their Midst, C 634
"The Provider," AA 4, C 617
Publishers' Weekly, A 1.1.a, A 1.1.e, A 1.1.h, A 2.1.a, A 3.1.y_1, A 5.1.a, A 5.1.m, A 7, A 8.1.a_1–a_2, A 9.1.a, AA 1, AA 2, C 641
Pulitzer Prize, A 3.1.y_2, A 3.1.dd
"Pulitzer Prize Edition," A 3.1.a, A 3.3.b
"Pulitzer Prize Limited Edition," A 3.3.a–b, A 3.16

Queensland Braille Writing Association, A 5.1.e, A 8.2.a

Radnitz, Robert B., Appendix 2.4
Randon House, A 3.7.a
Rao, Kommuri S., E 103
Rascher (publisher), E 108
Readers Book Club, A 8.4
Reader's Digest, C 602, E 99
The Reader's Digest Assciation Ltd., A 3.20, A 5.1.a
"Reader's Digest Edition," A 3.20
"The Real Thing," C 37
"The Reforming of a Mala Puella," C 14
Reginald Saunders (publishers), A 3.1.y_2, A 5.1.d
"Regional Literature of the South," C 613
"Regular Edition," A 3.5.f
"The Reincarnation of Miss Hetty," C 10, C 21
Reinhart and Co., C 637, D 5–6
"Residue," A 5.1.a, A 5.2.a
Restrup, Kirsten, E 6
"The Rev. Clinton Wunder Is Pioneer Efficiency Pastor," C 80
RHI Entertainment, Appendix 2.5
Rice, Alice H., C 48
Ritt, Martin, Appendix 2.4

"A River That Flows Through Florida History," C 627
Road to the Sun, D 6
Robert E. Lee High School, A 3.10.a
Robert M. McBride and Co., B 12
Robertson, Archibald, A 8.1.a_1
Rochester Evening Journal, C 78, C 81, C 83
Rochester Sunday American, C 76, C 79–82
Rochester Times-Union, C 88–175, C 177–587
Roczniak, E 88
Rollins Animated Magazine, C 602, C 608, C 614
Rollins College, C 608, C 614
"A Romance," C 30
"Romance of Fifty Years Ago," C 81
Rosenman, Leonard, Appendix 2.4
Rowohlt, E 46, E 116
Royal Blind Society, A 3.1.a
Royal Institute for Deaf and Blind Children, A 3.8.b
Ryōhei, Koiso, E 57

"Sad Story of Little Pip," C 18
Saint Lawrence University, C 646
"A Sanitorium Without Mud Baths or Mineral Water," C 68
San Marco Book Store, A 2.a.f, A 4.1.g–h, A 9.1.f–g, AA 2
Sa Sang Ke Sa, E 80
Saturday Evening Post, C 596, C 602, C 610, C 612, C 635, C 639, Appendix 1.2
Saturday Review, C 616
Schmidt, Harold von, C 599
Schnittkind, Henry T., Appendix 4
Scholastic Magazine, B 12, C 597, C 601–602, C 607, C 619
Scholastic Scope, C 650
"School Edition," A 3.1.a, A 3.5.a–p
Scientia (publishers), E 12
Scribner, Julia (see Bigham)
"Scribner Classics," A 3.1.zz
"The Scribner Library, Contemporary Classics," A 1.5
Scribner Press, A 1.1.a, A 2.1.a, A 3.1.a, A 3.3.a–b, A 4.1.a, A 5.1.a, A 6.1.a, A 8.1.a_1
Scribners Archive, A 1.1.a–b, A 1.2

Index

Scribners File-Cards, A 1.1.a, A 1.4, A 2.1.a, A 3.1.a, A 4.1.a, A 5.1.a, A 5.2.a, A 8.2.a
"Scribners Illustrated Classics," A 3.3.d
Scribner's Magazine, C 588, C 590–591, C 593–595, C 597–598, C 600–C 601, C 606, C 648
Scribners Records, A 1.1.a, A 1.1.c, A 2.1.a, A 3.1.a, A 3.1.c–f, A 3.1.h, A 3.1.k, A 3.1.m–q, A 3.1.s–z, A 3.1.bb–cc, A 3.1.jj, A 3.1.mm, A 3.3.a–b, A 3.3.d–e, A 3.3.g, A 3.5.a, A 3.5.d, A 3.5.g–o, A 4.1.c, A 4.1.e, A 5.1.a, A 5.1.i, A 8.1.a_1–a_2, A 8.1.d, 9.1.c–d
The Secret River, A 9, E 121–124
Segawa, Shinobu, E 70
Seinen-shobo, E 52
Sekai no ehon, E 57
Selected Letters of Marjorie Kinnan Rawlings, A 10
Self, Edwin, Appendix 2.5
"Sellandra," A 1.1.o, A 5.1.p, A 8.1.i
Serra, Beatrice B., E 5
Seven Gothic Tales, D 5
Sheean, Vincent, A 3.1.y_2
"The Shell," AA 2, AA 4, C 629
Shenton, Edward, A 3.1.a, A 3.1.y_1, A 3.1.z, A 3.1.dd, A 3.5.a, A 3.10.a, A 3.12, A 3.20, A 4.1.a, A 5.1.a, A 5.1.p, A 5.1.r, A 5.2.a, A 5.4, A 5.5, A 5.8.a_1
"Shenton Edition," A 3.1.jj
Shigen-sha, E 51
Shigeo, Hisashi. E 65
Shincho-sha, E 55
Shogaku-kan, E 65a, E 78
Shoptalk, A 3.1.a
Short Stories from the New Yorker, B 5
Short Stories of Marjorie Kinnan Rawlings, AA 4
Shu hu chu pan, E 28
Shumara Press, E 22, E 125
Shunyodo Shoten, E 67
Shuppankyoudousha, E 129
Sibley, Celestine, A 3.18
Sigbert Mohn, E 123
Silverthorne, Elizabeth, Appendix 1.2, 3
Simon and Schuster, B 5, B 14
"The Singer," C 40
Sisk, Robert, Appendix 2.1
Slatkin, Charles E., B 13

smf Holiday Network, Appendix 2.1
"Society Divides Between Opera and Wrestling," C 86
The Sojourner, A 3.8.c, A 8, C 644, C 647, E 111–120
Solens born, E 1
"Songs of a Housewife," C 88–175, C 177–587 (499 poems, each with a separate title, are not listed individually)
Sorensen, Virginia, D 2
"The Southern Classics Library," A 3.18
Southern Folklore Quarterly, C 648
Southern Living Gallery, A 3.18
South Moon Books, A 5.8.a_1–a_3
South Moon Under, A 1, A 2.1.c, A 3.1.a, A 3.1.y_1–y_2, A 3.1.dd, A 3.3.b, A 4.1.a, A 4.2, AA 2, E 1–17
Souza, Augusto, E 89
"Spring at the Creek," A 5.1.a, A 5.2.a
Spur unter Sternen, E 3–4
Sribhumi (publisher), E 18
Step Down, Elder Brother, D 5
Still, James, C 618
Stinehour Press, A 11
The St. Johns, C 627
St. Nicholas Magazine, C 65
Stothart, Herbert, Appendix 2.1
Stratford Co., Appendix 4
Suigoumonogatri, E 110
"Summer," A 5.1.a, A 5.2.a
The Sun Comes Up, Appendix 1.1, 2.2
Sunrise: The Florida Magazine, C 592
Supplement to F. Scott Fitzgerald: A Descriptive Bibliography, D 1
"A Surprise," C 31
Süskind, Wilhelm E., E 11–12
Svenska Dagbladet, E 126
Svensson, Birte, E 121
Sverstniki, E 90
"Sweet Talk, Honey," 624

Ta Chung Su Chu, E 26
Takakashi, Yasukuni, E 130
"Taking Up the Slack," A 5.1.a, A 5.2.a, AA 2
Tampa Morning Tribune, C 603
Tannenbaum, Samuel, C 635
Tarr, Carol A., A 5.8.a_1
Tarr, Rodger L., A 5.8.a_1, AA 4, C 1, C 84
Tauchnitz, Bernard (publisher), A 3.4

"Tauchnitz Edition," A 3.4
Telephone Topics, C 61
Tellegren, Lou, C 76
Tender is the Night, D 1
This Is My Best, B 6
Thompson, George W., A 8.1.a$_1$
Thorn EMI Films, Appendix 2.4
Thorpe, Richard, Appendix 2.2
"Through Three Revolutions: A Woman's Experience in Modern Russia," C 66
Thryloitou dasous, E 48
Thuyêt, Tiêu, E 104
Tienfeng Press, E 23
Time Reading Program, A 5.5
"Toady-frogs, Lizards, Antses, and Varmints," A 5.1.a, A 5.2.a
Today's Woman, C 602
Todd, William B., A 3.4
To Have and Have Not, A 1.1.j
"To James Whitcomb Riley," C 24
Tokyosougen-sha, E 60
Tompkins, Fred, C 596
Topsoe, Soffy, E 1
"Tragic Drama at the Corinthian Stirs Rochester's Elite," C 84
Transatlantic, C 628
"The Traveller," C 6
"Trees for Tomorrow," C 626
Trumpet Club, A 3.1.yy
Tsoukala, G., E 48
Tsugiko Aizawa, E 67

Uchiki, Muraji, E 63
Ueda, Satoshi, E 53
Uj Elet Floridaban, E 14
University of Florida, A 1.1.a, A 3.1.a, A 11, Appendix 3
University of Florida Address, A 11
University of Florida Press, B 17
University of Miami Press, A 7
University of North Carolina, D 7
University of Oklahoma Press, C 634
University of Pittsburgh Press, D 1
University of Virginia, A 3.1.a
University Presses of Florida, A 10.1.a–c
University Press of Florida, AA 4
"The Use of a Sitz-Bath," C 636
USIS, E 91, E 111

Václav Petr, E 29
"The Vagrant of Romance Finds Large City Harsh," C 77

Valentino Bompiani, E 5, E 15–16, E 50, E 109, E 117
"Varmints," A 4.1.a, A 4.2, AA 4, C 601
Vidheshi S. Grandhamul, E 103
Viking Press, C 618
Vilmos, Juhász, E 49
Virtude Selvagem, E 89
Virtud Salvaje, E 96
Vogel, Joseph, A 3.2.a
Vogue, C 609, C 622, C 624
Vogue's Fireside Book, B 7
Vogue's First Reader, B 6
V pomladi Življenja, E 93

Washington Post, C 1–11, C 13, C 15–20, C 22, C 24, C 26
Weisenfeld, Joe, Appendix 2.5
Weisgard, Leonard, A 9.1.a, A 9.1.d, E 121
A Welfare Worker (pseudonym), C 67
Werner Söderström, E 8, E 35, E 114, E 128
Western, C 12, C 14, C 23, C 25, C 27–30, C 32
Wheelock, John H., C 641
"When the Muse Knocks," C 38
When the Whippoorwill—, A 3.1.y$_1$, A 4, A 5.2.a, AA 2, E 105
"Who Owns Cross Creek," A 5.1.a, A 5.2.a, C 621
"Who Will Take This Money," C 34
"The Widow Slater," A 5.1.a, A 5.2.a
Wiegand, Anita, E 108
Wilhelm Goldmann, E 13
Wilkon, Józef, E 88
Windmill Press, A 2.2, A 3.2.a, A 4.2, A 8.2.a
Wings: The Literary Guild Review, C 644
"Winter," A 5.1.a, A 5.2.a
Wisconsin Literary Magazine, C 36–60
Wisconsin Magazine, C 34–35
"Witter Binner and Vachel Lindsay," C 56
"Wives' School First Aid for Peeved Hubbies," C 79
Woman's Home Campanion, C 617, C 623
Woman's Magazine, C 63
"Women Are Spoiled," C 76
"Women as Constructionists," C 64
"A Word About My Life as a Novelist," AA 3

Index

Words to Live By, B 14
World Books, A 3.2.h–i
"World Books Edition," A 3.2.h
World Distributors, A 2.3
World Magazine, C 176
World Publishing Co., A 2.1.c–e, D 3
Wright, Richard, A 1.1.l
Wuppertal, Erich R., E 122
Wyeth, N. C., A 3.1.z, A 3.3.a–b, A 3.3.d, A 3.3.o, A 3.16, A 3.18, A 4.1.a
Wyman, Jane, A 3.1.hh

Xiao, Yuan, E 27

Yamada, Kotoko, E 73
Yamanushi, Toshiko, E 64
Yamaya, Saburo, E 55, E 59
Yazaki, Setsuo, E 75
The Yearling, A 1.1.k–m, A 2.2–3, A 3, A 4.1.a, A 4.2, A 5.1.a, A 5.2.a–b, A 6.1.a, A 6.2, A 8.1.a$_1$, AA 2, AA 3, C 604, C 607–608, C 650, E 18–104, Appendix 2.1, 2.5
Ying, Taiwan, E 23
Yoshida, Kinetaro, E 57, E 60
Young, Darlene, Appendix 2.4
Young, Owen D., C 636, C 646
"You Reckon This Mought Be the Same Man, Elmer," C 603
Yukimuro, Shunichi, E 66
Yukyoungsa, E 80a

Zoltán, Horváth, E 14
Zsolnay, Paul, E 116